# A WORKING THEOLOGY OF LABOR

"This book begins with a simple but profound premise: 'God is pro-worker.' From that insight, a host of implications follow, including the idea that the people of God should be pro-worker too! This book covers pressing issues related to human dignity in the marketplace and helps Christians think theologically about the meaning of work and the link between a right theology of labor and the pursuit of justice. Gustine gives us all much to consider."

—**Esau McCaulley**, Wheaton College

"God loves the worker. But do we grasp why and how our work fits into God's design? *A Working Theology of Labor* offers an approachable, loving, and theologically deep dive into the gospel perspective on work. It encourages us to see Christ in laborers whom the modern economy ignores and marginalizes. This book will convict you to see 'all who labor' the way God sees them."

—**Meghan Sullivan**, University of Notre Dame; founding director, Institute for Ethics and the Common Good

"Evangelical workers once helped to power the rise of the labor movement—and precisely because the Bible told them to do so. In *A Working Theology of Labor* Adam Gustine makes the case that contemporary believers have much to learn from their example. Drawing not on party politics but on the very best of evangelical theology and biblical study, Gustine underscores why Jesus followers should resist the siren call of upward mobility and instead rejoin the fight for economic justice. A timely and compelling read."

—**Heath W. Carter**, Princeton Theological Seminary

"Evangelical discourse on work has been contradictory, emphasizing the intrinsic dignity of work while also allowing exploitative labor conditions to persist. This leads many to leave the church because it seems as if evangelicals side with Pharaoh. Gustine traces the historical and theological origins of the contradiction, charts a faithful theological path forward, and restores evangelical Christian witness."

—**Robert Chao Romero**, UCLA Department of Chicana/o and Central American Studies

"How often do we pause to examine the 'social hierarchy of labor' and the subtle ways it shapes—perhaps even distorts—our own perspective? Adam Gustine offers a fascinating and much-needed theological reflection on labor, reminding us of God's deep love for the worker and our shared calling to pursue a kingdom vision of redemptive work and the common good."

—**Paul Hawkinson**, executive director and cofounder, Transform Capital

# A WORKING THEOLOGY OF LABOR

## JUSTICE, DIGNITY, AND THE COMMON GOOD

ADAM L. GUSTINE

Baker Academic
*a division of Baker Publishing Group*
Grand Rapids, Michigan

Published by Baker Academic
a division of Baker Publishing Group
Grand Rapids, Michigan
BakerAcademic.com

Printed in the United States of America



Library of Congress Cataloging-in-Publication Data
Names: Gustine, Adam L., 1982– author
Title: A working theology of labor : justice, dignity, and the common good / Adam L. Gustine.
Description: Grand Rapids, Michigan : Baker Academic, a division of Baker Publishing Group, [2026] | Includes bibliographical references and index.
Identifiers: LCCN 2026013597 | ISBN 9781540969286 paperback | ISBN 9781493456062 ebook | ISBN 9781493456079 pdf
Subjects: LCSH: Work—Religious aspects—Christianity
Classification: LCC BT738.5 .G87 2026
LC record available at https://lccn.loc.gov/2026013597



Cover design by Chris Kuhatschek

Baker Publishing Group publications use paper produced from sustainable forestry practices and postconsumer waste whenever possible.

26 27 28 29 30 31 32 7 6 5 4 3 2 1

To my kids: Josiah, Levi, and Nina.
I hope you find the deeper beauty of good work
and learn to celebrate the dignity
that dwells in every person.

# CONTENTS

# PREFACE

Of all the heirlooms I've inherited from my family, my favorite is my grandfather's old chore coat. It has his company's logo (he sold animal feed to local farmers) stitched on the chest, and it is just retro enough to be very cool today. By some stroke of fate, it ended up in my closet. I wear it mainly for yard work during the fall and winter months. But if it weren't for that coat, this project might not exist. The framing and concept came to me while wearing it, sparked by some reflections and questions I had not previously thought to consider.

My grandfather was a blue-collar worker his entire life. Aside from him, I had very little contact with blue-collar communities. I grew up in a white-collar home, as did the overwhelming majority of the people I knew. Trying to understand the lives of working-class families was not something that ever really occurred to me. Despite the fact that my own grandfather was working class, I was not inclined to consider his experience in any serious way. I didn't feel bad about my grandfather's working-class status; I didn't feel any sort of way about it at all. Over the years, as my writing interests homed in on moral and theological questions about economics and justice, that chore coat has become a kind of symbol and source of pride for me. Not that I gain any working-class cred when I put it on, but it reminds me that I am proud of him, proud that he was my grandfather. I've learned to respect the way he carved out a life in the world, even though it was far different from the life I'm carving out for myself.[1]

1. In the early stages of this project, I found that people unacquainted with the labor question might puzzle a bit at the terminology used in this book. The classic definition of "the working class" is that they are people who have to sell their labor for a wage and do not own the means

And I started to ask questions about the disconnect I felt from his experience. My life has been nearly the opposite of his. He was in school only through eighth grade. I was in school with few gaps into my thirties. He worked outside his whole life, and he would have hated spending as much time as I do behind a desk plodding away at a keyboard. Honestly, I would not have been very good in his line of work either. I've worked very few jobs that could be described as physically demanding. My summer mowing gigs in high school were probably the closest I came to manual labor, and they solidified my desire to do anything but sweat on the job.

My grandfather has been gone for over twenty years now, but I still think about him often. He and I never had any heart-to-heart talks, so I really don't know what he thought about the questions I'm asking about his life now. When I visited him, we would play cards, and he would tell war stories and wake me up early to go have ice cream for breakfast. He'd ask my mom if her car's oil had been changed recently enough for his liking, and he'd call a few days in advance of our visiting to talk about the weather and whether we should play it safe driving due to any impending storms. I realize that in the pages that follow I do a fair bit of hypothesizing about his life, his experiences, and the feelings he had about that life and those experiences. In the absence of answers to my questions, conjecture is all I have. Yet the scraps of stories and thoughts he'd toss around here and there, and the reflections from others—like my mom—who knew him better than I did, suggest that the questions I intend to explore in this book were indeed relevant to him, even if he didn't let anyone in on whether or how he struggled with them.

I spend many of my days trying to understand how the kingdom of God might shape and reshape our economic lives in all manner of spaces. But I never asked those kinds of questions about my own life, nor about how the stories of those who came before me shaped my life. I had not seriously considered the economic realities of my family's previous generations, so starkly different from my own.

---

of production, so they have little to no authority within the labor structure. This is why labor discussions often center on the relationship between workers and owners. The experience of those in the working class is largely dependent on the actions of those belonging to an outside group—the owner class. In this classic definition, the working class includes both blue-collar workers and white-collar workers. Somewhat alternatively, "working class" has also come to refer more specifically to those employed in what have traditionally been considered blue-collar jobs—those that don't require college degrees and that typically pay an hourly wage. These are workers who often face significant barriers to the kind of economic benefits that white-collar workers receive as a matter of course. Sometimes you will see me referring to "workers" or to the "working class" in this sense.

And I'm not alone. Far too few Christians think theologically about the labor issues that dramatically impact their lives. I think we need books like this because, throughout my life in every Christian space I inhabited, the topic of labor and the experience of workers *never* came up. That may seem like an exaggeration, and admittedly I can't prove that beyond a shadow of a doubt, but as I search my memories and experiences I cannot remember a single time at a local church level or at a national conference I attended where the topic of labor and justice for workers was considered. There were, of course, conversations about ministry *to* mistreated worker groups—like the day laborers who congregated outside the doors of the church I pastored in Brooklyn, or the racist rhetoric directed at immigrants who supposedly came to America illegally to "steal our jobs," or the undocumented immigrants forced to work in sweatshops in my neighborhood—but none of those conversations were really about the labor itself, or the systems of labor through which the seeds of exploitation and injustice germinate. Perhaps the closest I got to conversations around this topic was when "fair trade" became an en-vogue topic for Christians, or when the public became aware of a certain big-box store relying on government-subsidized healthcare for their workers instead of offering employee health plans. But very few of those conversations ever found their way to a theologically animated space—a space where we were reflecting on the theological implications of the labor realities we were discussing.

There are reasons for the silence on these issues, and various chapters of this book explore some of those. But, in short, my experience was shaped by growing up in predominantly evangelical spaces,[2] which have been largely unconcerned about labor and the working class for the better part of the last

2. Because there are so many ways to understand the term "evangelical," it is a term ripe for confusion. Adding to that, the moniker has been redefined dramatically in the past two decades. Instead of a descriptor of a broad religious movement with common political dispositions, the term is now more often deployed as a political signifier of religiously infused political conservatism. So, rather than a way to signal a common set of religious beliefs, "evangelical" is commonly used to identify the religious stream of an increasingly nativist political movement. This makes the term tricky and unwieldy. The risk in using the term, of course, is that its recent connotations will color the way it is interpreted throughout this text. Certainly, we did not arrive at today's understanding of evangelicalism in a vacuum, and the story of fundamentalism/evangelicalism in the United States reveals reasons why the evangelical movement might have been particularly prone to such shifts. But I have not found a term that better describes the religious movement that created the void this book is meant to begin to fill. As I use it, "evangelical" describes the broad Protestant faith traditions that prioritize (a) personal conversion experience and religious practice, (b) commitment to Scripture as normative for faithful Christian life, and (c) the centrality of Jesus's life, death, and resurrection for the life of faith. Those specific theological commitments tend to be present across the movement irrespective of other theological, political, cultural, or social factors. Evangelicals are, in this way of describing them, a very large swath of (predominantly White or White denominational) American Christians who do not

eighty years. With some notable exceptions, the broadly defined evangelical church in the United States has concerned itself with other topics.[3]

I've come to see my grandfather as an example of the way work becomes a primary arena where we wrestle with big questions of our own dignity and worth. It is fair to say that his life was a struggle—a struggle in which questions of labor and economics were inextricably bound together with questions of what it means to be human and to have a good life. His experience was also a microcosm of the larger systems of exchange we call "economies" that have serious impacts on the lives of workers—not always, but often, for ill. Labor is a primary context for injustice: the exploitation of workers and the pursuit of profits that disregard the well-being of people and the planet. These are serious issues, very worthy of our time and attention. I wonder if he felt like he was under the thumb of uncharitable forces outside his control. He certainly was, but did he realize it?

At the same time, I hope to avoid lionizing his experience. That seems to me one of the dangers of a project attempting to establish the moral urgency of social questions that impact people we care deeply about. Theological work attempting to center the experience of folks on the margins can uncritically reduce their plight into abstractions that serve some larger theological claim. This is especially true when writing from outside that lived reality. My experience is not working class, so idealization is certainly a danger. To be sure, my grandfather's life, and the lives of countless millions like him, was often one of struggle and precarity without a payoff or happy ending. My gradual awakening to these topics is not a badge of honor so much as a revelation of my blindness. Still, what the social gospelers might have called a "theology of allyship" related to labor has its place, as its aim is to awaken the moral imaginations of readers who may not have considered these issues either.[4] This is how I locate myself in the context of this work. Chances are decently high that you, the reader, have a similar experience and that you have not encountered much in the way of a theologically animated view on the major labor issues facing us today.

---

consider themselves Catholic, mainline, or Pentecostal. In the absence of a better descriptor, I will use this term in the broadest possible sense, and I will try to limit my use of qualifiers.

3. Miroslav Volf, *Work in the Spirit: Toward a Theology of Work* (Wipf & Stock, 2001), 6–7.

4. Dan McKanan, "George Lippard, Ignatius Donnelly, and the Esoteric Theology of American Labor," in *The Pew and the Picket Line: Christianity and the American Working-Class*, ed. Christopher D. Cantwell, Heather W. Carter, and Janine Giodano Drake (University of Illinois Press, 2016), 23.

# ACKNOWLEDGMENTS

I owe a deep debt of gratitude to my grandfather, Clarence Eldred Denney, as his life and labor were a source and guide of this project. He modeled good and true virtues that were lost on me in the time he and I had together, and only now, decades after he's gone, do I see the good life at work in the memories and anecdotes that mark the pages of this project. Rest well.

I'm grateful to the many wise and thoughtful conversation partners who shaped ideas and concepts in this book, even if many years ago. David Swanson and Andrew Gates have been constant companions throughout the work. José Humphreys, who cowrote my previous book with me,[1] pushed my thinking throughout that project and left me continuing to think about how our theological commitments land in the labor space. Kelli Reagan Hickey has been a great conversation partner over the years, and her thoughtful engagement with me on these topics has been invaluable. Aaron Kuecker has been an incredible support and generous reader of this project along the way. Sara Hendren was not only a great encouragement but also a fantastic interlocutor on some of the initial framing of this project—in particular, on the section on labor and disability.

I would not have come to this topic in a substantive way without the many colleagues and friends at the University of Notre Dame who introduced me to serious labor theology, helped me see and hone my vision for the moral urgency of the labor question, and taught me so much along the way. First of all, my research assistants Matthew LaPorte and Dani Tutani played an essential role in background research for this project. Thank you for your

1. Adam Gustine and José Humphreys III, *Ecosystems of Jubilee: Economic Ethics for the Neighborhood* (Zondervan, 2023).

commitment and excellent work. Thank you to Dan Graff, who taught me the fundamentals of the labor question and whose feedback in the early stages of this project was a great gift. Thank you to Meghan Sullivan, Angie Appleby Purcell, and my colleagues at Notre Dame's Institute for Ethics and the Common Good. The mission to grapple with the ethical questions pressing our world is inspiring, and I'm glad for our shared work together. Very special thanks to Dustyn Keepers and the team at Baker Academic for believing in the value and importance of such a book and for seeing the possibility of an applied theology of labor in a fraught and fraying world.

Finally, thanks to my wife, Ann. I'm inspired by the way you model to me (and everyone you meet) how to see and celebrate the dignity of each person and how to cultivate a resilient hope that the common good is worth our life's labor.

# INTRODUCTION

I was constantly astonished by the extraordinary dreams of ordinary people. No matter how bewildering the times, . . . those we call ordinary are aware of a sense of personal worth—or more often a lack of it—in the work they do.

—Studs Terkel[1]

"Labor is a dog." Someone said that to me once, and I think it's telling. They meant, mainly, that the topic of labor doesn't have much juice, that it doesn't get people's blood flowing, and so they didn't think it is the most strategic plank of a justice-oriented agenda. But if in fact labor is a dog, that says a bit more about societal lack of concern than it does the arena of labor and the lived experience of workers. The economic systems we inhabit today generally disregard workers' well-being. That disregard is revealed in disrespect toward those in so-called dirty jobs. It is revealed in vindictive manipulation, in abuse of power toward employees, and in unsafe or compromising working conditions. It is revealed in superficial expressions of solidarity in response to substantive examples of inequality. It is revealed in the rush toward automation that eliminates the need for flesh-and-blood humans, and in casual indifference, where workers are discarded when they are no longer deemed useful. In other words, labor is a dog because too many workers are treated like dogs (and not the breeds we carry around in handbags). Labor is a dog because society doesn't think righteously and live justly. Disregard is just one

1. Studs Terkel, *Working: People Talk About What They Do All Day and How They Feel About What They Do* (Pantheon, 1974), xxiv.

sign of our collective moral failure when it comes to the labor question and the working class. That disregard extends to our churches, especially White evangelical congregations, where the labor question has largely been unasked and unanswered for at least half a century.

The "labor question" is really a set of compelling and urgent moral questions about the practices and structures of our businesses and economies, in particular as those practices and structures aid or impede the well-being of workers. Economic inequality and the mistreatment of workers raise important questions about our economic practices, structures, and systems as well as about the cultural values and beliefs that give rise to them. It is regrettable that our evangelical churches have largely ignored the labor question up to now.

But if the topic of labor supposedly comes up in evangelical circles only rarely, why are there so many resources out there that talk about work from a broadly evangelical perspective? Importantly, there is a difference between *considerations of faith and work* and *a theological framework for engaging the labor question*. Work is something we all engage in, whether paid or not. But we usually work in codified systems of labor. Those systems and the outcomes they produce in the world are what we've largely ignored. Other traditions have had at least some thread of concern for working-class folks, and we will draw heavily on them as we move forward. Most notably perhaps, since at least the 1880s the Catholic Church has made the dignity of work and the rights of workers significant parts of its social theology.

By contrast, evangelicalism gave birth to a Faith and Work movement. This movement has dominated the last several decades of evangelical thought on work, producing hundreds of books, resources, centers, conferences, and local chapters of Faith and Work–style organizations across the country. As we will see, there are many helpful contributions to the theological exploration of work. But as it relates to labor, many of those have misfired and distracted us from significant core issues.[2] While the movement has produced helpful resources for Christian people attempting to think about what personal Christian faithfulness in the workplace looks like, it has proven mostly

2. There is one outlier text that is worth highlighting here as an exemplar: Miroslav Volf's *Work in the Spirit: Toward a Theology of Work* (Wipf & Sock, 2001) has proven to be a wonderful conversation partner in the development of this project. Volf, though not an evangelical himself, has had a profound influence on evangelical leaders during his career, and this text is no different. He speaks about critical problems, like alienation and exploitation, and has stretched my thinking along the way. Writing a broad theology of work—and also landing it in working-class realities—as he has is an example of the very thing evangelical thinking on work has largely been unable to do. Even though Volf does not treat working-class issues at length, he does some, and it is clear that his work drives his thinking toward the experience of workers rather than away from it.

unwilling to engage—something Adam Joyce, a veteran of the Faith and Work movement, describes as a "blindness" to—serious labor questions that arise from the working-class experience in America.[3] Interestingly, over the past decade or so, there has been a growing recognition of the gap, the need for recalibration on this issue, and an awareness that our theological work has not appropriately engaged working-class issues. There is a small, growing corpus highlighting the ways evangelicals have missed the boat on working-class questions.[4] I'm hopeful that this project will continue to help fill that gap in the literature.

## Why We Need a Working Theology of Labor

Set against the decades-long evangelical silence on the labor question is . . . *the Bible*. Any thoughtful and honest survey of the Scriptures reveals a fundamental truth that lies behind every chapter of this book—*God is passionately pro-worker*. As we move through this project, a close reading of the biblical text will make that reality apparent again and again. Scripture's inner logic and normative expectations when it comes to labor are so clear that a disregard for the labor question sticks out as an anomaly based on evangelicalism's own methodological commitments in biblical interpretation and theology. In other words, an abiding concern for labor issues and justice for workers holds up against the long-standing theological standard that we be guided by Scripture. Then, when we put the biblical text in conversation with scholarship from other theological streams from the past century and a half, we find a deep and meaningful theological foundation that might animate a renewed imagination for labor and a deeper concern for the lived experience of the working class.

If God is passionately pro-worker, then God's people should be too. This is particularly the case when we consider the many ways labor provides the context for dehumanization and abuse of people who experience many of life's vulnerabilities. Pope John Paul II said that work (labor) is "at the very

3. One notable, and commendable, exception is the Theology of Work Project, which has long-form online essays treating a number of topics related to working-class issues. I find their reflections compelling and worthy of time and attention. See https://www.theologyofwork.org/; and Adam Joyce, "Theology for the One Percent: The Problem with the Evangelical Faith and Work Movement," *ABC Religion and Ethics*, October 21, 2019, https://www.abc.net.au/religion/theology-for-the-one-percent-the-evangelical-faith-and-work-mov/11625040.

4. In addition to Joyce's article, see also these representative examples: Ken Estey, "The Faith and Work Movement Stops Short of Class," *Working-Class Perspectives*, January 27, 2020; Jeff Hanaan, "God of the Second Shift," *Christianity Today*, October 2018; and Elesha Coffman, "Do They Know It's Labor Sunday?," *Christianity Today*, August 19, 2009.

centre of the 'social question.'"[5] An overriding concern for the labor question provides a unique and "new" way to enact the hopefully still-growing evangelical passion for justice.

An authentically Christian view of the labor question might help counter factors that have historically prevented evangelicals from giving vulnerable populations the same priority of place and concern that Jesus gave them. In other words, *exploring the labor question helps us love our neighbors*. This is because labor issues affect every corner of society, cutting across race, gender, nationality, socioeconomic status, and so on. Perhaps more than any other issue, grappling with the labor question—at theological and practical levels—allows Christians to engage with the lived experience of their neighbors and with the most pressing issues of the day. This is not to ignore the specific ways that issues of race impact discussion of labor. Indeed, issues of race inform many of the particular issues we discuss: wages, power, treatment of workers, asset building, and so on. Nor is it to dismiss the many ways that gender shapes the way we consider the labor question, as we will see clearly when touching on topics common to women in the workforce: discrimination, unpaid labor abuse, and (again) wage disparity. What we find is that for any large social issue (race, gender, immigration, poverty, the environment, etc.), focusing on labor provides us with a unique angle to consider those other issues afresh. We may find some critical commonalities in the structures of injustice that prove helpful as we seek to build a more just society.

In that sense, this is a project in Christian social ethics, intent on uncovering the moral demands of Scripture and exploring their implications for the way people of faith engage their neighbors and their world. It is also an attempt to make the theological conversation around labor something much more robust than what is typical. The ethical demands of Scripture invite a more comprehensive response than the overly simplistic and highly individualized responses to working-class concerns so often proffered in Christian circles: be nicer to the checkout person, tip your server better, hire differently, shop local, and so on. Those things are not bad (I'm not suggesting we tip less!), but they are insufficient. Scripture offers a view of labor that implicates each of us individually but is also highly concerned about the systems and structures that perpetuate injustice and misdeeds toward the working class.

This project will also re-narrate what we think constitutes a "good" job. Work is probably a top-three issue for every person. It engages the time and attention of humanity more than nearly any other thing. It is only logical

5. John Paul II, *Laborem Exercens*, September 14, 1981, §2, https://www.vatican.va/content/john-paul-ii/en/encyclicals/documents/hf_jp-ii_enc_14091981_laborem-exercens.html.

that we would devote a great deal of time, attention, and resources to the theological and practical exploration of work. It is fundamental to our daily lives, an elemental space where we work out something of what it means to be human. So, we will look for different ways forward, with the labor question as our guide. Building out a theologically informed understanding of *labor* emphasizes important and unique conclusions about the nature of *work*. I believe we need to find a way to shift the discourse to a view of work that is much more fundamental to our humanity. When we consider the nature of work alongside the labor question, we come away with a more expansive view of the value of work; we're able to see the goodness and beauty of labor in many sectors that are ignored and disregarded by church and society. That opens a window to a different perspective on the dignity of our work, no matter what kind of work we do. I hope we come away with a deeper appreciation for the way the biblical text offers a profound counternarrative to the values and norms of everyday society.

That profound counternarrative to social norms and values is an urgent need for the church, because the conventional value system related to work is deeply damaging to the human person. It degrades our capacity to build societies where everyone can truly flourish. This is what I'm calling "the social hierarchy of labor." The social hierarchy of labor is an often unspoken, but concretely enacted, set of social values that bestows value and worth on particular types of jobs—and the people who do them—over others. This hierarchy is pervasive and impacts nearly every corner of society related to labor. It not only creates an artificial socioeconomic caste system that perpetuates socioeconomic inequality; it also justifies all the ways we shame, marginalize, exclude, exploit, and otherwise injure those on the lower rungs of the ladder in this hierarchy. The social hierarchy of labor has a number of inflections that come into fuller relief depending on the particular topic at hand. A major aim of this book is to help us all better identify, and then begin to dismantle, the social hierarchy of labor. We will return to this idea throughout as we seek to understand the ways this value system creates and perpetuates something other than God's desires for us when it comes to labor.

## Important Initial Concepts

Before we get too far into the body of this project, I want to sketch out a few preliminary ideas that undergird my main arguments. Specifically, I want to quickly outline four premises that I take to be true as a matter of course.

Unless we share them (or at least I name them), it may be hard to navigate the larger trajectory of this book.

Conversations around economic justice in general, and labor issues in particular, have historically been maligned from within the evangelical movement based on a supposed connection with far-left political ideologies (i.e., communism, socialism, etc.). The reasons for this are, from my view, overwhelmingly historical and social as opposed to theological. So, the first premise I want to highlight is that there is nothing inherent in a theological exploration of economic justice, the labor question, and the poor and working classes in the United States that renders it unfaithful to the text of Scripture. Dismissing such theological exploration outright as unfaithful to Scripture is not an intellectually serious engagement with the core questions being asked. Of course, one *can* advocate for extreme and/or leftist ideas when doing theology of labor, but it is not a foregone conclusion that doing theology of labor *will* lead to such advocacy. A good-faith reading of this book will resist such flimsy rhetoric and, instead, exhibit a willingness to examine the values, structures, and practices of the actual systems we inhabit in the United States with an eye to biblically animated reform. Where Scripture challenges us, we should allow it to, and we should wonder together about ways of being that would be more faithful to God's ideals as laid out in Scripture. Critique, as well as creating space for interrogation by normative questions, is the modus operandi of theological work applied to the world and any particular social issue.

I also want to emphasize, second, that I do not maintain a favorable view of the notion of "upward mobility." As I use the term, "upward mobility" is more of a social value than a descriptor of a person's, or family's, economic progress. It is a value that conditions most of us to view economic ascendancy as an amoral goal. I am not against the accumulation of resources/assets in a de facto way. That would be hypocritical and naive. In fact, I'll argue strongly that asset accumulation is essential to any notion of the good life connected to economic vitality in the world we live in. But Miroslav Volf observes that "economic systems are only apparently value-free" and that "part of the job of an economist seems to be to make sure that no 'subjective' ethical norms and value judgments interfere."[6] To my view, that makes upward mobility a universal theological problem. This means that anyone, on any rung of the socioeconomic ladder, can fall prey to the trap of upward mobility. No one is immune. The notion of upward mobility leads to uncritical attachment to economic resources and breeds avarice and distrust. It poisons our ability to live good economic lives in communities, as it incentivizes isolationist and

6. Volf, *Work in the Spirit*, 15.

hoarding behaviors that corrupt even our best intentions. The social value of upward mobility is a vice and should be named, examined, and undermined at every possible turn.

Third, I have become convinced over the years of the Bible's internal logic regarding questions of poverty and justice, which guides the conclusions I draw about any topic but especially about economic justice and the labor questions we explore in this book. That inner logic is summed up nicely by what Jon Sobrino calls "the fact of the poor." He says that "the objective fact we are speaking of . . . is the fact of misery, oppression, and injustice in which millions of human beings live."[7] The poor are *everywhere* in Scripture; the biblical characters we encounter are, typically, poor and subject to powerful forces of oppression and injustice. Scripture paints a picture of God's clear and overriding desire to respond to the cries, and satisfy the needs, of the poor. Suggesting that God's salve on the wounds of the poor is only a spiritual response—that it has no tangible or real-world effect—simply does not match the biblical text. If we claim to be a people of the book, we should be honest enough to admit that that book is overwhelmingly on the side of the poor. We might say that the Bible was written with the underclass in mind. What's more, the fact of the poor calls the rest of us to account. Sobrino says that those who come to grips with the truth of the poor "have felt questioned and challenged by this objective reality."[8] The fact of the poor is a reality we are invited to not only accept but also respond to in some fashion.

That this idea lies in the background of this discussion is important because the labor question is ultimately a question about injustice toward, and exploitation of, the poor and working classes in society. I am well aware that there are many, many workers in the world who are in fact not poor. Many have carved out substantial economic toeholds in society with the labor of their hands. As we consider the experience of "the worker," however, I want us to keep in mind the classic definition of the worker: one who must sell their body/labor for a wage. This means that workers all too often labor from a vulnerable position, economically speaking—often because they are mistreated by those who are far less vulnerable than they are. "The fact of the poor" invites reflection and response toward those unjust realities. My hope is that the Scriptures deepen our sensitivities to the plight of those on the economic margins of society. Sadly, though, "the fact of the poor" usually elicits a very different response. Rather than compassion and righteous anger, there are far too many (those whom the Scriptures refer to as "the wicked") who view

7. Jon Sobrino and Juan Hernández Pico, *Theology of Christian Solidarity* (Orbis Books, 1985), 5.

8. Sobrino and Pico, *Theology of Christian Solidarity*, 5.

that reality as an opportunity for unrighteous gain. We live in a world that operationalizes the idea that "there is money to be made at the expense of the poor."[9] The Scriptures counter and condemn this as a height of evil, yet these practices of exploitation are oftentimes too embedded in disembodied economic practice for us to recognize them, much less resist or reject them.

Fourth, "the fact of the poor" informs the language I use throughout this project. I wrestled with how to describe certain people and groups and which classifications best fit various ideas. In the end, you'll note a variety of purposeful linguistic decisions. In some cases, I've chosen to use the descriptions commonly employed by society: blue/white collar, working class, and so on. In using those conventional labels, I am not rendering a value judgment. I am, instead, using the terms as a statement of the facts Sobrino names. There is, in fact, a class of people "lower" on the socioeconomic ladder than those at the top. A lower-rung worker is not, in my view, less valuable, but the term draws attention to real social constructs that shape our views and attitudes toward others. In other cases, I felt that the terms I wanted to use did not create enough clarity about my intentions. Terms like "powerful" and "powerless" are, in a sense, too ordinary to ensure that I am clear in my intent of use. In those cases, I have tried to draw attention to the intended nuance through unconventional spelling like "power-full" and "power-less." In doing so, the purpose, again, is to highlight the *fact* of power disparities between people and groups, not to cast some as being without agency. This approach is imprecise, but the goal is to create moments where the reader will trip on the language and so be invited to ponder the nuance intended.

## Structure

Part 1 of this book establishes the moral urgency of, and the need for, a theology of labor and provides a high-level overview of how we got to our present place of such need. In these chapters, we explore some of the historical and theological reasons why the evangelical movement has largely divorced itself from the working class and, in so doing, substituted an insufficient alternative to a robust theology of labor. The Faith and Work movement is that alternative. We analyze some of the major themes of that movement and consider ways that it leaves the evangelical theological imagination ill-equipped to wrestle with significant labor questions.

9. Walter Brueggemann, *Tenacious Solidarity: Biblical Provocations on Race, Religion, Climate, and the Economy* (Fortress, 2018), 90.

Part 1 also unpacks our core thesis—namely, that Scripture provides ample resources for the development of a working theology of labor. We will build this theology on two foundational ideas: the universal dignity of the human person and the priority of the common good. I argue that while these two notions are underdeveloped in the evangelical theological imagination, they are both thoroughly biblical and Christian. Human dignity and the common good also invite us to address other fundamental questions that will impact the way we apply these core concepts to particular labor issues in part 2.

The exploration of human dignity and the dignity of labor, in chapter 2, will challenge us to reconsider the fundamental nature of work and the idea of calling. It's my view that reform in our approach to questions of calling and vocation is essential. Chapter 3 explores this notion in depth and suggests alternative ways forward that better allow us to affirm the dignity of all labor. Connecting human dignity, the dignity of labor, and the biblical notion of calling sets the stage for exploring the purpose of work in a new way—namely, as contribution to the common good. Chapter 4 outlines the common good as a basic and essential Christian doctrine and sketches out the implications of such for an understanding of the nature and purpose of work.

Part 1 intends to highlight the theological significance at the intersection of what it means to be human and the purposes for which humans were created. That intersection invites a determined commitment to seeing ourselves as part of a shared calling of co-creation with God and one another toward the flourishing of the whole of our corner of the cosmos. Our aim is to expose the social hierarchy of labor as an ongoing violation of that calling and to imagine ways people of faith might begin to embody a different posture toward labor in the face of it.

Part 2 seeks to apply the fundamental ideas developed in part 1 to particular issues related to the labor question. Of course, the first and most obvious question to explore is the question of wages. Wages are a crucible, a crossroads where the faithfulness of the owner class is weighed against the lived experience of the working class. Scripture leaves little room to negotiate around the essential question of wages for issues of justice. Chapter 5 outlines a theological approach to thinking about wages that weaves human dignity and the common good together with the rest of the biblical witness.

Chapter 6 then considers the question of how we might think biblically, or Christianly, about the explicit negotiation of power between owners and workers. In real time, these negotiations make many evangelicals nervous or wary, fostering an overtly negative disposition toward most movements for workers' rights. There is no question that workers' rights negotiations are messy and vulnerable to corruption from any angle. Thankfully, the biblical text provides a pathway to view the negotiation of power that might help us re-narrate these issues.

Chapter 7 explores the question of worker agency and asset ownership. Part of the basic definition of "working class" includes the recognition of a lack of agency and asset ownership; that is, working-class people do not own, and therefore cannot direct, the means of production. Very practically, asset ownership is an essential ingredient of economic viability for those experiencing a lion's share of economic vulnerability. What's more, Scripture evidences the fact that the just and equitable distribution of goods (assets) is part of God's intention for how healthy societies function. The concentration of assets in the hands of an increasingly wealthy few is a recipe for societal breakdown, and this chapter explores this idea.

Chapter 8 is a response to some of the issues that arise when we seek to enact the theological convictions outlined in the project thus far. Our emerging theology of labor invites us to wonder about its implications for situations where the affirmation of dignity, the dignity of labor, and the possibility of the common good are called into question. Even though the topics are distinct, labor has a unique common intersection with the issues of uncompensated labor, disability, and artificial intelligence. For example, if work is a fundamental way we give evidence of the *imago Dei*, what does that mean for a person who labors outside the traditional paid economy, or someone who is differently abled? Also, throughout human history every major technological revolution has fundamentally redefined people's relationship to work in a way that frankly has caused disastrous consequences for marginalized populations of workers. As we stand today on the edge of a monumental revolution in technology, exemplified most directly in the rapid advance of artificial intelligence, how might our working theology of labor engage, challenge, critique, and resist the dehumanizing implications of such a revolution? These and other questions become front-burner issues for discernment for Christians engaging the labor question in modern society.

As a working theology of labor implies, there are a host of questions this project is meant to provoke but not necessarily answer. This one book will not unearth every way that labor systems create the conditions for injustice and inequity. I am neither a historian nor an economist, though those fields will inevitably come into play in what follows. That invites further scholarly reflection across disciplines that will inevitably round out our understanding of how God's Word intersects with labor in real-time in God's world. This project is meant to bring these ideas together in a generative way that provides a foundation and framework for further theological reflection and practical application in the field.

## Finally, My Hopes for This Book

The labor question is all around us. Labor made the clothes you put on this morning, transported you to work (or school) where you do your labor, and made the furniture you're sitting on to read this book right now. Labor questions infuse every action we take in the world with moral import, because behind every system of production and every commercial exchange is a river of humanity impacted by our collective choices and the systems that either celebrate or violate each person's dignity and either contribute to or detract from the common good.

And we are also surrounded by labor injustice. Workers are being underpaid, sometimes criminally so. They are subjected to all manner of humiliations on the job. They endure unsafe working conditions and environments waging war on their well-being. Workers are disregarded in too many discussions of economic policy, and their experience is often the last thing to be considered when the ins and outs of our individual and shared economic lives are evaluated.

If this book has done its job, you'll never engage a worker the same again. You (and I) will wonder about the lived experience of the person in the back of house washing the dishes at our favorite restaurant. We'll pause when we pass by the hotel worker on our way to sightsee in our favorite city. We may be more curious about the system of production that created the bag of frozen food we pull out for a quick dinner on Friday night. We may have more compassion for, or interest in, the unrest we observe in the fossil-fuel industry. It may strike us as relevant when we read news stories of Starbucks or Amazon workers attempting to unionize. And the people who build our roads, maintain our communities, deliver our mail, stock our shelves, drive our buses, teach our children, and fix our cars will take up new residence in our imagination. No matter what kind of job you do—be it blue, white, or no collar—I hope this book causes you to consider those around you who are vulnerable to violation in their labor.

Even in writing that last paragraph, it's obvious that I live on one side of the divide created by the social hierarchy of labor. As this book tries to navigate that very real divide while also attempting to dismantle it, my hope is that it won't read as a project that excludes but instead as one that advocates for a massive swath of society often overlooked and discounted. The biblical text connects imaginative sinews sufficient to animate a way of life for the people of God to cultivate the fruit of justice, righteousness, and peace. That sensibility can be applied to every issue facing us in our world. I believe God is keen to help us inhabit our world in a way increasingly reflective of what we might call "kingdom intent." I am also convinced this means God desires something different from the common lived experience of the working class. These are folks who are often socially or politically idealized, but in practice they are overlooked, ignored, or harmed. God does not intend for people to live under constant economic precarity, vulnerable to exploitation and usury. God does not intend for work to be the context for dehumanization and degradation. God does not intend for our labor to cultivate the fruit of conflict and competition at the expense of others, particularly those who experience life at the social margins. A cursory survey of our shared economic life reveals far too many ways that life serves these ends rather than something that God might recognize as holy and good. With that in mind, I hope this book reignites thoughtful theological reflection on the labor question. The moral imagination of the church is central to its prophetic witness in the world. The last two decades have seen a robust expansion of timely scholarly engagement with a variety of justice issues meant to shape that imagination toward the intentions of God. The lived experience of the working class is in many ways an urgent reminder of the need to continue that work into the future.

God wants our work to be good and to serve good ends. We are on good ground to contend that God expects, even demands, the reform of systems and structures that harm people and increase or capitalize on their vulnerability. These are gospel issues—arbiters of good news in a fraught world—because they are spaces intended for people to discover and deploy the fullness of their humanity, participating in and contributing to the good world God has given us stewardship over. If you are concerned about and committed to exploring and inhabiting the fullness of God's intentions in the world, cultivating the fruits of justice, righteousness, and peace, then my prayer is that you'll find this text a helpful companion in the journey. If you come to this project with a degree of skepticism, that's understandable. The culture of American Christianity has fostered a doubtful disposition in many of us. My hope is that you'll give this a good-faith reading, engage the questions, study the Scriptures, and wonder with me about what it means to engage the labor question with Christian fidelity.

# PART 1
# A WORKING THEOLOGY OF LABOR

# 1 IN SEARCH OF GOOD WORK

## Labor and the Church

It is a search . . . for daily meaning as well as daily bread, for recognition as well as cash, for astonishment rather than torpor; in short, for a sort of life rather than a Monday through Friday sort of dying.

—Studs Terkel[1]

I believe my grandfather would be suspect of much of the conversation around faith and work. Many of the best theologies of work produced over the past two generations are broad, beautiful, sweeping treatments that make sense in a perfect world. Unfortunately, though, we don't live in that perfect world, and so theologies of work are often irrelevant to the front-burner issues facing the working class. So I'm interested in exploring what would happen if we attempted to reflect on the theological nature of work from the ground up. If we allowed the issues, struggles, and questions working-class communities face to guide our reflections, could we build out a theology of work that helps account for the particularity of the working-class experience? Could we do that in a way that also helps us understand something new about God's overall intentions for the world of work?

For the next few chapters, we will try to do just that. We want the working-class experience to shape the *way* we think about work, because as we survey

1. Studs Terkel, *Working: People Talk About What They Do All Day and How They Feel About What They Do* (Pantheon, 1974), xi.

the Scriptures, we find that the biblical text reveals a God who centers the experience of the worker. God's vision for labor relations starts with the experience of the vulnerable working class, and we will attempt to integrate that same logic into the core questions we are asking about the meaning, value, and purpose of work. In each of the next four chapters, we will see that the labor question has a profound effect on the way we think about work at the cosmic and applied level. We begin by understanding why theologies of work, while helpful, tend to fall short of being able to take the working-class experience seriously enough.

## The Great Evangelical Divorce

American religious history shows us that working-class believers at one time found a home in congregations that were characteristically evangelical. Prior to the transformative effects of industrialization and urbanization in the half century that followed the Civil War, communities we'd recognize as working-class integrated well into this particular stream of faith.

But post–Civil War America signaled a sea change in the religious affiliation of blue-collar Christians. Over roughly the next one hundred years, these believers felt increasingly unwelcome, ill at ease, and not at home within the religious movement that came to be called evangelicalism.[2] By the end of the 1960s, American evangelicalism had little substantive connection to working-class people, including working-class Christians. These two streams now practiced faith in distinct spaces, firmly establishing a disconnect between evangelicalism and what became known as "working-class religion."[3] During this time, working-class religion had many expressions of robust faith, and faith that eagerly engaged social questions on behalf of blue-collar folks.[4] But evangelicalism was a different story. Certainly, evangelical writers and theologians touched on specific issues related to labor or dealt with labor ethics in measured ways, but on the whole it has been many decades since evangelicalism has made an attempt at a holistic theological treatment of the labor question. Generally speaking, by the 1980s and '90s—when the evangelical movement reached its fullest expression—there was little concern

2. See, e.g., the many firsthand accounts of working-class people in H. Francis Perry, "The Workingman's Alienation from the Church," *American Journal of Sociology* 4, no. 5 (March 1899): 621–29.

3. Matthew Pehl, *The Making of Working-Class Religion* (University of Illinois Press, 2016), 5.

4. Herbert G. Gutman, "Protestantism and the American Labor Movement: The Christian Spirit in the Gilded Age," *The American Historical Review* 72, no. 1 (October 1966): 74–101.

for labor-justice issues in the pews, in the minds of theological leaders, and in the pervasive evangelical subculture.

## Bedecked Belief: The Gilded Age of Evangelical Christianity

One of the most significant themes of the early days of what would become the evangelical movement—one that indelibly shaped the movement's capacity and concern for the labor question—is an affinity for affluence. Beginning in the Gilded Age (roughly from the end of the Civil War to the opening decade of the twentieth century), economic gain was seen as a clear sign of Christian regeneration—proof positive that this particular brand of Christian faith paid off.[5] Conversely, poverty was a sign of something else—namely, sin.[6] The famous preacher Henry Ward Beecher said as much in the years following the Civil War, arguing that "no man in this land suffers from poverty unless it be more than his fault—unless it be his *sin*."[7]

Given the strong, and quite public, aversion to economic struggle, it should come as no surprise to note that conservative Christianity in the Gilded Age "warmly embraced the rising industrialist," a nineteenth-century term for the powerful economically—and socially—upwardly mobile.[8] The nation experienced astronomical economic growth due to industrialization. Men like John D. Rockefeller, Andrew Carnegie, and many others oversaw industries in steel, oil, mining, and more, redefining what it meant to be wealthy in the United States. The Gilded Age was aptly named, as everything that the nation's upper class touched seemed to turn to gold. This included churches. The wealthy class in the United States enthusiastically engaged in, and funded, congregational life through philanthropy and the operations of local churches. They left their mark across the Protestant landscape at the turn of the twentieth century. (In my city, stories tell of a church paid for by one of our local "Rockefellers," whose portrait is enshrined in stained glass next to the apostles.)

Perhaps unsurprisingly, this new face of American church life was a far cry from the grassroots religion practiced by many in the decades leading up to industrialization. The austere disposition of this new-money religion must have seemed strange to those who worked in the factories that produced

5. Carl F. H. Henry, *Aspects of Christian Social Ethics* (Eerdmans, 1964), 62.

6. Gutman, "Protestantism and the American Labor Movement," 76.

7. Gutman, "Protestantism and the American Labor Movement," 76. Quoted in Henry F. May, *Protestant Churches in Industrial America* (Harper, 1949), 69.

8. Gutman, "Protestantism and the American Labor Movement," 77.

Rockefeller's wealth. Gutman continues to describe the religious disposition of the time: "The wealthy busied themselves . . . purchasing expensive church pews, . . . the middle classes chased wealth and . . . wage earners, busy laboring, found little time to ponder existential questions and felt separated from institutional Protestantism. Workers wandered from the fold, and the churches lost touch with the laboring classes."[9] These laboring classes felt the disconnect in significant ways. But that disconnect did not foster a corresponding despondency as much as it did a growing disdain for what was perceived to be a sinful lust for monetary gain. Said one woman at the turn of the twentieth century: "Until the church repents of its money-worship it is not a fit companion for the common people."[10]

Nonetheless, many found the opportunities and possibilities of a religiously infused rise in affluence appealing. Even though many working-class Christians were troubled by the development, popular sentiment was that economic gain was at least amoral if not an outright good that should be left alone.[11] Part of that attraction was a winsome notion that God desires a certain degree of upward mobility—essentially arguing that the American dream was God's dream for each person and family. One can easily see the appeal of such a claim in a world of rapid change from a preindustrial and agriculturally centered America to the explosive wealth for a relative few brought about by the Industrial Revolution.[12]

The rapid economic growth of the owner class in the United States, and the religious preoccupation with being in their company, did not end at the turn of the century. Public figures throughout the twentieth century—including well-known leaders like Billy Graham—were themselves enamored with, and apologists for, the special place of not just business and capitalism but also business leaders themselves. In 1954, Graham suggested that Jesus had profitable businesses in mind when he promised that everything would be "added to us" if one sought first the kingdom of God. "Graham helped introduce captains of industry to the incredible power of prayer," because for Graham, prayer became more than a spiritual exercise; it became "a tool to improve the public image of their companies." He presided over business events and industry conventions, eventually leading the *Daily Herald* of London to call him "the Big Business evangelist."[13]

9. Gutman, "Protestantism and the American Labor Movement," 77.

10. Perry, "The Workingman's Alienation from the Church," 624.

11. Gutman, "Protestantism and the American Labor Movement," 78.

12. Gutman, "Protestantism and the American Labor Movement," 92.

13. Kevin Kruse, *One Nation Under God: How Corporate America Invented Christian America* (Basic Books, 2015), 37–38.

Problematically, though, that meant these chaplains of big business were not in a position to thoughtfully consider the plight of the worker. As an early expression of a theme that became all too common, evangelical affinity for industry leaders made many of the movement's most prominent leaders skeptical of labor issues and antagonistic toward the lived experience of workers. As an example, in 1952 Graham described a vision of Genesis's Eden as "a paradise with 'no union dues, no labor leaders, no snakes, no disease'" and said that a "truly Christian worker 'would not stoop to take unfair advantage of his employer by ganging up against him in a union.'" Graham framed industry leaders as powerless victims and organized workers as victimizers. He thought labor unrest, and strikes in particular, "were inherently selfish and sinful." Graham went so far as to couple salvation with the rejection of labor disputes, insinuating that to sympathize with labor, and so also workers, was against the work of God. Real revival had to include a rejection of the labor question. He saw the rank and file as a mission field for evangelistic harvest, further confirming the profound separation evangelical leaders articulated and codified between the movement and the working class.[14] Graham is not an outlier in the twentieth century; prominent leaders across the movement took similar positions alongside industry leaders and so stood against working-class concerns in the midst of labor disputes.

Graham was making more public, and more influential, the coupling of religion and commerce that had taken off in the previous few decades. In the 1930s, Abraham Vereide began to convene gatherings of high-powered businessmen, first on the West Coast but eventually around the world, for prayer breakfasts. These breakfasts intentionally targeted executives—gathering a wide array of company presidents and politicians—for what would eventually be called the City Chapel movement. The expressed aim of City Chapel was to "develop a Christian nation" through an ever-growing cadre of industry executives.[15] Chapters sprung up everywhere, including in Washington, DC, a nod to this story's other theme: politics. The intertwined motivations of spiritual revival, economic superiority, and political power started to become a calling card of evangelicalism in the public square. City Chapel morphed into a national organization called the National Council for Christian Leadership, and the board was dotted with men of immense power in both politics and business.[16] The appeal of such a movement is obvious: high-powered (usually) men in positions of incredible influence gathering in the name of God and

14. Kruse, *One Nation Under God*, 37–38.
15. Kruse, *One Nation Under God*, 41–42.
16. Kruse, *One Nation Under God*, 45–46.

their collective business and political interests. The politicization of evangelicalism begins in earnest in this period of time and offers us a second window into the story of the divorce between evangelicals and the working class.

### Dead and Red: Evangelical Aversion to the Left and Labor

In 1949, the American public learned that the Soviet Union possessed an atomic arsenal.[17] As the Cold War played out across the country, an existential anxiety settled over the nation. This collective angst was searching for some kind of resolution, and again it was Billy Graham who had a solution. The evangelistic crusades with which Graham would become synonymous provided consolation for worried Americans and condemnation for their enemies. He said, "Communism . . . has decided against God, against Christ, against the Bible, and against all religion. Communism is not only an economic interpretation of life—communism is a religion that is inspired, directed, and motivated by the Devil himself who has declared war against Almighty God."[18]

Of course, communism and socialism had long been economic enemies of the capitalist system that produced the United States' incredible industrial growth. That made them direct ideological competitors to big business. Andrew Carnegie, titan of the steel industry, declared in his treatise *The Gospel of Wealth* that the socialist is "attacking the foundation upon which civilization itself rests."[19] A full-throated attack makes sense coming from Carnegie, but what accounts for the condemnations from Graham, and others, that caused millions of evangelicals to more fully solidify their break from "the left" and labor?

One of the characteristics of twentieth-century evangelicals and evangelical theology was a tendency to adopt a posture of skepticism and suspicion of streams outside their own, in particular those streams leaning toward "the left." There was often a fear of association with what was viewed as liberal theology or practice. That suspicion manifested itself in large-scale organizing of movements against any outside force seen as a threat to conservative Christian values (often framed as "traditional American values"). Historian Randall Balmer describes evangelicals as feeling "under siege," and so they began to fight back.[20] Over the course of the twentieth century, evangelicals demonstrated public opposition to all manner of perceived threats.[21] This is still at work today.

17. Kruse, *One Nation Under God*, 49.

18. Quoted in Kruse, *One Nation Under God*, 36.

19. Andrew Carnegie, *The Gospel of Wealth* (F. C. Hagen, 1889), 6.

20. Randall Balmer, *Bad Faith: Race and the Rise of the Religious Right* (Eerdmans, 2021), 16.

21. Clyde Wilcox, "Popular Backing for the Old Christian Right: Explaining Support for the Christian Anti-Communism Crusade," *Journal of Social History* 21, no. 1 (1987): 117–32.

The theological posture of suspicion and skepticism stems, in part, from a dispensational perspective that tended to view "the world" as evil, doomed to continued corruption until its eventual destruction.[22] The church was a lifeboat from the storms of the world. "In the middle decades of the twentieth century, evangelicals sought especially to shield their children from the depredations of that larger world."[23] The enemy-ization of the world may not have been an outright objective of early twentieth-century evangelicalism, but it is undoubtedly a major consequence.

The anticommunist stream of conservative Christianity mirrored that theological and practical disposition. The seeds of anticommunism had been around for decades by the time Billy Graham came around. The firebrand Billy Sunday once said, "If I had my way with these ornery wild-eyed socialists and IWW's [pro-labor organization], . . . I would stand them up before a firing squad."[24] Sunday typifies the intensity with which evangelicals attacked those deemed to be adversaries of American values. This extended well into the twentieth century to the height of the "red scare" era. In this era, there was no middle ground in the fight for the soul of America. Anticommunist Reverend David Noebel was quoted as saying, "A special place in hell is being reserved for people who believe in walking down the middle of the political and religious road. It will be their privilege . . . to fry with Eleanor Roosevelt and Adlai Stevenson."[25]

So it is easy to see how the more measured, but equally intense, Graham could stand in the decades-long stream of anticommunist preachers and put his finger on the existential anxiety brought about by the Cold War with a salvation message that commended traditional American values *and the American economic system*. It is no wonder that his Los Angeles crusades at the end of 1949 (in the immediate aftermath of the public realization of Soviet atomic strike capability) drew around 350,000 people. Over the course of the next few years, Graham wove together a message of individual salvation, anticommunism, and American patriotism in which he couched an explicit disdain for the labor question.[26] Because labor unions and worker movements had long been associated with left-leaning politics, the fervor with which the

22. Balmer, *Bad Faith*, 14.

23. Balmer, *Bad Faith*, 18.

24. Quoted in Michael Lienesch, "Right-Wing Religion: Christian Conservatism as a Political Movement," *Political Science Quarterly* 97, no. 3 (1982): 407.

25. Quoted in Lienesch, "Right-Wing Religion," 408.

26. Kruse, *One Nation Under God*, 36–38. For more on the history of political affiliation and evangelical faith, see also Darren Dochuk, "Christ and the CIO: Blue-Collar Evangelicalism's Crisis of Conscience and the Political Turn in Early Cold-War California," *International Labor and Working-Class History*, no. 74 (Fall 2008): 76–100.

nation responded in opposition to the Soviet Union and the spread of communism all but sealed the divorce between evangelicalism and the working class.

Working-class evangelicals then had a choice "between their class and their faith commitments." It was a choice that reflected one's theological orthodoxy, one's patriotic fervor, and one's economic values and aspirations. Attempts to bridge the divide between evangelical Christians and blue-collar labor flamed out. Even if there was some reluctance, many working-class evangelicals eventually embraced the larger culture of conservative Christianity.[27]

So, are there no working-class evangelicals? Of course there are. I grew up in an evangelical church with a large population of working-class folks. I'm sure most readers could readily identify churches that hold strong evangelical commitments and have many blue-collar congregants. Many churches that could be characterized by this "working-class religion" still hold to the traditional tenets of evangelical faith. The critical nuance here is to recognize the divide between working-class Christians and the evangelical *movement*. That is, the major organizations, leaders, and public theologians that galvanized and shaped the broader evangelical landscape have not paid much positive attention at all to the working class. "The gap is wide between the day-to-day work of rank and file evangelicals on the shop floor and the operational imperatives of even the best-intentioned advocates in national evangelical organizations."[28] Carl Henry observed this reality in the 1960s. Lamenting evangelicalism's inability to connect to workers, he reflects that the "absence of evangelical challenge to workers at the labor level explains why the evangelistic thrust has found so little response among the laboring class as such, and especially among organized labor."[29] What accounts for the disconnect?

## Evangelicals and Work, Not Labor

By the second half of the twentieth century, evangelicalism in the United States found itself in a new social location, one marked by increased affluence and a firm commitment to political power,[30] something Andrew Lynn calls the "embourgeoisement process of American evangelicalism."[31] This led the

27. Dochuk, "Christ and the CIO," 78.

28. Ken Estey, *Labor Evangelicals: Faith, Authority, and Resistance at Work* (Palgrave Macmillan, 2024), 6.

29. Henry, *Aspects of Christian Social Ethics*, 41.

30. David French, "The Christian Right Is Going Extinct," *New York Times*, May 1, 2025, https://www.nytimes.com/2025/05/01/opinion/trump-evangelicals-republicans.html.

31. Andrew Lynn, *Saving the Protestant Ethic: Creative Class Evangelicalism and the Crisis of Work* (Oxford University Press, 2023), 25.

movement to begin to think about work in a markedly different manner. That new way came to be known as the Faith and Work movement, and it developed into a significant area of Christian thought and practice in the United States.[32] In short, the Faith and Work movement explores and advocates for the integration of Christian faith in the workplace.[33] Arising in response to an observed lack of engagement with the topic, and in perhaps stereotypical evangelical fashion, the Faith and Work movement's intended audience is the *individual* Christian, and its goal is the application of faith to that individual's job.[34]

Even though the Faith and Work movement as we know it today really took off after World War II, its seeds are scattered throughout the first half of the twentieth century.[35] The early decades of the 1900s saw a rise in social awareness across all Christian streams. Because the gospel mandate to make disciples of all nations should extend to society, a Christian's faith must engage the world, but primarily for the purposes of saving individual souls.[36] The integration of evangelism in the workplace became a hallmark of the Faith and Work movement. During this time, there was an observable rise in "special purpose groups" that functioned similarly to what we might today call a parachurch ministry or organization. Prior to the twentieth century, groups like the YMCA emerged, as did groups dedicated to particular issues like anti-slavery or temperance. In the early twentieth century, we begin to see groups thinking about the integration of faith and the workplace. Joseph Oldham—who would later write *Work in Modern Society*—remarked that the church had a responsibility "of restoring the lost unity between worship and work."[37] These groups continued to grow and gain popularity, pointing to both the theological emphasis and laity-led hunger for discussion and action on the integration of faith and work.

However, it was during the 1950s and '60s that the movement really began to pick up steam. The Full Gospel Business Men's Fellowship International, the Laity Lodge, the Fellowship of Companies for Christ International, the

32. The Faith and Work movement has no governing denominational bodies and no organizational structures working out one particular strategic emphasis. Tracking and tracing the various threads of what we have come to call the Faith and Work movement requires a significant amount of historical and sociological research that falls outside the scope of a working theology of labor. Thankfully, good work has been done in that area by scholars like Andrew Lynn, in *Saving the Protestant Ethic*, and David W. Miller, in *God at Work: The History and Promise of the Faith and Work Movement* (Oxford University Press, 2007).

33. Miller, *God at Work*, 6.

34. Lynn, *Saving the Protestant Ethic*, 32.

35. Lynn, *Saving the Protestant Ethic*, 91–98, provides a fairly comprehensive timeline of the movement, including key figures, texts, organizations, and so on.

36. Miller, *God at Work*, 29.

37. Miller, *God at Work*, 31–32.

International Christian Leadership group, and the Pittsburgh Experiment—among many, many others—are all examples of organizations launched to bridge the world of faith and work. David W. Miller calls this period a time of emphasis on the "ministry of the laity." This ignited generations of growth, as the number of these organizations has doubled every decade since the 1960s.[38] Alongside these start-up organizations came a wave of devotionally oriented resources that came to characterize the movement. *Faith at Work* magazine launched in 1956. Books like *A Theology of the Laity* (1958) named what defines so much Faith and Work writing—the divide between Sunday and Monday in the lives of Christians.[39] In the 1970s, leaders like William Diehl—interestingly, a retired executive from Bethlehem Steel—took the mantle of advocating for the integration of Christian faith in the workplace. Over roughly the next twenty years, Diehl wrote several books and founded the Coalition for Ministry in Daily Life, another parachurch ministry dedicated to faith and work.[40]

As the emphasis on the integration of faith and work grew stronger, the 1980s, 1990s, and early 2000s saw a flood of publishing on the integration of faith and work—with topical bibliographies growing by over 500 percent in five years in some cases.[41] Today there are scores of books on the topic of faith and work. In addition to the explosion of resources from the Christian publishing industry, denominational and mission-oriented groups also took interest in the topic. In 1983, the World Evangelical Fellowship convened a consultation at Wheaton College emphasizing the need to bring Christian mission and evangelism to all the world. This is an extension of the same line of thinking that came from the seminal Lausanne Conference in 1974, which declared the intrinsic link between evangelism and the Christian responsibility for social engagement.[42] In 1983, InterVarsity initiated its first MBA-specific ministry. The C12 group, an organization dedicated to equipping business executives for excellence, was founded in 1992.[43] In 1995, Focus on the Family—perhaps the most influential evangelical parachurch organization in twentieth-century America—launched the CEO Forum.[44] Seven different annual conferences on faith and work have launched since 2002. The early 2000s saw a renewed focus on Christian cultural engagement,

38. Lynn, *Saving the Protestant Ethic*, 1.
39. Miller, *God at Work*, 42–50; Lynn, *Saving the Protestant Ethic*, 22.
40. Miller, *God at Work*, 53–55.
41. Lynn, *Saving the Protestant Ethic*, 2.
42. Miller, *God at Work*, 42.
43. Lynn, *Saving the Protestant Ethic*, 91–92; see www.joinc12.com.
44. Miller, *God at Work*, 87, 124, 140; Lynn, *Saving the Protestant Ethic*, 93.

and coupled with a steep rise in urban ministry by historically White denominations, a new stream of evangelical leadership developed a unique contribution to the movement. Two of the more influential projects have been Redeemer Presbyterian Church's Center for Faith and Work, founded in 2002 in New York City, and the Theology of Work Project, founded in 2007. Seeing the benefit of movements like this, the Kern Family Foundation funded both the Made to Flourish Network and the Oikonomia Network, which is dedicated to helping evangelical seminaries and colleges continue to develop resources for use in the local church around the integration of faith and work.[45]

## The Theological Legacy of the Faith and Work Movement

Every entry into the Faith and Work discussion begins with a common question: *Why does work matter?* While there are countless ways to describe the movement's various ways of answering that question, those responses can in general be divided into two major categories: articulating a vision and motivation for how God works (1) *in* people through their work (discipleship) and (2) *through* people in their work (mission).

The most significant contribution of the Faith and Work movement is a vision for our work as a context for discipleship, a place where God works in us.[46] Work as an expression of what it means to be human and the original human vocation are strong emphases in this area, as is the way work provides a unique possibility for positive spiritual formation. Key themes here include bridging the gap between Sunday and Monday, the gospel demand to live out one's faith in the public sphere, and—as we will explore more fully in the next chapter—to more fully live into the image of God.

Tangentially connected to this theme is a self-help perspective on faith and work. Christian faith still has an effect on the worker, but here faith helps a person do better on the job. Christian faith might help a person be more disciplined or productive,[47] perhaps embolden them to take more risks (as

45. Lynn, *Saving the Protestant Ethic*, 1–2, 94–95, 113.

46. Tom Nelson, *Work Matters: Connecting Sunday Worship to Monday Work* (Crossway, 2011); R. Paul Stevens, *Work Matters: Lessons from Scripture* (Eerdmans, 2012); R. Paul Stevens, *The Other 6 Days: Vocation, Work, and Ministry in Biblical Perspective* (Eerdmans, 2000).

47. Matt Perman, *What's Best Next: How the Gospel Transforms the Way You Get Things Done* (Zondervan, 2014); Jordan Raynor, *Redeeming the Time: 7 Biblical Principles for Being Purposeful, Present, and Wildly Productive* (Waterbrook, 2021); or David Goetsch and Karen Moore, *Christian Women on the Job: Excelling at Work Without Compromising Your Faith* (Fidelis, 2020).

an expression of faith),[48] or encourage them to develop a mastery of some particular field.[49] The workplace self-help genre is a logical next step from workplace discipleship, and writers are keen to highlight the many ways one's faith can help someone be more tangibly successful, often economically so. In other words, work infused with faith produces qualitatively, and often quantitatively, better results and an increase in personal wealth and social location.[50]

A second major branch of the Faith and Work canon is the intersection of work and Christian mission—what God might want to do in the world *through* work.[51] An extensive resource catalog helps Christians embrace their jobs as opportunities to spread the gospel and equips them to become more effective workplace evangelists.[52] The aforementioned Carl Henry took pains to emphasize the evangelistic potential of the workplace.[53] One formal expression of this theme is the Business as Mission movement (BAM).[54] BAM emphasizes the means by which business might be deployed for kingdom purposes. Attempting to take the Great Commission seriously, BAM animates a missional imagination that partners well with the entrepreneurial spirit of many aspiring and established business leaders who want to see their business acumen aid the "cause" of Christ.

Beyond interpersonal evangelism or business as a strategy for such, some writers focused on the way work contributes to social transformation. This includes significant attention to social entrepreneurship and other business strategies aimed at producing *direct* social good. That might include microlending institutions, work-development programs, or business start-ups aimed

48. Jordan Raynor, *Called to Create: A Biblical Invitation to Create, Innovate, and Risk* (Baker Books, 2017); Andrew Hanna and Mona Hanna, *The Kingdom Entrepreneur Devotional* (Ark House, 2022); or Henry Kaestner, J. D. Greear, and Chip Ingram, *Faith Driven Entrepreneur: What It Takes to Step Into Your Purpose and Pursue Your God-Given Call to Create* (Tyndale Momentum, 2021).

49. Jordan Raynor, *Master of One: Find and Focus on the Work You Were Created to Do* (Waterbrook, 2020).

50. Lynn, *Saving the Protestant Ethic*, 132. See, e.g., John D. Beckett, *Loving Monday: Succeeding in Business Without Selling Your Soul* (IVP Books, 2006).

51. Tom Nelson, *Why Your Work Matters: How God Uses Our Everyday Vocations to Transform Us, Our Neighbors, and the World* (Baker Books, 2025).

52. One example of this is at the Theology of Work Project. See the blog posts at https://www.theologyofwork.org/key-topics/evangelism-sharing-the-gospel-at-work-overview/. This type of short-form equipping and blog-post-style resourcing is pervasive across many Faith and Work platforms.

53. Henry, *Aspects of Christian Social Ethics*, 61.

54. See https://businessasmission.com/. See also C. Neal Johnson, *Business as Mission: A Comprehensive Guide to Theory and Practice* (IVP Academic, 2009); or Gea Gort, *BAM Global Movement: Business as Mission Concepts and Stories* (Hendrickson, 2018).

at some transformative effect. Amy Sherman's *Kingdom Calling: Vocational Stewardship for the Common Good* is a great example of theological reflection that emphasizes not only the *possibility* of work to produce transformative effects in the world—social justice and so on—but also the *responsibility* people of faith have to take this possibility seriously. In other words, Christian faith creates a mandate to orient one's work around the transformation of society in tangible ways.

A nuanced version of this same line of thinking is present in the broadly Reformed emphasis on gospel-centered cultural renewal.[55] Tim Keller, famously the founding pastor of Redeemer Presbyterian Church in New York City and Redeemer's Center for Faith and Work, was well-known for his vision for how God works to renew the world through gospel-centered people taking seriously the call to broad cultural engagement. In this way of thinking, the church lives to proclaim to the world God's promise to restore the fallen creation. This is clear at Redeemer's Center for Faith and Work, which "exists to form Christians into agents of renewal who integrate their faith and work for the peace and prosperity of the city."[56] Keller's seminal work on work, *Every Good Endeavor: Connecting Your Work to God's Work*, is exemplary, as is Andy Crouch's *Culture Making: Recovering Our Creative Calling*, a vision for faith-informed influence in culture that points toward the ultimate redemption of God's kingdom. The possibility of cultural engagement and influence highlights our shared responsibility to take work seriously as a "sacred stewardship."[57]

## Theologies of Work Are Great, but They're Insufficient

It would be a mistake to read this book as an attempt to disregard the very real contributions made by so many through the Faith and Work movement. If, as David says in Psalm 24, "the earth is the Lord's, and everything in it" (v. 1), then it is right and proper to give serious time and attention to the kingdom of God in our workplaces. The individual believer *should* seek to saturate their daily work with their Christian faith. The values of God's kingdom *should* permeate the lives of Christians to such an extent that the gospel is made explicit in and through our work. In my review of resources developed through this movement (what is presented here only scratches the surface), I encountered beautiful treatments of faith and work and thoughtful

55. Lynn, *Saving the Protestant Ethic*, 210–22. Lynn refers to this as Kuyperian humanism.
56. See www.faithandwork.com.
57. Henry, *Aspects of Christian Social Ethics*, 31.

theological reflection that has borne significant fruit in the lives of believers, which will benefit the church for generations.

Still, while we can affirm that many of these treatments are good contributions, we can also say that, on the whole, theologies of work are insufficient to treat the labor question in a significant way. To start, there is little evidence within the movement that evangelicals have thought seriously about working-class concerns and the kind of systemic issues (wage injustice, exploitation, worker vulnerabilities, etc.) that arise when thinking theologically about labor.[58] The frontline issues facing the working class are functionally ignored, and the topics addressed are too abstract or individualistic to make sense in the labor conversation. On the whole, the Faith and Work movement opens us up to theological claims or commitments that work against good-faith attempts to engage the labor question on its own terms.

## Intrinsic vs. Existential Value of Faith-Animated Work

As an example, the major themes of the Faith and Work movement open us up to the claim that work infused with faith is *intrinsically* more valuable than work on its own terms. Carl Henry said as much when he claimed that "a disciple of Christ . . . has greater potential for service."[59] In context, Henry seems to be arguing that a Christian can do better work than someone who is not a Christian. But this gets the essential theological idea backward. Instead of the idea that integrating faith with work helps you become a more faithful—or, crassly, better—Christian, this notion suggests that integrating faith and work helps you become a better worker. This is not a hypothetical issue; it is the exact logic of the scores of self-help books attempting to leverage faith, or biblical principles, toward more effective work.

Arguing that faith-infused work has more intrinsic value essentially forces us—as in, it's almost unavoidable—to make comparative judgments about the relative value of people's labor. For example, in the next chapter we will consider a case study of sanitation workers. The question is: *Is a Christian's garbage collection more valuable than a non-Christian's garbage collection?* Here we are speaking of the *actual* labor itself. If we argue that faith-infused work has more intrinsic value, we find ourselves having

58. Adam Joyce, "Theology for the One Percent: The Problem with the Evangelical Faith and Work Movement," *ABC Religion and Ethics*, October 21, 2019, https://www.abc.net.au/religion/theology-for-the-one-percent-the-evangelical-faith-and-work-mov/11625040.

59. Henry, *Aspects of Christian Social Ethics*, 61. In context, "service" is a reference to a person's work, not Christian service.

to argue that the Christian garbage collector is doing more valuable work than the unbelieving garbage collector. But of course, there is no material advantage to being a Christian doing this job. The collection of garbage is not a more valuable contribution to society when done by a Christian. Similarly, it is impossible to argue that there is a Christian form of bus driving, plumbing, farming, teaching, business owning, and so on. Can a Christian police officer assure my safety *better* than a non-Christian one? That is a difficult claim to defend. There may be *ways of working* that are more or less compatible with Christian values, but those ways of working are not exclusive to Christians. We've also certainly seen the tragic evidence of ways Christian workers are capable of doing work that is unethical, unjust, or sinful. In fact, a nonbelieving person can be just as excellent in their work as a believing person.

Instead of arguing that faith infuses work with more intrinsic value, a better emphasis might be the existential value of faith-infused work. Instead of faith making one's work intrinsically better, we come to see that work understood through the eyes of faith is an incredible gift of grace. Over the next few chapters, we will consider the nature of work as an expression of the original human vocation where every person, Christian or not, has the same calling: participating in God's world and making a positive contribution to it. The gift of faith-infused work might be, simply, knowing that's true. What better way to engage one's work each day than to know that you are participating in God's original intention for creation. What's more, because God is always and everywhere at work, when I go to work each day I stand to witness the possibility of God's redemptive action in the world. Writers who emphasize the possibility of the renewal of creation through work highlight this very idea quite well. The person with faith-infused work can give their conscious and willful consent to that divinely collaborative project. There is a precious gift in being able to say yes to God's invitation to participate in something divinely designed for such good purposes.

A counterargument here might be that this claim does not account for the ways God's Spirit is actively regenerating a Christian's life and that the ongoing sanctification of that person might actually make the work they do better. Miroslav Volf, reflecting on the notion of *charisms*—gifts given by the Spirit—argues that those gifts are directly connected to the way Christian people work in the world.[60] There is an important conversation here about the way God's Spirit inhabits the people of God in the world of work. However, I think this limits our ability to see work's original intention as a way

60. Volf, *Work in the Spirit*, 111–14, 124–25.

for every person to participate in and contribute to the world.[61] For example, Volf thinks about work as "cooperation with God."[62] A question I want to ask is, Must a person be inhabited by the Spirit (must they be a Christian) to cooperate with God in their work? Must they *know* they are cooperating with God to cooperate with God? They might not be able to give their conscious and willful consent, but that does not mean they cannot cooperate. Think about how many civil and social codes a person abides by in a typical day without knowing they are doing so. The normal functioning of society depends on our unconscious cooperation with all manner of systems and structures. The same is true with a person's ability to cooperate with God in their work in the world. That is a gift of common grace—bestowed to all—and not a pneumatologically contingent gift.

It is, of course, true that sin corrupts human capacity for faithfulness to God's intentions and that Scripture explicitly names the struggles of human labor as a by-product of sin in the world. Yet, while the regenerative work of God's Spirit in a person's life might increase their capacity to honor God in every arena of life—including their work—there is nothing in that claim that forces us to assign value to labor *comparatively*. If a person's work is transformed by the power of God through the Spirit (say, they become more ethical in their dealings with customers), that does not mean their work has more intrinsic value than the work of a non-Christian—particularly because the non-Christian is perfectly capable of *not* defrauding customers in the first place. So, a person might become more virtuous, but that does not make their work intrinsically *better* than someone else's. Instead, it reinforces the idea that work is a context for discipleship. Allowing faith to lead us to comparative judgments at all—something assigning intrinsic value inevitably does—is an unhelpful path to walk. In fact, Jesus's parable of the Pharisee and the tax collector in Luke 18:9–14 invites us to resist thinking about faith as providing permission for comparative value judgments between people of faith and those they deem to be without.

Here's why this distinction is so important: If, instead of recognizing the distinction between the intrinsic and existential value of work, we uncritically assign more value to work done by people of Christian faith, our assessments regarding the dignity of work begin with theologically sanctioned hierarchy of labor. When Faith and Work themes reinforce the idea that Christian work is more intrinsically valuable, or that faith gives a person some kind of

61. I am less inclined to put as much emphasis on the relationship between Spirit-empowered sanctification and human labor, precisely because I think we have yet to take the original human relationship to work seriously enough.

62. Volf, *Work in the Spirit*, 114–15.

advantage in the workplace, we cannot affirm the full dignity of labor performed by unbelieving people, and we will marginalize people who do not share our faith. This is inherently problematic, but it is all the more so when one considers the affluent target audience for the Faith and Work movement and the way working-class communities have been excluded from the discourse and from evangelical spaces. We are left with a pseudo-spiritual class system that makes it difficult to resist unhelpful, and inaccurate, assumptions about the spiritual lives of working-class people and privileging Christian work in a way not supported by the biblical text.

## Prioritizing the Value of Impact

Another reason why the Faith and Work movement can't engage the labor question substantively is its overwhelming emphasis on *impact*. The scholarship demonstrates that the organizations and industries driving the movement have centered on the executive, power broker, knowledge economy, and "creative class" Christian to the observable exclusion of the working class.[63] There are multiple motivations for this, but, generously, reaching the person at the top of the corporate ladder is a priority because of their impact potential. Viewing impact through a Faith and Work lens confers "religious significance over more influential positions of power," which spiritually incentivizes obtaining a high-powered and influential job.[64] Being in "the room where it happens" is seen as a gift that increases one's ability to use one's job as an expression of a kind of divine calling. So it is not only the current executive or power broker whose work is emphasized but aspiring ones as well.

This is a logical outcome for a movement that pays so much attention to the missional possibilities of work. If work is an arena for evangelism, it is important to seek out work with a large relational reach. If work is an arena for cultural renewal or social transformation, positions of power and influence are essential. So even if the movement didn't intentionally target executives and power brokers, the theological train of thought would have led to the boardroom eventually. And it goes without saying that the working class never goes into the boardroom—except to clean it during the night shift.

So there is a value judgment baked into the Faith and Work movement that preferences executives and those with an upwardly mobile career trajectory.

63. Lynn, *Saving the Protestant Ethic*, 2, 26, 27, 34, 36, 133, 162, 164. The pervasiveness of this observation only highlights the many ways the overt focus on this demographic is seen across the movement in both theory and practice.

64. Lynn, *Saving the Protestant Ethic*, 133.

This is a real blind spot for the movement. When "impact" is a governing value, it delegitimizes the lives and contributions of those who occupy social spaces that do not, according to the conventional wisdom of "impact," have as much potential. Faith and Work ends up reinforcing a culturally conditioned social hierarchy of labor. This inevitably demeans the working class.

One example of this is found in Daniel Doriani's *Work: Its Purpose, Dignity, and Transformation*. In many ways, Doriani is making an important contribution to the theology of work. He clearly rejects the sacred/secular divide that preferences Christians' work as intrinsically more valuable. Importantly, he recognizes that any particular job's value is socially conditioned in a way that devalues the contributions of many workers. He says, "The esteem and compensation given to farmers, physicians, drivers, teachers, salespeople, entertainers, carpenters, pastors, domestic laborers, and engineers rise and fall according to the social needs and economic perspectives of each era."[65] He also notes the inherent duplicity in that social esteem. For instance, even though politicians are typically held in higher regard than garbage collectors, he rightly asks: If they all "disappeared simultaneously, whom would society miss first?"[66] He then draws attention to the fact that there are jobs that don't honor the dignity of people very well, a topic we will consider in the next chapter. In his words, "Indeed, some work is so shoddy and trivial that it barely seems to matter."[67] Throughout his work, Doriani has a clear and explicit sensitivity to the plight of the working class that is commendable. He is quick to highlight ways the working class can be exploited and mistreated, and he advocates for reforms that restore humane treatment to workers in many sectors. In his reflections on the notion of calling, a topic we take up in chapter 3, he affirms the value of all manner of contributions to human systems. The idea that contributions to society, no matter how "small," are important is a fundamental notion connected to a Christian vision for calling because it creates the possibility for affirming the dignity of labor in a more expansive way.[68] A theological disposition that fosters real compassion for the working class is important to highlight.

And yet, even though Doriani recognizes and critiques the socially conditioned value of work and some of its ill effects, an emphasis on impact potential creates an argument that ultimately reinforces the structures of the social hierarchy of labor. This is partially because the logic of impact potential creates permission for comparative value judgments about labor.

65. Daniel Doriani, *Work: Its Purpose, Dignity, and Transformation* (P&R, 2019), 5.
66. Doriani, *Work*, 9.
67. Doriani, *Work*, xiv.
68. Doriani, *Work*, 109–12.

We see a good example of this in his claim that saying "'All work matters' invites the *motivational* but *imprecise* thought that stock clerks matter as much as executives."[69]

This is a comparative value judgment in action. The executive *matters more* than the stock clerk. Doriani continues later: "The saying 'All work is equal' is true from one perspective, but empty rhetoric from another. All work is equal in that a stock clerk and an executive can *please God* equally. And every honest job has equal dignity. But an executive shapes a company, and even society, in a way that a stock clerk never will, and it's ludicrous to pretend otherwise."[70]

It's curious to me that affirming the value of the executive requires demeaning the stock clerk. The comparative value judgment is a clue that the value of work is rooted in its supposed impact potential. In this sense, a job is only worthwhile insofar as it can "make a difference" and have a scalable impact on the world/others. And this connection between impact and importance is apparently so obvious that taking issue with the claim is "ludicrous." Anyone suggesting otherwise is being disingenuous to the lower-level worker because "in our zeal to motivate individual workers, we act like cheerleaders, shouting, 'Your work matters! It lasts forever, whatever you do.'"[71] Interestingly, Doriani indicates he has personal experience at both the lowest and the highest rungs of the ladder. Reflecting on his own story, he says, "I'm sure I did more good with a strong sermon for a thousand people than I did when I put olives in the most convenient spot for a low-ranking cook."[72] Not only does this compare the value of various jobs he's had; it also makes a value judgment about the importance of the "low-ranking" cook. Summing up his argument, he concludes, "Yes, all work is important, but leadership is more important."[73]

This logic is the natural result of equating labor's value with impact potential, so it's perfectly understandable that these are the claims and conclusions presented. But it is ultimately problematic because prioritizing impact potential will quickly brush aside the inherent dignity of "lesser" work and will dismiss notions about the universal value of labor as trite motivational speak. This is a glib dismissal of the value of working-class labor, and it reflects an unbecoming economic pride of place. David H. Jensen calls these dismissive arguments "as economically vain as [they are]

69. Doriani, *Work*, 9 (emphasis added).
70. Doriani, *Work*, 10.
71. Doriani, *Work*, 9.
72. Doriani, *Work*, 10.
73. Doriani, *Work*, 10.

theologically misguided."[74] Granted, the possibility of impact does invite conversation about the kind of responsibility one possesses in a particular job. But even if the language in his initial claim about an executive *mattering more* than a store clerk was an imprecise attempt to compare the work (and not the actual people), the (Freudian) slip is telling—it highlights just how easy it is to fall into the trap of demeaning workers based on the labor they perform.

Of course, there is no question that a business executive has more *power* than a grocery clerk. That power can be used, or abused, by the executive. The grocer does not have the same kind of power at their disposal. However, acknowledging a power differential between the two positions does not require us to equate power with importance. This comparison is jarring when set alongside biblical accounts. Consider the incarnation of Jesus, which Paul explicitly calls a rejection of power, or the feeding of the five thousand, where Jesus takes the "meager" offering of an "insignificant" child and multiplies it to feed the masses. Rather than disparaging the stock clerk, the biblical witness about power and the value of any given person's contribution should make us wonder and delight in them.

Doriani suggests that the idea that "all work matters" is for the purpose of motivating individual workers, as though the affirmation of the dignity of work is not actually accurate but is only useful to motivate people who have jobs that—according to his definition—don't matter as much as those of "leaders." But what if individual motivation is not the reason for claims about the universal dignity of labor? As we will see in the next chapter, it is at least equally plausible that these claims are aimed at challenging dehumanizing labor systems as they are about helping lower-rung workers bear up under the strain of their undervalued labor.

Finally, why is this even a question we are "answering"? Who is the audience and what is the motivation for this excursus on the relative meaninglessness of lower-rung jobs? What business executive is asking about whether they matter more, or less, than a stock clerk? We certainly don't live in a world where CEOs are vulnerable to substantive hits to their sense of value and worth. The argument articulated here certainly doesn't challenge any idolatrous social status quo. In fact, it provides theological credibility to the existing social hierarchy of labor, reinforcing culturally conditioned values about the importance of "the elite." I'm hard-pressed to imagine a scenario where Jesus would think that telling a stock clerk their work is less valuable

74. David H. Jensen, *Responsive Labor: A Theology of Work* (Westminster John Knox, 2006), 56.

than a CEO's is a good use of time, much less a demonstration of gospel love. Instead, in the same way theology has been used to solidify the hierarchy of men's dominance over women or White dominance over non-White people(s), it seems we find ourselves—again—using theology in service of power brokers to the defamation of the relatively power-less. The fact that this line of reasoning is even present in the book suggests Doriani is writing with the CEO as his audience and using the stock clerk as a straw man—one who, we have to assume, won't be reading the book. At least hopefully not.

This is how valuing impact potential, as the Faith and Work movement generally does, demeans the working class. It creates a situation where telling a worker that their job is important actually sets up a larger argument demonstrating that it, in fact, is not. In the end, when impact potential has too much control over our imagination related to the value of work, we can easily end up in a tedious back-and-forth. We can't sustain an assertion about the dignity of all work because our commitment to equating value and worth with impact potential leads to the ultimate disparagement of "low-level" workers.

Contrast that argument with Tim Keller's in *Every Good Endeavor*. Keller would likely affirm the importance of impact—particularly as it relates to influence and cultural renewal—and so he opens himself up to the same possibility of disregard for the working class. Yet despite that frame, Keller refuses to engage in comparative value judgments that exacerbate the divide between the power-full and the power-less: "Western societies are increasingly divided between the highly remunerated . . . and the poorly remunerated . . . , and most of us accept and perpetuate the value judgments that attach to these categories. . . . Often people who have made it into the knowledge classes show great disdain for the concierges, handymen, dry cleaners, cooks, gardeners, and others who hold service jobs. The biblical view of these matters is utterly different. Work of all kinds, whether with the hands or the mind, evidences our dignity as human beings."[75] There is a markedly different disposition guiding this way of evaluating the dignity and value of work. The evaluation begins with a theological premise that rejects comparative value judgments that solidify social hierarchies. To Keller's point, God invites something wholly other than the superficial priority of impact potential. Keller continues: "The current economic era has given us fresh impulses and new ways to stigmatize work. . . . But in Genesis we see God as a gardener, and in the New Testament we see him as a carpenter. No task is too small a vessel to hold the immense dignity of work given by God. Simple physical labor is God's work no less

75. Timothy Keller, *Every Good Endeavor: Connecting Your Work to God's Work* (Dutton, 2012), 47–48.

than the formulation of theological truth."[76] So, in the end, stocking shelves and sermonizing are good work—full stop, no need to compare.

Keller confirms our instinct that comparative judgments about the value of work based on impact potential do not hold up to biblical scrutiny and the fundamentals of Christian theology. Scripture does not commend impact as a worthy value. Even the parable of the talents (Matt. 25:14–30), a passage sometimes read as supporting a value for impact potential, is better read as an invitation to steward well the things God has entrusted to us. The master of the house does not *value* the larger contribution of the one good and faithful servant over the smaller contribution of the other good and faithful servant; instead, both servants are commended for having put what was invested in them "into play." Return on investment—even in a missional kingdom sense—is not a value affirmed by Scripture. Instead, the biblical text consistently affirms the virtue of stewardship, of planting seeds and entrusting the "return" to God.

Giving preference to the executives and the power brokers in society disregards ordinary labor. So, the Faith and Work movement has a hard time affirming the intrinsic value of work that serves a neighborhood and not an entire city. It struggles to celebrate the people who provide services that support the well-being of people but don't have an obvious career trajectory. It certainly suggests that sermons are more valuable if they are given to congregations of thousands instead of congregations of dozens. This line of thinking implies that the vast majority of people go to work in jobs that are somehow less than. When *impact* controls our determinations about the value of particular jobs, it turns out very few of us have jobs that matter. Most people are left with no option but to aspire to something "more" from their work, because almost everyone *could* be more impactful working somewhere other than where they currently work.

It also demonstrates a disregard for laborers. If we prioritize impact potential, focused on the needs of the executive, it seems hard to imagine a scenario where we would not be automatically predisposed to side with ownership when conflict arises. We will naturally trust ownership because we've been working to affirm their pride of place all along. The experience and concerns of ordinary workers are not as important, just as their work is less important. That gives too much power and permission to the owner class, and it's a position we do not find God taking anywhere in the biblical text.

Finally, judging the value of work based on so-called impact potential forces us to disregard other groups of people and their contributions to society. How can we authentically value the contribution of a stay-at-home parent

76. Keller, *Every Good Endeavor*, 49.

if their impact potential extends only as far as the number of children they are raising? What about differently abled people who do not assimilate well into existing labor structures? What about workers displaced by an uncritical embrace of AI? In each of these cases, a devotion to impact potential leaves us little choice but to demean the contributions of each, and we'll consider this in chapter 8.

The evangelical divorce from the labor question is regrettable. Evangelicals left working-class issues behind not for theological reasons but for economic and political ones. To the detriment of their neighbors, generations of conservative Christians have written off blue-collar problems and the injustices faced by the working class as ideologically suspect. At the same time, the movement—cozying up to power brokers in both business and the GOP—became enamored with economic gain and political power. Over the past two or three generations, the Faith and Work movement has dominated the evangelical discourse on work. As a hyperpersonal and devotionally driven movement, it has proven unable to address the lived experiences of workers in substantive ways. As a result, the social hierarchy of labor remains intact and fortified by theological defenses. For a theology of labor to animate a different kind of disposition toward the working class, it will have to attack the social hierarchy of labor head-on, exposing its idolatries, highlighting our theological complicities, and motivating us to try to dismantle the hierarchy wherever we find it in operation. Our shared capacity to see and celebrate the dignity of each person and the good work they do depends on it.

# 2 A JOB IS AN ASSERTION OF DIGNITY

## Labor and the *Imago Dei*

Is it any wonder that . . . status rather than the work itself becomes important? Thus the prevalence of euphemisms in work. . . . The janitor is a building engineer; the garbage man, a sanitary engineer; the man at the rendering plant, a factory mechanic; the gravedigger, a caretaker. They are not themselves ashamed of their work, but society, they feel, looks upon them as a lesser species. So they call upon a promiscuously used language to match the "respectability" of others, whose jobs may have less social worth than their own.

—Studs Terkel[1]

My grandfather was supremely proud that I was preparing to go into vocational ministry as a young adult. He liked to tell everyone who would listen that I was going to be a "preacher." I always found this strange because he was a committedly irreligious person. He limited church attendance to weddings or funerals, and that was rare as well—he didn't even go to church for his own funeral. He spoke nothing of God in day-to-day life, and I doubt he had the first clue about what church life and ministry entailed. It seems peculiar to me that someone who cared so little for "the things of God" could be so proud of a grandson preparing for a life in ministry. Why would he care so much?

1. Studs Terkel, *Working: People Talk About What They Do All Day and How They Feel About What They Do* (Pantheon, 1974), xvi–xvii.

My best guess is that he saw the job of pastor as a socially honorable profession, a respectable vocation in the social hierarchy of jobs. I think his excitement about my career path might have also been a sign of his feelings toward the perceived value of his job as a feed salesman in rural Illinois. Did he think that my path represented a "step up" in the world? I wonder whether he harbored feelings of being "less than," as someone who graduated only eighth grade and whose job didn't require advanced education to perform. I wonder whether someone had ever told him that people who preach sermons mattered more than people who sell feed to farmers.

I know I won't get answers to these questions, but it's at least plausible to assume as much. It would mirror the way our world bestows value and meaning to certain types of jobs over others. The social hierarchy of labor is powerful and ever present. But is it the only option? Hardly. Scripture offers a profound counternarrative to the social hierarchy of labor and empowers us to make bold and challenging claims about the dignity of work and of those who labor across all sectors of society.

## I Am a Man

In early 1964, Black workers in Memphis were under the thumb of exploitation. Eighty percent of the low-wage labor in the city was done by the Black community.[2] A grassroots movement developed around a sanitation-worker strike. The strike was sparked by the deaths of two workers who—in the course of their duties—were crushed by the compactor of the garbage truck they drove. Black Memphians gathered together, demanding recognition and reform of gross labor inequality, a problem that is ongoing today.

Beyond obviously dangerous industries like mining,[3] unsafe labor conditions still plague the working class, often with deadly results.[4] But conditions do not have to be deadly to wage war on workers. Poor conditions are rampant in warehouse work,[5] construction,[6] and the food-packing industry, to name just a

2. Michael Honey, in Martin Luther King Jr., *"All Labor Has Dignity"* (Beacon, 1986 and 2011), 167–68.

3. See https://www.nytimes.com/topic/subject/mining-disasters.

4. John Keilman, "Factory Workers Are Dying Because Machines Aren't Being Turned Off," *The Wall Street Journal*, October 3, 2024.

5. Max Nesterak, "Amazon Warehouse Cited for Unsafe Working Conditions—and Other Labor News," *Minnesota Reformer*, June 28, 2024, https://minnesotareformer.com/2024/06/28/amazon-warehouse-cited-for-unsafe-working-conditions-and-other-labor-news/.

6. Jennifer Rodriguez, "Worker Is Buried Alive in Construction Site Accident, Iowa Suit Says. 'Please Save Me,'" December 10, 2024, https://www.kansascity.com/news/nation-world/national/article296886644.html.

few.[7] Let us not forget that these are not distant and disconnected stories; they are case studies of current, everyday realities for many millions of workers.

The 1964 strike in Memphis was aimed at union recognition. It was a quest by the sanitation workers for protection from mistreatment and hopefully a guarantee of the basic rights and necessities that should be provided to laborers. James Lawson invited Martin Luther King Jr. to Memphis to lend support. A few weeks before his assassination, King came to the city and gave a speech at the Masonic Temple in front of fifteen thousand people.[8] In his speech, he said, "Whenever you are engaged in work that serves humanity and is for the building of humanity, it has dignity and it has worth. . . . All labor has . . . dignity."[9]

This is the most fundamental claim of this entire project. *All labor has dignity*. It is my conviction that this is not just a nicety, a motivational statement, or a sentimental platitude. It is a statement of theological fact—one that shapes nearly every idea we posit as Christians concerning labor-related issues. It is irreducibly important.

But that King *had to say* that all labor has dignity reveals another fundamental fact: We live in a world where "dirty jobs" are disrespected. He is, of course, not alone in this insight. Carl Henry observed this in 1964: "As with the gods, so with men: thinking is nobler than manual labor, according to the Greeks. Moreover, these activities differentiate two classes of men, namely the philosopher or the man of leisure, and the slave destined for the menial tasks of life. This tendency to disparage non-intellectual pursuits is already evident in Egypt as early as the time of Israel's sojourn. When the Egyptians, who disdained agricultural pursuits, discovered that the Hebrews were an agricultural people, they assigned the captives to the distant land of Goshen, where the Jews soon were in bondage."[10] In 1960s America, in ancient and biblical times, and in our modern day, society looks down on scores of jobs (and job classes). There is a labor underclass into which "undesirable" jobs and those who do them are tossed and labeled "unclean" and "undignified." The garbage collector is perhaps the perfect example of a so-called dirty job that is looked down on by many. A feed salesman might fit that description as well.

7. Kate Gibson, "Mar-Jac Poultry Plant's 'Inaction' Led to Death of Teen Pulled into Machine, Feds Say," *CBS News*, January 16, 2024.

8. Taylor Branch, *The King Years* (Simon & Schuster, 2013), 174. *The King Years* is a streamlined volume that synthesizes Branch's epic trilogy of the civil rights movement. In it, he provides a narrative that opens up the broader context of the sanitation workers strike and King's involvement.

9. King, *"All Labor Has Dignity,"* 171–72. The redaction here eliminates text that indicated audience response. King's exact words were "All labor has dignity."

10. Carl F. H. Henry, *Aspects of Christian Social Ethics* (Eerdmans, 1964), 49.

King contrasts these jobs with "so-called big jobs." He said, "You are demanding that this city will respect the dignity of labor. So often we overlook the work and the significance of those who are not in professional jobs . . . , of those who are not in so-called big jobs."[11] King speaks a prophetic corrective into society's value system. To say that all labor has dignity calls into question the social hierarchy that attaches higher value to certain jobs over others. He challenges its basic premise, pronouncing a moral judgment on the status quo. Agreeing with King requires admitting this status quo is wrong. Admitting such is not something many were, or are, willing to do.

## Work and Human Dignity

Saying that all labor has dignity is well and good, but staking a theological claim in favor of the dignity of labor is a slightly different matter. However, when we tease out King's notion and consider its theological underpinnings, we find such a statement to be not only accurate but also a theological imperative.

The dignity of labor finds its genesis in Genesis 1:26–28, where we encounter the story of God giving the original humans, Adam and Eve, their primary assignment:

> Then God said, "Let us make mankind in our image, in our likeness, so that they may rule over the fish in the sea and the birds in the sky, over the livestock and all the wild animals, and over all the creatures that move along the ground."
>
> So God created mankind in his own image,
> in the image of God he created them;
> male and female he created them.
>
> God blessed them and said to them, "Be fruitful and increase in number; fill the earth and subdue it. Rule over the fish in the sea and the birds in the sky and over every living creature that moves on the ground."

The connection between work and human dignity is animated in at least two ways by this passage. First, work is an expression of the original human vocation. In the act of creation, we encounter a God who labors. Work originates with God, who extends to humanity the complementary tasks of ruling, being fruitful, and filling and subduing the earth. This idea,

11. King, "*All Labor Has Dignity*," 171.

at the heart of so many Faith and Work themes, shapes our understanding of work's importance. Work, as an expression of God's intentions for us as humanity, is an intrinsic good. It "is not solely a means to an end."[12] Work does not have to contain *added* layers of purpose in order to be a fundamental good. If our work is a way of living out God's intentions for us, then even the most mundane tasks can find new depths of meaning. This idea stretches back to at least the sixteenth century, when Martin Luther famously said to a hypothetical milkmaid, "God even milks the cows through you."[13]

Luther is keen to emphasize that all work matters to God because it reflects God's design and glory. Work is a pre-fall reality, inextricably bound with humanness itself.[14] The capacity for and call to work is one of the ways this text informs our understanding of what it means to be human. So when Martin Luther King Jr. says that all labor has dignity insofar as it serves and builds humanity, he is in line with the claim that labor is a reflection of, and a way of making good on, this original human vocation. All labor that builds and sustains community is dignified because it takes God's words in Genesis 1 seriously. Carl Henry argued similarly: "Through his work, man thus shares the creation-purpose of God in subduing nature, whether he be a miner with dirty hands, a mechanic with greasy face, or a stenographer with stencil-smudged fingers. Work is permeated by purpose; it is intended to serve God, benefit mankind, make nature subservient to the moral program of creation."[15] In chapter 4, we will unpack the idea that we are called to work that builds and sustains community.[16]

## Inhabiting the *Imago Dei*

The other fundamental reality that Genesis 1 makes clear is that human beings are made in the image of God, the *imago Dei*. The image of God is a nuanced sense of God's creative intention unique to humanity, which differentiates us from the rest of creation. Walter Brueggemann says that a person "is the only

12. Kim Hawtrey, "The Oxford Declaration on Christian Faith and Economics," *Transformation* 7, no. 2 (April/June 1990): 3.

13. Quoted in Henry, *Aspects of Christian Social Ethics*, 43.

14. For an example of this kind of thinking see Henry, *Aspects of Christian Social Ethics*, 45–47.

15. Henry, *Aspects of Christian Social Ethics*, 48.

16. This precise phrasing was given to me by a coconspirator, Kelli Reagan Hickey, who is the coauthor, with Clemens Sedmak, of *Counting the Cost: Financial Decision-Making, Discipleship, and Christian Living* (Liturgical Press, 2023).

creature, the only part of creation, which discloses to us something about the reality of God."[17]

As such, innate human dignity based on the *imago Dei* is a basic building block of a robust theological anthropology, with wide-ranging implications. It is an essential Christian doctrine. It is essential because it is *fundamentally* true. Bearing the image of God is the *first* thing that is true about someone. The image of God is an antecedent reality to all other truths about an individual person and humanity in general. Before anything else can be said about humans, it is true that they bear God's image. Similarly, it is essential because it is *universally* applicable. Bearing the image of God is true of every human person. Irrespective of a person's station, circumstance, religious belief, or actions, they bear the image of God. There are no segments of humanity that do not bear the image of God, and there are none who bear it fundamentally more than others. It is also essential because it is indispensably *formative*. A robust sense of identity grows from a deep exploration and integration of one's *imago Dei*-ness. It is just as critical as grappling with the impact of sin, redemption, and restoration. That every person's story starts with the image of God has major implications for the way one lives day-to-day. The invitation to everyone is to inhabit this fundamental truth.

In these ways, we recognize the connection between the idea of the *imago Dei* and the dignity of every human. Many have rightly pointed out that this means that dignity cannot be taken away. If a person has innate dignity because they bear the image of God, then no one can rob that person of their dignity. It also means, as many have also said, that one cannot give dignity to another person. Dignity does not reside in someone like a balance sheet with corresponding transactions—debits and credits of value and worth depending on how a person acts or is treated. It is not possible to add to or subtract from this innate reality.

Yet even though the *imago Dei* is a matter of our identity, the fact that we are made in the image of God invites our active response. It is meant to shape the way we live in the world. The extent to which we act on, and out of, our identity is the extent to which we inhabit the image of God faithfully in the world. This impacts any discussion of labor, as Genesis 1 makes a clear connection between the *imago Dei* and work. God says, "Let us make mankind in our image, in our likeness, *so that they may rule*" (v. 26, emphasis added)—that is, God intends for us to take up God's creative vocation. In one sense, work is a primary reason humanity is created in the image of God in

17. Walter Brueggemann, *Genesis*, Interpretation: A Bible Commentary for Teaching and Preaching (John Knox, 1982), 32.

the first place. As Pope John Paul II said, "Work is a good thing for man—a good thing for his humanity—because through work man . . . becomes 'more a human being.'"[18] Work is a way we can enact our fundamental identity, a way we inhabit the image of God more fully.[19]

Because work is a primary way we inhabit the image of God, anyone who engages the labor question from a Christian perspective must take the *imago Dei* seriously. In a way that will become increasingly evident as we move forward, the *imago Dei* gives us a frame to celebrate the ways every person, irrespective of job type, gives expression to their fundamental identity through their labor. Just as Martin Luther affirmed the labor of the milkmaid—someone surely on the lower rungs of sixteenth-century society—and Martin Luther King Jr. affirmed the labor of sanitation workers in the 1960s, the connection between labor and the image of God affirms the dignity of all work. Certainly, the type and character of our work matters, but the *imago Dei* challenges the values and assumptions that undergird the social hierarchy of labor. Work enables any and every person to inhabit a fuller sense of their identity as an image bearer of God. We are not mere mirrors of God's glory; the image of God is in our bones.

The question, then, is not *whether* a person asserts their dignity when they work. Instead, we wonder about the extent to which that dignity is seen, celebrated, honored, and treated well. King's 1968 speech is a recognition of what those Memphis sanitation workers already knew to be true: Their labor had dignity because they had dignity. They were challenging the rest of society to take note and act accordingly. These were the very workers who walked the picket lines with indelibly prophetic signs declaring "*I AM A MAN!*" Those famous signs made explicit what was theologically true all along: Their labor was an assertion of their dignity. By pulling on their worker's denim each day they inhabited their identity as they stepped out into the world to serve and build humanity. King's speech simply affirmed the dignity they were asserting all along. *This means that every job is an assertion of dignity.*

The problem is, instead of being an arena of dignity, labor is too often an arena of dehumanization. Because even though dignity cannot be given or taken, it *can* be violated. Dignity can be ignored, denied, maligned, denigrated, and abused. Almost every form of injustice can be traced back to a dishonoring of the *imago Dei* in a person or people group. The mistreatment of the *imago Dei* creates a situation where one or more person(s) is living outside

18. John Paul II, *Laborem Exercens*, September 14, 1981, §9, https://www.vatican.va/content/john-paul-ii/en/encyclicals/documents/hf_jp-ii_enc_14091981_laborem-exercens.html.

19. Henry, *Aspects of Christian Social Ethics*, 51.

God's ultimate reality; it creates a situation where what is most true—what is fundamentally, universally, and formatively true—is not the animating idea. But Christians challenge those injustices by taking the *imago Dei* seriously. Instead of ignoring the image of God, we truly see it. Rather than denying and denigrating, we affirm and celebrate the image of God. Instead of abusing it, we cherish it as God does. Doing so issues the same corrective to society that King issued.

The battle between dignity and dehumanization always takes concrete form. In the case of sanitation workers in 1968, the battleground was safe and respectable working conditions, among other grievances. Today, it might be the same battle that the sanitation workers were fighting. It might also be something unconsidered in the 1960s, such as employee privacy or extreme forms of monitoring workers. No matter the issue, it seems that the battle typically circles back to the basic question of human dignity versus practices that deny the dignity that dwells in each of us. This forms the basis of most justice work—creating normative patterns of thinking and acting in alignment with human dignity at a personal, communal, and societal level. This is not an easy task, but it is an essential one, animated by fundamental, orthodox Christian beliefs.

One of the challenges we must face is that, strictly speaking, the connections we've established between the image of God and human dignity have not proven capable of engaging the labor question in a way that authentically challenges the forces of dehumanization in society. But if we lean further into our exploration of the *imago Dei*, we'll find that we have only scratched the surface of the implications of the image of God for labor and human dignity.

## A More Robust *Imago Dei*

It's my contention that our thinking related to labor and the *imago Dei* has not taken the trinitarian identity of God seriously enough. Anytime we speak of God in a truly Christian sense, we are speaking of a God we know through the persons of the Father, the Son, and the Holy Spirit. Volumes can, and have, been written about the nature and identity of God as Trinity—this isn't the place to survey that scholarship. Instead, we want to explore the ways the trinitarian identity of God might shape the way we think about the relationship between the *imago Dei* and labor.[20]

So, to begin, among the many ways we might speak of our trinitarian God, we affirm the basic idea that the three persons of the Trinity are bound together

20. For a differentiated sense of the trinitarian implications for work, see David H. Jensen, *Responsive Labor: A Theology of Work* (Westminster John Knox, 2006), 49–51.

relationally. This is perhaps best on display in the ways Jesus describes his relationship to the Father throughout the book of John. In John 10:30, Jesus says, "I and the Father are one." In John 14:11, he says, "I am in the Father and the Father is in me." Jesus describes their relationship as one of love, of shared mission, of deep knowledge of the other, of submission to the other, and of many other characteristics that give us a sense of the whole and holy relationship that exists *within* God. This way of describing God's nature, the *social Trinity*, understands God's identity through the relationships between various persons of the Trinity.

Jurgen Moltmann says, "The trinitarian Persons are not 'modes of being'; they are individual, unique, non-interchangeable subjects of the one, common divine substance, with consciousness and will. Each of the Persons possesses the divine nature in a non-interchangeable way; each presents it in his own way. . . . But since the trinitarian Persons are unique, they cannot merely be defined by their relationship to their common nature . . . [but rather must be informed by] the character of relation with respect to the other Persons."[21] This is an admittedly dense passage, but the fundamentals of a social Trinity are present. Social trinitarians highlight how the identity, role, and purpose of each person is defined by the loving relationship that person has with each other person of the Trinity. That means God is a being in communion.[22] God exists in a relationship characterized as whole, dynamic, mutual, and rooted in the flourishing of each person.[23] For God, or each person of the Trinity, to flourish, we mean that—perhaps like a seed planted in the ground—God bears the full fruit of God. There is nothing impeding or threatening God's capacity to do what God can do. Beyond that, each person of the Trinity is fully committed to each other person's capacity to do the same. We see that concern on display in the life of Jesus and the way he and the Father relate to one another. Flourishing is a state of full fruitfulness that reflects God's character and capacity.

The implications for people—created in the *imago Dei*—are immense because God includes us in that divine relationship. Just after Jesus describes the togetherness he experiences with the Father, he says, "I am in my Father, and you are in me, and I am in you" (John 14:20). Jesus reminds us that an essential part of our identity as humans is bound up in the nature of our relationships with God *and* with one another. That reality should shape the

21. Jurgen Moltmann, *The Trinity and the Kingdom* (Harper & Row, 1981), 171–72.

22. Catherine Mowry LaCugna, *God for Us: The Trinity and Christian Life* (HarperSanFrancisco, 1973), 249.

23. Moltmann, *The Trinity and the Kingdom*, 174–76.

way we think about ordering our community life and society,[24] and it should also impact our thinking about the nature of families, neighborhoods, cities, and, yes, even places of work. Catherine LaCugna argues that it is God's nature "to-be-for, to-be-toward, to exist as persons in communion," which seems a nice way to frame an organizing principle of any human community.[25] *Anytime* we exist in community, we do so *for one another*, championing one another's flourishing. We do so *toward one another*, moving deeper into relationship, even across boundaries. And we live in the world *in communion with one another*. Miroslav Volf speaks to this also, noting that because the *imago Dei* reminds us of our fundamental sociality as humans, the doctrine carries with it a sense of "responsibility to the whole human community."[26] Meghan Clark argues that any conception of the image of God "must also be *imago* trinitatis."[27] In other words, the Trinity provides a normative, or moral, model for human relationships that serves not just to critique but also to set the standard for all relationships everywhere.

## Trinitarian Implications for Labor

This way of thinking about God's nature allows us to make new claims about the way we evaluate the relationship between work and human dignity. Consider the earlier example of Martin Luther's hypothetical milkmaid. Does milking cows glorify God? Does that work allow a person to more fully inhabit the *imago Dei*? Well, in a perfect world, our emerging theology of labor and human dignity would say, "Yes!" But, of course, we do not live in a perfect world and so our answer has to be, "Maybe?" We do not yet know enough to be able to say whether this labor might give expression to—or violate—human dignity. This means we might have to answer the question, Does *this* labor have dignity? with an emphatic, "No!"

Ultimately we are forced to grapple with the question of labor and dignity in a more expansive way. We cannot answer that question for any one particular person, nor can we adequately assess the extent to which that person is flourishing and thriving outside of their relational/social/societal ecosystem. For a theology of the *imago Dei* to adequately grapple with labor, it cannot foreground the infinitely unique and creative capacity of humanity without

24. LaCugna, *God for Us*, 258.

25. LaCugna, *God for Us*, 354.

26. Miroslav Volf, *Work in the Spirit: Toward a Theology of Work* (Wipf & Stock, 2001), 147 (italics removed).

27. Meghan Clark, *The Vision of Catholic Social Thought: The Virtue of Solidarity and the Praxis of Human Rights* (Fortress, 2014), 6.

simultaneously increasing one's deep appreciation for interconnection with others.[28] Bearing the image of God *presumes* participation in a mutually beneficial system committed to the flourishing of each part. When you add this relational layer to the evaluation of specific forms of labor, it becomes easier to identify forms of work that are actually demeaning, ways work might devalue someone, and ways it falls short of the ideal as a primary means of inhabiting the *imago Dei*. So, what makes work demeaning to the *imago Dei*? I'll suggest the following three categories as a starting point for evaluation.

First, labor that disregards the relational demands of the *imago Dei* is a violation of dignity. Volf calls this violation "alienation."[29] If to be human is to be relationally connected to others, and if identity is shaped through those interconnections, then work that isolates people from those connections prevents a person from more fully inhabiting the image of God.[30] By isolation, we do not mean to say that it is always a violation of the image of God for a person to work by themselves. Instead, isolation implies a relational disregard for or the removal of a person from a supportive and collaborative system or ecosystem. We are thinking of work situations where people are left to fend for themselves because concern for their participation in a broader work community is lacking. There are, of course, countless ways to create working conditions marked by a general disregard for the relational layer of a person's humanity. Disregard for workers often increases their individual and collective vulnerability. We can imagine work where disregard extends to issues of safety, or the overt permission for violence against workers. We can also imagine ways this isolation and disregard could widen a person's exposure to exploitation because they do not have a relational support structure to protect them from such.

This is how we might begin to evaluate the relative justness of the work done by Luther's milkmaid. Is this milkmaid vulnerable to exploitation, susceptible to manipulation or oppression? If so, we have an obligation to label the work as ripe for violations of human dignity.[31] Consider this modern-day example: Hotel workers, and in particular women, are often exposed to unwanted harassment and overt acts of violence. In a 2016 survey by

28. Andy Crouch names this insight directly in *Culture Making*—though related to the idea of creativity broadly defined, not specific to labor questions. It is interesting to note the way his connection of the social implications of the *imago Dei* is applied to environmental questions. Crouch, *Culture Making: Rediscovering Our Creative Calling* (InterVarsity, 2023), 105.

29. Volf, *Work in the Spirit*, 160. He speaks to this dynamic throughout *Work in the Spirit*.

30. David Hollenbach, *The Common Good and Christian Ethics* (Cambridge University Press, 2002), 192. See also Jensen, *Responsive Labor*, 57.

31. See Esther Reed, *Good Work: Christian Ethics in the Workplace* (Baylor University Press, 2010), 7–8.

Chicago-based hotel worker union Unite Here Local 1, 49 percent of female hotel housekeepers reported "having had guest(s) answer the door naked, expose themselves, or flash them." Over 60 percent of respondents reported sexual harassment of some kind—nearly twice as many as reported workplace sexual harassment in a general survey conducted by a national women's magazine.[32] Any time a woman experiences workplace sexual harassment, it is a violation of the *imago Dei* and should be adamantly condemned by people of faith. But the fact that female hotel workers experience it at nearly double the rate of the rest of the population indicates that these women are a particularly vulnerable population of workers, suggesting that there may also be systemic issues at play that help account for these gross violations. Our more robust conception of the image of God enables us to more ably critique this disregard in a substantive way that accounts for both individual acts of violence *and* the larger systems that permit their persistence. A trinitarian conception of God can more vigorously protest the isolation of these workers by better recognizing and naming their susceptibility and exposure to exploitation and abuse.

Second, work that creates or reinforces systems of unhealthy codependency is a violation of the *imago Dei*. A trinitarian understanding of God is always cognizant of the fact that the relationships between the persons of the Trinity are mutual and exist in an ecosystem of shared flourishing. Work as an expression of the *imago Dei* should intentionally increase a person's capacity to participate in community in that mutually beneficial and interdependent way. Work should not highlight or increase a worker's codependence—unhealthy attachment to some other person or system—and thereby increase their social vulnerability. Work situations that increase systems of codependence and vulnerability are often the result of larger issues that reify systems of inequity and the exploitation of workers.

One example of this was the sharecropping system (mostly) of the American South. On the surface, sharecroppers appeared able to exercise will and agency in their farming; but in reality, sharecropping increased economic vulnerability by fostering an intentional system of economic codependence. Sharecroppers were forced to take on millstone-like debts just to survive, which further guaranteed that their work would primarily benefit their debt holders. Sharecropping made poor and working-class Black families economically dependent on an owner class of White families who often had little to no concern for the Black families' well-being.

32. Unite Here Local 1, "Hands Off Pants On: Sexual Harassment in Chicago's Hospitality Industry," July 2016, 3–4, www.handsoffpantson.org.

Today, we see huge swaths of the American labor force in working situations that highlight economic vulnerability that can trap them in perpetual poverty, unable to break free or get ahead. One example of this dynamic is caretaker arrangements in US agriculture. I have an uncle who used to live on land owned by a farmer who employed him in a kind of rent-for-labor arrangement. This kind of tenant farming is still a common practice. (In fact, these cases are not dissimilar to pastors who live in church-owned parsonages.) Not all of these arrangements are bad; in many cases they make a lot of sense and represent sound and creative financial relationships. At the same time, by directly coupling housing with in-kind labor, they also increase the economic vulnerability of people like my uncle. These arrangements likely give tenants little to no recourse in the case of a situation that turns sour. That possibility alone increases the likelihood of (even subtle) worker exploitation. (It might also suggest looking for alternatives to church parsonages.)

Third, work that fails to cultivate or highlight a sense of skill or substance fails to take the image of God seriously enough to celebrate the dignity of workers. This is the most common way the connection between work and the image of God is discussed today, and it is a critical layer to our assessments. Pope Francis argued that work should "be the setting for . . . rich personal growth, where many aspects of life enter into play: creativity, planning for the future, developing our talents, living out our values, relating to others, giving glory to God."[33] We must admit that much of the world of work does not provide that for workers. Certainly, there are jobs that are more routine than others, and jobs centered on maintaining systems could become monotonous over time. This is not exactly what we are questioning here. Instead, it calls to mind a question raised by Carl Henry about assembly-line workers and whether the tasks required for the work have the potential to honor the dignity of workers. Henry quotes Alexis de Tocqueville, who asks, "What can be expected of a man . . . who has spent twenty years of his life in making heads for pins?"[34] This is an important question precisely because it doesn't interrogate the supposed intellectual or physical capacity of the worker but instead questions the effects of particular tasks on a person created in the image of God. The question is, Does *mindless* work have ill effects on a worker who might otherwise demonstrate a fuller sense of the creative and generative image of God? Henry continues:

33. Francis, *Laudato Si*, May 24, 2015, §127, https://www.vatican.va/content/francesco/en/encyclicals/documents/papa-francesco_20150524_enciclica-laudato-si.html.

34. Henry, *Aspects of Christian Social Ethics*, 54.

> How . . . can a person sit hour after hour in a factory, turning the same screw, or stapling the same box, and maintain the dignity of personality, the sense of creatively investing his talent to the glory of God? If the assembly line necessarily degrades men into machines, and robs them of their destiny as sons of God in the world of work, then Christianity has no alternative but to condemn the assembly line. . . . If the assembly line destroys man's conviction of being a fellow-worker with God, if it dissolves his personal and spiritual well-being, then Christian social ethics must condemn it.[35]

Henry is putting his finger on one of the great challenges for any theological reflection on labor—that is, affirming the fullness of human dignity alongside the dignity of work in ways that do not subtly preference the upwardly mobile over those who labor in the types of conditions Henry decries. Henry is arguing that labor that treats a person as a cog in a machine—or "values efficiency over human creativity"—should be condemned precisely because it dehumanizes the worker.[36] This is not reserved only for the conventional notion of assembly-line factory work. The spirit of the assembly line—"stupefyingly simple actions done with monotonous regularity"—has spread to all types of workplaces in the name of efficiency and uniformity.[37] Henry invites us to ask important questions about all those types of jobs: If work is a way that a person inhabits the image of God, then should society promote and perpetuate work that reduces people to interchangeable parts? Should we celebrate work where people participate in systems of standardized production that keep them uninformed about the true ends of their labor or that fail to create space for evaluating the virtue of what is being made or consumed?[38]

This is a tension point for theological reflection on the labor question because of the ever-present temptation to demean working-class people by inviting them to aspire to work higher up the social hierarchy of labor. It is, of course, not wrong to aspire to some vocational goal. The problem lies in the tacit endorsement of a set of social values that delegitimize working-class jobs as somehow less worthy than the "so-called big jobs" King spoke about. Centering the *imago Dei* in our argument allows us to identify and call out ways that labor fails to meet the standards of human dignity without that critique inadvertently reinforcing the values of the social hierarchy of labor.

Luther's milkmaid did not live in an automated world full of continuous technological advances that rapidly remove the human element from work

35. Henry, *Aspects of Christian Social Ethics*, 57–58.
36. Jensen, *Responsive Labor*, 103.
37. Volf, *Work in the Spirit*, 39.
38. Volf, *Work in the Spirit*, 187.

long considered to be meaningful. Henry, though, put his finger on a sensitive but inevitable question: In what way does our ever-modernizing economic system and practice change the way we think about work and the way that individual jobs do or do not reflect an appreciation for human dignity? Miroslav Volf argues that this kind of "work is an assault on human *creativity* and is dehumanizing."[39] Perhaps this is why there is so much labor unrest in sectors that rely on automation, repetitive menial tasks, and assembly-line work. Perhaps this is what leads to the strong push for unionization in those same sectors, where the future of the work itself creates a diminishing confidence that one's labor will be worthy of one created in the image of God.

Ultimately, this third category returns us to the question of whether the tasks of labor are humanizing or dehumanizing.[40] Do the tasks involved turn someone into a kind of machine where the only focus is increasing efficiency and decreasing error? Does the work reflect a commitment to creativity and agency?[41] Does the work allow the worker to more fully contribute their particular gifts and skills to the world? These are important questions that allow us to examine labor questions well beyond a superficial pivot to relational considerations. Charles Eisenstein poses the problem along these lines as well: "Ever since the dawn of the industrial era, we have borne an ever-present anxiety that we will be replaced by machines. . . . To be taken over by a machine, the job one is doing must have been mechanical to begin with. As society as a whole became more mechanized, more and more jobs took on the machine's characteristics of uniformity, routine, and standardization. . . . Herein lies a much deeper source of our anxiety: not that we will be replaced by machines, but that we will *become* machines, that we will live and work like machines."[42]

Taken as a starting point, we can begin to see how a more robust appreciation for the *imago Dei* gives us new ways to evaluate whether a job affirms the dignity of a worker. In the end, we are able to more fully affirm King's idea because we must readily admit that there are a multitude of jobs that do not meet the standard set by the *imago Dei*. In such cases, we should expect a person to feel the urge to stand up and assert the dignity that is being violated by the work they are being asked to do. We do not merely invite them to see the violation of their dignity as an opportunity for further sanctification, as some have done throughout church history. Instead, while they honor God and

39. Volf, *Work in the Spirit*, 39.

40. Charles Eisenstein, *Sacred Economics: Money, Gift and Society in the Age of Transition* (North Atlantic Books, 2011), 281.

41. Volf, *Work in the Spirit*, 170.

42. Eisenstein, *Sacred Economics*, 272–73.

others, we affirm the impulse to long, and call, for a kind of work that more fully reflects the image of God they seek to inhabit in the world. A person need not know about or care at all for the doctrine of the *imago Dei* for us to affirm their desire for dignity. When they stand up to declare *I AM A MAN!*, we are able to join the chorus of that assertion of dignity.

## Jesus, Dignity, and Work

Obviously, not every important idea from the Old Testament gets borne out in practice in the New, but in many cases the social and communal implications of God's intentions for humanity do find expression in one way or another in the New Testament. So we might anticipate finding something in the New Testament narrative that affirms humanity's *imago Dei* identity in a way that disrupts some kind of first-century class system. To that end, the ministry of Jesus lends credibility to our arguments around labor and dignity by upending an existing social hierarchy of first-century Jewish society.

Arguing that Jesus's ministry actively upends a social hierarchy of labor depends on there actually being a social hierarchy to upend. And, in my view, Jewish society did affirm a social hierarchy that blended together both socioeconomic and religious elements. The most powerful people in first-century Jewish society were the chief priests, a group known as the Sadducees.[43] More than merely a job title, the chief priests operated as a kind of ruling class, particularly in Jerusalem. Theirs was an exclusive group, reserved for what the ancient historian Josephus described as "only a few males" who were "foremost in worthiness."[44] They constituted a powerful socioeconomic and political class that included some non-priestly aristocrats as well. The chief priests' way of life was governed by aristocratic norms.[45] This social class interfaced with the Roman government and held primary responsibility for managing Jewish society, which was under the thumb of Roman rule. This would not have been true of every priest in Jewish society—many of them lived and worked in relative obscurity—but for this class of chief priests, it is clear that they lived at the very top of the religious, political, and economic food chain.[46] At the very top of this chain was the high priest, a highly desired office, one appointed by political rulers—thereby solidifying the interconnection between the religious and political.[47]

43. E. P. Sanders, *Judaism: Practice and Belief 63 BCE–66 CE* (SCM, 2005), 318.
44. Quoted in Sanders, *Judaism*, 318.
45. Sanders, *Judaism*, 327–32.
46. N. T. Wright, *The New Testament and the People of God* (Fortress, 1992), 210.
47. Sanders, *Judaism*, 319–27.

Opposite the chief priestly class, then, were *the people*. As is also the case in our modern day, the poor population far outnumbered those at the top of the socioeconomic ladder. The stratified economic hierarchy consisted of (excluding the priestly class) a relatively small number of landowners at the top, a middle class (though perhaps not what we mean when we say "middle class" in the United States) made up of all manner of jobs we'd associate with blue-collar work today, and an expansive lower class who "struggled . . . to avoid being crushed between two millstones of local exploitation and foreign overlordship."[48] This economic class system was, as we've said, intertwined with religious and political dimensions. N. T. Wright argues that "the party divisions in first-century Judaism clearly reflect socio-economic divisions directly."[49]

The *people* represent everyone outside the priestly line. Membership in the priestly class was hereditary, which on its own is a confirmation of the concrete divide between priest and commoner.[50] That divide extended beyond the vocational and naturally took on concrete religious dimensions, such as differentiated access to various parts of the temple.[51] Ordinary folks, excluded from the socioeconomic-religio-political center of Jewish society, were referred to as "the people of the land."[52] Throughout Judaea and Galilee, the majority of the populace maintained a livelihood through agriculture—working either their own farms or the farms of others. And those who lived around the major seas typically made a living from fishing.[53] Either way, the name "people of the land" still fit. Notice how both of these social classes were labeled by their labor. Tying social station to specific forms of labor is a hallmark of the social hierarchy we've been describing all along. Even if the term "people of the land" was not pejorative in Jesus's day,[54] these common folks were often culturally disregarded, as evidenced by the relative lack of detail about them in the historical record.[55]

Our primary concern is noting the distinctions drawn between social classes. There were elite power brokers and *everyone else*, those who lived in response to the whims and movements of the social elites. They were divided along lines of religion, economics, and labor—different descriptors of the

48. Wright, *The New Testament and the People of God*, 169. See also Sanders, *Judaism*, 118–45.

49. Wright, *The New Testament and the People of God*, 169.

50. Sanders, *Judaism*, 49–50.

51. Sanders, *Judaism*, 70–76.

52. Wright, *The New Testament and the People of God*, 214.

53. Sanders, *Judaism*, 121.

54. Wright, *The New Testament and the People of God*, 214.

55. Sanders, *Judaism*, 48.

same line of social divide. That dividing line came to represent the identity of the two groups.

This is the world Jesus enters, announcing the kingdom of God. Reading through the Gospels, we come to see the many ways the kingdom of God challenges the status quo of society. It interrupts conventional ways and wisdom and interjects a new way, one that questions or critiques what is through the cultivation of something new. The kingdom of God has been called an "upside-down kingdom" because of this very dynamic.[56] In light of that, a good hermeneutical practice when studying the life and ministry of Jesus is to ask ourselves, *Is there something happening here that is flipping the status quo on its head?* And Jesus's calling of the disciples is representative of his intent to upend this social hierarchy.

Let's remember the story of Jesus calling the first disciples to follow him. In Matthew 4:18–22, Jesus calls his first four disciples: Peter, Andrew, James, and John, all four fishermen. Beyond these initial four, it is only Matthew (Levi) whose occupation—tax collector—is known (Mark 2:14). What we do know is that all the disciples were chosen from among the "people of the land." Yet these are the disciples who will be handed enormous authority in the nascent religious community and in the establishment of the church for the next few decades. This confounds conventional practice, as the established status quo typically conferred religious leadership on a hereditary class of socioeconomic and political elites.

It's possible to conclude that the leadership Jesus confers on the disciples is a mere "spiritual" reality. However, the same realities that governed Jewish society governed early Christian society as well. That is, both communities were organized around a religious center (Israel maintaining a kind of institutionalized theocracy, and the early church operating in a more informal manner) that was often lived out under the civic rule of a foreign power. That foreign power was generally comfortable with these communities organizing their common life together according to their religious convictions—as the mere presence of a Jewish governing class proves. The narratives of the early church in Acts reveal the same dynamics, where religious and civil concerns of the fledgling community are worked out by this new leadership structure instituted by Jesus. Indeed, Jesus calls these disciples to occupy the same social position within the Christian community as the chief priests do within the Jewish community, albeit in a more informal way. This new Christian community is forced to work out its "civil code," and in the New Testament we encounter a range of examples that deal with normative Christian expectations for not only religious but also political and economic issues.

56. D. B. Kraybill, *The Upside-Down Kingdom*, rev. ed. (Herald, 1990).

Given this, the calling of the disciples represents a disruption of the social hierarchy of labor in two major ways. First, by choosing ordinary Jews to be the leaders of this community, Jesus disrupts a social status quo where the aristocratic class maintains a sanctioned pride of place in society. Jesus's call uniquely affirms the working-class identity of the disciples. Being a "mere" fisherman is not a disqualifying feature, and Jesus honors the profession by calling those who labor in that sector to this new accompanying role. There is no distinction in Jesus's mind between "big jobs" and "dirty jobs." There is a recognition of the value of each person within the role they play in society. Rather than the socially conditioned manner in which certain forms of work reflect well or poorly on individuals, the reality of the innate human dignity of each person is on full display. In doing this, Jesus disconnects the link between labor and social location. No longer will particular roles be filled by certain social and economic classes. Instead, the disciples are examples of the great equalization movement of God's kingdom.

Second, this move redefines the spiritual significance of traditional social indicators like bloodline, wealth, or power and challenges any notion that suggests there are forms of work that are more, or less, godly. And, rather than simply transferring that power to ordinary folks at the exclusion of the aristocratic class, Jesus establishes a community where those socioeconomic indicators are not considered in the conferment of roles within the community. There is no privileged class for which spiritual leadership is reserved. Instead, there is a recognition of the equality of people within the kingdom of God.

Theologically, Peter drives this point home in 1 Peter 2:9 when he calls all the believers together "a royal priesthood." Against the backdrop of a priesthood (representing not just religious but also economic and political power) that excluded huge swaths of society, Peter is the prototypical *person of the land* challenging the status quo of the society out of which the church is born. Authority, agency, and leadership are democratized in ways previously unheard of. Going forward, the "job" of spiritual leader will be filled mostly by those who work out their livelihood in other ways. Rather than a system whereby ordinary folks support the needs of the priestly class, the church is established in a way that does not separate out the clerical class as existing *above* the ordinary class. Instead, spiritual leadership is integrated across the spectrum of labor and socioeconomic status. Notice how Jesus's actions recontour the connections between religion, labor, and economics.

As Jesus calls the disciples and upsets the status quo of society, he affirms the dignity of an entire economic class and questions what it means to be "foremost in worthiness." These initial twelve disciples represent, in more ways than one, the communal nature of the kingdom of God. In a very real way, when Jesus calls the disciples, he declares "He is a man!" to the world that does not recognize those disciples as such. They are no longer faceless "people of the land"; the calling of the disciples humanizes each individual.

In sum, when Jesus calls a cadre of disciples from the social classes most vulnerable to exploitation and oppression and bestows on them positions typically held by aristocratic elites, there is a disruption of the status quo. That disruption is best described as an affirmation of human dignity, a recognition of the *imago Dei* that dismantles an entrenched social hierarchy. A robust embrace of human dignity challenges and undermines social hierarchies wherever they are found.

## Dismantling the Hierarchy

Consideration of the triune inflections to our understanding of the image of God, and reflection on the life and ministry of Jesus, allow us to see the social hierarchy of labor for what it is: an active and ongoing violation of human dignity that must be dismantled in large and small ways. As followers of Jesus—who affirms dignity when others deny it—we Christians have a moral responsibility to refute and resist violations of dignity when we witness them.

As an example, let's return to Carl Henry's *Aspects of Christian Social Ethics*.[57] It's important to recognize the significance that Henry would even address labor questions in 1964. This would have been an unpopular topic in American evangelicalism at the time. So Henry can be applauded for taking direct aim at these critical labor issues. He addresses unfair wages, the mistreatment of workers, and the hierarchy of labor. He says, "Life's variety of callings implies *no distinction in the respective value or dignity of those engaged therein*; God's purpose in the calling is the discriminating factor and *not man's superiority or inferiority*."[58] He notes how Jesus's trade as a carpenter lends credence to the idea that manual labor is not less than other forms of labor. For Henry, the invitation to the church to pursue labor justice is not a matter of small changes; rather, it calls the entire system of labor into question.

57. Henry, *Aspects of Christian Social Ethics*, 31–72.

58. Henry, *Aspects of Christian Social Ethics*, 44. Interestingly, there are a few places where Henry seems to contradict his own argument by suggesting that working-class folks might be more spiritually empty than middle-class folks, insinuating something close to the interconnection of salvation and upward mobility. That logic would naturally predispose people to value upward mobility in a spiritual sense, looking down on those lower as potentially less spiritually mature.

Henry also nods to questions about labor at large. He seems willing to say that perhaps certain jobs *don't* allow workers to express their dignity as deeply as they could precisely because of the kind of work they are being asked to do. He says, "[The] chief target of this criticism is the assembly-line operation. Here the work seems completely stripped of all creative significance. Depersonalized monotony seems to demote him to a subhuman cog in a gigantic machine. . . . That this process raises the general standard of living by lessening production costs and bringing commodities within the purchasing power of lower income groups is hardly an adequate compensation for 'debasing' the worker."[59] Henry is willing to criticize a labor system that prevents a person from expressing the fullness of their dignity through their work. This kind of theological reflection is an example of how to question the way society assigns value to various forms of labor. Now, an overly reductionistic consideration of this question might subtly reinforce a value system that disregards the real contributions of blue-collar workers to society. Henry doesn't do this. We need the kind of sustained and wise discourse today that Henry provided in his. Christians possess, or can conceivably possess, a particular sensitivity and appreciation for the value and worth of each person when it is on display as they do their work. It is possible to develop a keener sense of how human dignity is violated in the world of work and to contribute a unique and theologically animated voice to the conversation.

And that contribution begins by—at the very least—offering what I think is the most important response to labor that violates human dignity. We can champion the notion that *God does not call people to submit to their own dehumanization, humiliation, and exploitation.* We will return to this idea in the next chapter, but for now we can state that there is no theologically defensible support for the idea that some people should just "stick it out" in situations where they are being actively demeaned, devalued, or otherwise violated. Yes, there may be a difference between perceived and real violations of dignity, and there is always need for discernment when these matters connect to the cultivation of virtues like patience and resilience. But here we are saying that in the countless ways humans fail to recognize and affirm the dignity of others, they create the conditions for abuse and exploitation that no one should have to accept as "part of God's plan."

Surely, the image of God at some level demands that people *not* submit to their own exploitation. Surely, the image of God requires one to push back against violations of their dignity and assert, "*I am a man!*" Surely, the image

59. Henry, *Aspects of Christian Social Ethics*, 53–54.

of God requires each of us individually, and all of us together, to demand more of a society that uses labor to demean and exploit others. If the *imago Dei* is a reality every person is called by God to inhabit to the fullest sense possible, then it is a terrible injustice when our systems and structures of labor prevent that from happening. Certainly, we Christians are called to love everyone, even our enemies. When that enemy is a boss or business owner, the charge is the same: Love. But loving one's enemies should not be conflated with welcoming one's own dehumanization. The sanitation workers in Memphis had it right. They asserted their dignity in a world that was living outside the *imago Dei*. They were inhabiting the image of God in a powerful way. Anyone in a similar work situation should likewise be free to assert their dignity, demanding that their humanity be taken as seriously and preciously as everyone else's. This is why asserting one's own dignity and loving one's enemies are compatible and can be practiced concurrently—because both are ways of taking the image of God in humanity seriously.

Importantly, the assertion of dignity is a call to the community that demands a response from the community. In other words, *the assertion of dignity is everyone's calling*. It is risky to assert one's dignity in a context where it is being denied or violated. To do so can jeopardize financial security, professional connections, and—tragically—even the physical safety of oneself and others. We remember, though, that no one inhabits the *imago Dei* in isolation. Instead, we do so as people in community, and so the support and, frankly, risk in asserting each one's dignity belongs to us all. In the end, the call to affirm assertions of dignity is a call to economic and relational solidarity.

## Celebrate the Dignity of All Labor

To that end, what might the people of God have to say or do in a world that fails to affirm human dignity and the dignity of labor? We ought not settle for anything less than enacting a Christian imagination for the dignity of all labor. The church should be on the front lines of the public conversation related to worker issues that impact, specifically, lower-rung workers. A finely tuned theological lens should sharpen our capacity to name violations of the *imago Dei* and give us a deeper creativity for ways of responding with substance. Christians should vigorously defend, and then celebrate, the notion that *a job is an assertion of dignity*. The dignity being asserted in the various labors of every individual, social sector, economic class, and so on should be highlighted, respected, and defended not just as a matter of Christian compassion but as a fundamental expression of basic Christian anthropology.

But do Christians do so? I think there is a strong connection between evangelical *disengagement* with labor issues and the substantive core of this question. It's my contention that, in practice—both theological and embodied—evangelicals don't adequately affirm the dignity of labor. Instead, and likely unknowingly, the dominant culture of American evangelicalism works at cross purposes with dignity. And I am increasingly convinced that it is partially rooted in the conventional ways we have come to think about the meaning of work and the question of calling. We have been ineffective, or inactive, in the work of dismantling the social hierarchy of labor in part because our vision of calling actually lends it support. In the very churches where working-class folks should be able to find meaning, purpose, and celebrations of their dignity, it appears that they do not. Instead, "contractors and plasterers, tailors and truck drivers, secretaries and domestics seem unable to identify their work in terms of 'divine calling.'"[60] This misshapen conception of calling is a problem we must address. A refreshed sense of why we work is in order. We turn to that topic now.

60. Henry, *Aspects of Christian Social Ethics*, 41 (see 40–41).

# 3 RECLAIMING CALLING

## The Privileging of Vocation

Nora Watson may have said it most succinctly. "I think most of us are looking for a calling, not a job. Most of us, like the assembly line worker, have jobs that are too small for our spirit. Jobs are not big enough for people."

—Studs Terkel[1]

Did my grandfather have a good job? Certainly, his day-to-day labor had dignity. It is hard to come away from an extended exploration of the connection between work and human dignity and say otherwise. But deciding whether any particular job is a *good* job is a slightly different question.

For many people, a good job is one that has a sense of purpose that gives work—and life—meaning. I've encountered scores of people throughout my life who experience personal angst, or even fear, rooted in an overwhelming desire for their lives to matter. Admittedly, I have worked in university settings for a large part of my career, so perhaps my experience is skewed by the fact that college students are likely to be fixated on questions of purpose and meaning. But eighteen-to-twenty-two-year-olds are not the only ones asking these questions. It is an expected human desire. It is normal to want your work to matter. It is normal to worry about whether or not it does. And it is

1. Studs Terkel, *Working: People Talk About What They Do All Day and How They Feel About What They Do* (Pantheon, 1974), xxiv.

normal to find something else to do if you determine that your current work doesn't matter as much as, or how, you want it to. The quest for meaningful work is a widespread human problem.

In this chapter, I want to problematize that problem. I think our quest to make meaning out of our work is misguided, but not irrevocably so. If we consider the issue carefully, we can find off-ramps from the path many people take on the quest for meaningful work.

For example, our commitment to human dignity and the dignity of labor challenges a foundational assumption of this widespread search for meaning. The anxious search for work that matters rests on an assumption that there is work that does *not* matter. Even taking into account, and eliminating, jobs we'd frame as a violation of human dignity, there are still scores of jobs likely to be cast aside as meaningless or unimportant—like feed salesman or stock clerk. If all work mattered in the grand scheme of things, the anxiety around meaningful work would basically be put to bed. Yet that battle rages on for countless people who wake up every day afraid that their lives won't amount to much if they do not find a way to do a job that "counts." The fact that we see this assumption playing out in the lives of countless people, and for people of faith in particular, indicates that we have a *long* way to go to free ourselves from the grip of the social hierarchy of labor.

The quest for meaning in work is often framed around the idea of calling. There are many inflections to a definition of "calling," and we will explore several along the way in this chapter. But in the most general sense, a calling is something you are *supposed* to be doing. The reason why it's so central to our exploration of labor is that calling is almost always applied to the world of work. Theologically, and in most Christian circles, calling is not simply a question of one's job; but it rarely if ever excludes it. It is that particular angle—calling applied to job/career path—that I want to focus on in this chapter.

For people who wonder whether their work matters, or who want their work to make a difference in the world, the idea that they might be called to a particular field is compelling. If I can say that I am called to a particular job or career path, the internal angst about finding work that matters resolves itself. Finding and doing the work we feel called to is a primary way we infuse our labor with meaning day-to-day. And we hear people use the language of calling related to their work all the time. Saying a job is "tailor-made" for someone is apt, giving a sense that work should *fit* well, like a custom suit. We "wear" our jobs as outward signs of inward realities and dispositions, thinking our work should say something about who we are, what we care about, and where we are going in life. That may be one reason why people seem to be so afraid of so-called *dead-end jobs*—because they are jobs that are "going nowhere," with little to no room for advancement.

Conventional wisdom suggests that if a job does those things—gives a sense of meaning and opens up a path to a better future—then it is a *good* job. That's the kind of job one finds *fulfilling*. Fulfillment is a feeling of satisfaction that pushes back against our angst and anxieties and provides a deep sense of peace. It leaves the worker feeling that their job allows them to do work that matters.

But personal fulfillment in one's work is in short supply. And this is not only a working-class crisis; it impacts everyone. Across the workforce—in service, manufacturing, corporate, and knowledge-economy spaces—millions of Americans intuit that their jobs lack meaning and purpose.[2] David Graeber theorizes that technological advancement has led to an explosion of white-collar positions that could accurately be described as "bullshit jobs," or the kind of automated, mindless widget making that the technological revolution was meant to save society from.[3] Zena Hitz, reflecting on Graeber's work, says "what is fascinating . . . is how deeply unhappy . . . workers are, people who have money and status without having to work for it. It seems that their hearts long for real work, for service, for connection with their communities."[4] The claim that such "bs" jobs matter surely sounds discordant with the everyday experience of people toiling away in so many lines of work. It is a great sadness that so many long for a sense of fulfillment from their work and yet intuit an abiding meaninglessness that robs them of any sense of purpose in their labor. That would suggest there are in fact very few *good* jobs. Given this way of describing them, I bet my grandfather would say he didn't really have a very good job.

People tend to respond to this crisis in one of two ways. Some resign themselves to work that is simply a means to an end. Miroslav Volf calls this the instrumental value of work: Work's value lies in what it does for you.[5] So, people's primary concern is the paycheck. Others adopt a kind of nomadic approach, wandering from job to job in the hope that they will find fulfillment. I fit the description of this second type well, looking for the perfect job, the right fit, under the assumption that fulfillment has been hidden from me

2. Carl F. H. Henry, *Aspects of Christian Social Ethics* (Eerdmans, 1964), 60.

3. David Graeber, "On the Phenomenon of Bullshit Jobs: A Work Rant," *Strike Magazine* 3 (August 2013), strikemag.org/bullshit-jobs/. Also see Graeber's larger work on the topic, *Bullshit Jobs: A Theory* (Simon & Schuster, 2019).

4. Zena Hitz, "What Is Time For?," *Plough*, August 16, 2023, https://www.plough.com/en/topics/life/work/what-is-time-for.

5. Miroslav Volf, *Work in the Spirit: Toward a Theology of Work* (Wipf & Stock, 2001), 197.

and that I might find it by finding the right job. I'm guessing you might find yourself in one of these two camps, and I'm quite sure you've met people who represent both of these understandable responses to the crisis of purpose and fulfillment in work.

This crisis is further evidenced by the trove of resources aimed at helping people navigate the search for purpose and fulfillment in work. A huge swath of the Faith and Work literature is dedicated to a theological perspective on this crisis. But this is not a question only for people of faith, and the response comes not only from Christians. Stanford University's Life Design Lab is just one example of how people marshal all manner of resources into the work of helping people find meaning and purpose through work. The promise of the Life Design Lab, along with its courses and resources, is that a person can engineer a worthwhile life. In other words, a good life can be charted ahead of time, and the class offers to help students do just that by giving them, as one student noted, "'permission' to dream."[6]

For many, the overwhelming attention we pay to finding work that matters has turned our lives into a quest for meaning and purpose. But I find myself wondering whether that quest is quixotic. Is the journey toward a fulfilled work life something that promotes a good life, or does it leave us tilting at windmills? What if a fixation on fulfillment is actually the reason why so many feel unfulfilled? What if work was never meant to fulfill us the way we want it to, if our jobs and our labor are unsuited to the task of relieving our angst and fear about whether our lives truly matter?

Before we start to explore these questions, I want to examine some of the ways Christians have sought to respond to the question of meaning and purpose in work. The church world has invested significant resources trying to give people vision for how work provides an abiding sense of fulfillment. Unfortunately, many of those responses have blind spots that shore up the social hierarchy of labor and leave people of faith ill-equipped to respond to labor questions in a substantive way.

## We Were Meant to Live for So Much More: Christian Responses to the Crisis of Purpose

In the early 2000s, the Christian rock band Switchfoot released an album titled *The Beautiful Letdown*. The album's opening track, "Meant to Live," captured the zeitgeist of evangelical youth culture at the time. The refrain, "We were meant to live for so much more!" perfectly encapsulates the angst

6. Stanford Life Design Lab, https://lifedesignlab.stanford.edu/dyl.

and aspiration common to the crisis of purpose we are exploring.[7] Switchfoot's contribution to our collective quest for fulfillment is a great example, and cultural artifact, of some of the ways the church responded to people's quest for meaning and purpose. In the main, Christian responses to the crisis of meaning in work can be sorted into two main categories: the discovery of calling (particularly in Christian colleges) and the possibility of mission in and through the workplace. We will explore ways these provide a meaningful contribution to the church but also reinforce the social hierarchy of labor in substantive ways.

## Calling in College

One of the first seeds of what we could call the "calling in college" movement was Programs for the Theological Exploration of Vocation (PTEV), born in 1999. Launched among a consortium of colleges and universities, PTEV aimed to develop programs across higher education to help students wrestle with major faith and vocational questions. By 2007, eighty-eight institutions participated in the initiative to the tune of over $218 million.[8] As a result, the last few decades witnessed an extraordinary rise in vocation- and calling-related work on the campuses of faith-based colleges and universities. All across the country, universities created centers, departments, and institutes to help students identify and pursue their calling and purpose in life. Discernment programs abound. Career centers are now Calling and Career Centers—further linking the concept of calling with the pursuit of career. At this point you would be hard-pressed to find a Christian college or university that does *not* use the language of vocation and calling as part of their curricular and cocurricular aims. For faith-based institutions, this is essential work. In the same way that human dignity is an essential doctrine, these institutions operate with a mindset that suggests issues of calling and

7. "Another leader observed that he primarily saw young adults gravitating toward the movement due to 'a real existential struggle' related to questions of calling and being in the right job. Questions of this sort tend to be taken up in a lifestage that only some workers in the contemporary labor market pass through: a college or post-college phase of discerning one's calling, generally at a stage that narrows relational or geographic commitment and thereby grants the worker more agency to undertake vocational discernment. These are the phases in which college ministries and 'vocational programming' guided by Faith and Work resources swoop in to provide pastoral guidance." Andrew Lynn, *Saving the Protestant Ethic: Creative Class Evangelicalism and the Crisis of Work* (Oxford University Press, 2023), 164.

8. Leslie Schwartz, "Expanded Vocational Understanding: Lilly Endowment Programs for the Theological Exploration of Vocation," *Spirituality in Higher Education Newsletter*, November 2007, 1–3.

purpose are fundamental to life, universally applicable, and indispensably formative in the development of Christian young adults. This is how a person comes to terms with their vocation.

The idea of vocation has a kind of logic to it—namely, that due to the infinite uniqueness of each person (their combination of gifts, skills, passions, and experiences), there is a particular way they can *best* spend their life. This is not necessarily to say that there is only *one* good way to orient and live one's life; rather, it is to say that there is a *best* way. This outlook is summed up well by Frederick Buechner's famous definition of vocation: God calls you to "the place where your deep gladness and the world's deep hunger meet."[9] Notice what Buechner's definition of vocation includes. First, it contains a divine appointment. Vocation is not first about a person's desires; it is about God's desires for that person. A person's vocation has serious gravitas. Second, vocation taps into a person's greatest joys. To discover your calling is to find that which is most fundamentally fulfilling to you as an individual. Third, notice how Buechner's definition suggests that one's vocation carries an inspiring and redemptive possibility. It is a source of great satisfaction, perhaps conveniently so, that somehow God designs and calls each one of us to the exact intersection of what we love and what the world's brokenness needs most. And, if we remain committed to discovering this sense of vocation, it should help us resist the pulls of social pressure, ego, and self-interest.[10]

This is an inspiring idea. Who could be against helping young people along this particular journey of discovery? In the sense that college is a time for emerging adults to expand their horizons and give shape to their values and aspirations, I can think of many worse ways of doing that. After all, if you are preparing to be a doctor, it's good to consider how you might practice your "calling" among often-forgotten populations. If you are being trained to teach, it is honorable to consider teaching in a context where you could shape the lives of kids who live in vulnerable situations. And the formative potential of programs that foreground calling and vocation can instill many meaningful values and virtues in students. Parker Palmer writes about ways the discovery of vocation teaches people how to listen, or to cultivate dispositions toward contemplation, when he writes, "Before I can tell my life what I want to do with it, I must listen to my life telling me who I am. I must listen for the truths and values at the heart of my own identity, not the standards by which I *must* live—but the standards by which I cannot help but live if I am living my own

9. Frederick Buechner, *Wishful Thinking: A Seeker's ABC* (HarperOne, 2003), 119.
10. Buechner, *Wishful Thinking*, 118.

life."[11] In Parker's view, vocation is ever present and ever speaking, waiting for the individual to learn to quiet themselves and their strivings enough to hear its voice clearly. Not unlike the still, small voice of God, vocation longs to be discovered by a person, and a person needs to discover their vocation in order to most fully understand themselves and their reasons for being.

I have engaged in programs like this—for college students in particular—in multiple contexts throughout my adult life. In fact, I direct several calling-related programs today. And, recognizing that the fullest theological expression of vocation is a very comprehensive notion, I'm a proponent of these kinds of programs for people of all ages. The issue arises, in my mind, where vocation intersects with work/career. While I have seen firsthand the ways students can be inspired, how they can gain vision for a life shaped by aspirational values, and how they can start to make decisions for their futures informed by these reflections that they encounter in vocational-discernment programs, I have also encountered a few complications and pitfalls for such programs.

First, some of the scholarly literature around this kind of programming in higher education suggests that vocation is not discovered but developed. In the common language of purpose and vocation, it is often implied that a person's calling is fixed, or set. That fixed purpose is also, strangely, somewhat difficult to find. The quest to discover one's calling is not totally unlike the idea of looking for the pot of gold at the end of the rainbow. But this is not the best way to help students cultivate a sense of purpose or vocation. Instead, people cultivate purpose through personal growth and development over time.[12] This suggests that vocation and purpose are not static ideas to discover once and then "do" forever. Instead, vocation and meaning can be cultivated throughout life, which means they might grow, shift, or even redirect over time.

These vocation-oriented programs, aimed at helping students answer questions related to meaning and purpose in their lives, can also cultivate the exact angst and anxiety they aim to resolve for students. When I put myself in their shoes, it makes sense, because if my vocation lies at the intersection of my deep gladness and the world's deepest need, then there is an unavoidable moral urgency to the discovery of my vocation. But what if I don't know what my vocation is? What if the process of discernment only muddies the waters? What if, God forbid, I get it wrong? Even as we would affirm the notion that vocation involves much more than a person's job, the intersection of "calling" and "career" is too ubiquitous to ignore or downplay. The flip side

11. Parker Palmer, *Let Your Life Speak: Listening for the Voice of Vocation* (Jossey-Bass, 2000), 4–5.

12. Anne Colby, "Purpose as a Unifying Goal for Higher Education," *Journal of College and Character* 21, no. 1 (2020): 21–29, esp. 24.

of the inspirational message of vocation is a unique kind of pressure placed on students that I find to be counterproductive.

Third, we further misguide students when we couple that discernment work with the stories of "calling" we find in the Bible—something I think the conventional wisdom in calling/vocation programs does, even if implicitly. When you line up the stories of Abraham, Moses, Samuel, David, the disciples, Paul, and many others next to one another, it is easy to come away thinking of these stories as normative. This must be how God works, so a student concerned to discover their calling looks for signs and wonders akin to what we read about in Scripture. We are going to examine the overall concept of calling in Scripture later, but for now I'll note that one major difference that seems to go unaccounted for in vocation programming is that these stories of God's calling are incredibly specific and clearly related to their intended results. These characters did not go searching for meaning and purpose. Instead, they were given very clear calls with very clear invitations to obedience. And in fact, many of these stories of calling run counter to the idea that a person's unique design *fits* right where God wants them. Many of these calls suggest just the opposite. Think about how ill-suited Moses was to his calling; only divine intervention made him successful. That might be worth exploring as we ponder the future of calling and vocation programs in higher education.

## Calling Is a Privilege, but It Shouldn't Be

There is a larger, underexplored issue that connects directly to our concerns about labor, something we might call the privileging of calling. This privileging bears heavily on our capacity to engage the labor question. So it benefits us to come to grips with the ways that "calling" may widen the gap between folks at different points on the socioeconomic spectrum. We see this at work in at least three ways within the "calling in college" movement.

First, the "calling in college" movement privileges calling because its participation is essentially restricted to those pursuing a particular form of higher education. Programs so often developed for use on college campuses necessarily exclude the vast swath of society that does not pursue higher education, as well as those who do not pursue the specific form of higher education that affords the time, space, and attention to vocation-oriented programming. If we were to describe the DNA of the colleges and universities that create and support the work of vocational discernment among the student body, we would likely find that they are primarily affluent and/or liberal arts institutions, as faith-based colleges and universities tend to be. Technical schools, community colleges, and state institutions are, on the face of it, less likely to have such programs, though campus ministry organizations engaging those campuses likely focus on these questions explicitly. "Calling in college" programs work very well in institutions that serve students who have the resources and overall stability to dedicate their time and attention to big, often abstract conversations around the nature of vocation and purpose.

It should not surprise us to learn, then, that there is a growing apprehension about the cultural embeddedness of most of these "calling in college" programs, regarding ways that "the literature on vocation, meaning, and purpose designs a narrative for a specific person: white, middle socioeconomic level, and professional class."[13] Susan L. Maros's book *Calling in Context* is an important engagement with the ways a person's social location informs and shapes their ability to engage in vocational formation. The vocational literature, birthed in middle-class (and up) contexts, is rooted in a "fundamental underlying assumption: that individuals are free to choose their vocational path. . . . This assumption establishes the relative socioeconomic privilege of the authors and their intended audience. To be able to consider one's inclinations, passions, and desires as a primary factor of vocational guidance assumes there are few economic pressures at work."[14] Maros, reflecting on Parker Palmer's aforementioned seminal book, *Let Your Life Speak*, says, "Embodied in that work is the social space Parker has as a white man with sufficient resources to make it possible for him to spend extended seasons of time waiting for the open door."[15]

In that sense, these programs are a luxury that many people cannot afford to engage in. Working-class populations who do send students to college often do so from a position of economic precarity, making efficient education not really a value but an essential condition of participation. "When the conditions are so dire, life-threatening, and oppressive, thriving may feel like nothing more than trite expressions, like 'living the American dream,' 'You can be whatever you want to be if you work hard,' or 'Follow your dreams.' These sayings only apply to those with privilege who do not have to face the threat of extinction."[16] There are plenty of examples of these programs failing to account for the particular challenges faced by working-class students and

13. Patrick B. Reyes, *The Purpose Gap: Empowering Communities of Color to Find Meaning and Thrive* (Westminster John Knox, 2021), 4.

14. Susan Maros, *Calling in Context: Social Location and Vocational Formation* (InterVarsity, 2022), 114.

15. Maros, *Calling in Context*, 114.

16. Reyes, *The Purpose Gap*, 1.

students from marginalized communities.[17] It is important to name the way the movement *tends* to frame one particular social location as normative and so fails to adequately take other life situations into account. Esther D. Reed suggests that coupling vocation and work so closely creates the conditions where "vocation rapidly becomes the domain of the middle class."[18] This blind spot excludes certain socioeconomic classes of people from meaningful participation in the discernment of vocation and the cultivation of calling.

Problematically, the movement can equate calling *with* college, meaning the jobs typically associated with "calling" are *also* jobs that require advanced degrees. Jobs that do not require postsecondary education (which includes nearly every working-class job) are the jobs people rarely, if ever, associate with calling. Even more than that, working-class jobs are often pitted against the very idea of calling, as if they were somehow settling for something less than a calling. After all, "'serious students' don't hang Sheetrock."[19] What Patrick Reyes calls "the purpose *gap*" is perhaps even a "purpose *caste system*" that, unsurprisingly, fits near perfectly atop the social hierarchy of labor. This dynamic is surely an unintentional by-product of common practice. Even in affirming the *need* for programs related to calling and vocation on college campuses, this expression of the privileging of calling invites deep reflection on the ways these programs subtly reinforce social norms related to the relative worth of jobs and the dignity of certain forms of labor.

Second, this new class system—a fusion of calling, education, and economics—ties vocation and calling to upward mobility. It centers affluent norms, and so the "calling in college" movement privileges those for whom upward mobility is a realistic aspiration. There is a convenient connection between "calling" and affluence, blurring the lines between vocation and aspiration. What someone might refer to as their calling could just as easily be an expression of that person's interests, personality, disposition, and/or ambition. There is nothing automatically immoral about pursuing your career interests or ambitions; they just aren't the same as vocation and calling. But when we blend these together, calling can serve to sanctify the pursuit of self-interest, preventing us from asking hard questions about values and priorities. It may be that we've fallen into patterns of allowing calling to cosign the uncritical pursuit of upward mobility, and in an inequitable way.

17. Reyes (*The Purpose Gap*) and Maros (*Calling in Context*) both provide a litany of case studies that demonstrate the way that calling-oriented programs fail to take the particularity of social location into account, to the detriment of non-White, non-male, non-affluent students.

18. Esther Reed, *Good Work: Christian Ethics in the Workplace* (Baylor University Press, 2010), 89.

19. Maros, *Calling in Context*, 109.

Very, very rarely have I encountered people who articulate a sense of calling to blue-collar, working-class, or manual-labor jobs. Those are the jobs a sense of calling "saves" you from. Consider the underlying message behind the above sentiment: "Serious students don't hang Sheetrock." This suggests that if you are a serious student—a student with real ambition and drive—you don't "settle" for manual labor. You set your sights *higher*. There is a not-so-subtle idea in the "calling in college" movement that draws a straight-line connection between education, the discovery of calling, and socioeconomic advancement. (To be fair, this is a promise of higher education writ large, not just one embedded in vocational programming.) Reading through Reyes's and Maros's analyses of the issues of calling and purpose programming for student populations on the social margins, it becomes clear that this idea is at play there. Even as they share case studies of students from working-class backgrounds struggling to navigate higher education, they acknowledge that education is prized because of its potential to help students escape working-class jobs.

On the one hand, this is entirely understandable. If you have the opportunity for education that might open up more doors of economic opportunity, it makes sense to pursue it. The idea that students, particularly those from economically vulnerable backgrounds, would reject the opportunity to attain more financial security is not only naive but would also be a privileged and arrogant suggestion (particularly coming from me). The individual student making the most of their educational opportunity is not at issue here. Rather, I want to demonstrate the connection between "calling in college" programs and the cultural value of upward mobility. People do not typically feel "called" to lower-income work.

The evidence for this point is somewhat circumstantial, and the factors that impact a person's sense of call are myriad, so it would be reductionistic to argue that "calling in college" programs only cosign upward mobility. But what are we to make of the fact that this conversation attracts people pursuing careers in fields that are "up and to the right"? When the language of calling, and the vision of purpose and meaning that characterize the Faith and Work movement as a whole, cosign and encourage those types of careers, it makes sense that Christians would uncritically conflate the two. As Andrew Lynn says, "For workers who approach their careers in this manner, the Faith and Work movement provides particularly good news: the work that already matters a great deal to you also matters a great deal to God."[20]

Also, what do we do with the fact that concrete upward mobility is actually incredibly rare? Stats suggest that less than 50 percent of people from the

20. Lynn, *Saving the Protestant Ethic*, 161.

bottom 20 percent of the socioeconomic spectrum ever make it to even the middle class, and only 5 percent ever make it to the top.[21] The unlikelihood of economic ascendancy should cause us to ask different questions about structural economic issues that contribute to and codify wealth gaps and overall economic inequality. Discerning a calling in college is not a guarantee of upward mobility, and, on the flip side, lack of access to vocational discernment programs is not the reason we have income inequality in our society. The social hierarchy of labor that segregates working-class communities and affluent communities from each other will not be bridged through these types of programs. Instead, we might wonder whether these programs implicitly center the lived experience of the upwardly mobile such that the "ideal" life is framed as much around wealth accumulation as it is around one's unique calling. Given that, it's worth asking whether "calling in college" programs might be a bit of a bait and switch—exacerbated by the fact that they layer big existential questions about meaning and purpose on top of real-world issues of structural economic inequality.

The overwhelming majority of people I have encountered in my life (like, nearly every single person) who articulate a sense of calling either (a) feel called to a "social good" job (something we will address later) or (b) feel called to a job we typically associate with upward mobility. That is, admittedly, anecdotal evidence, but it seems likely that my experience tracks across the world of faith-based higher education. Where does that leave people in lower-paying jobs? Are they not called? Are they ignoring God's call? Is there something about them that does not meet the standard to receive a calling? This is an expression of the dynamic that Martin Luther King Jr. was challenging in Memphis when he pointed out the difference between working-class jobs and the "so-called big jobs." There is almost no way to meaningfully dismantle the social hierarchy of labor when calling is so closely tied to upwardly mobile career paths.

We're on good ground to make these claims because, third, the "calling in college" movement encourages a protagonistic impulse in students that actively resists affirming the dignity of all labor. The protagonist of any story is the central character, the one through whose eyes we see the world, or the one around which the story revolves. The discernment of vocation and the discovery of calling is typically framed in such a way. Recall Buechner's definition of vocation being the intersection of a person's deepest joy and the world's deepest need. In his view, vocation centers each individual in a story of great redemptive possibility. The promise of vocation tells young people

21. Michael Sandel, *The Tyranny of Merit* (Picador, 2020), 23.

that the world *needs* them to show up with their unique gifts to make a unique contribution for a unique reason. That might be true in a certain sense, but framing vocation like this gives permission for each person to inhabit their life story as the hero. Reyes notes the concept of the "hero's journey," likening the discovery of purpose to something like the story of Frodo in *The Lord of the Rings*, an epic quest where the protagonist saves the world.[22] It is easy to see how easily the "calling in college" movement could put its metaphorical finger on the pulse of every student who wants their life to matter, tap into that desire, and generate momentum around the energy it creates. My experience in higher education confirms the suspicion that college students, as a group, want their lives and work to matter to such a degree that the concept of calling is a welcome solution to that inner ache.

"But what about those who are never called to some great journey by the universe or those who were left behind? What about those whose journey feels like a perpetual middle, a constant quest to overcome obstacles toward no clear end?"[23] Reyes is asking the right questions. Behind them is an acknowledgment that the natural end of much of the talk around calling and vocation is the eventual success, triumph, and victory of the hero. That's why vocation so easily centers the individual person. That's why it can so easily affirm the basic instincts of upward mobility. Every social indicator of success invites young people to turn calling into a personal challenge to make a mark, leave a legacy, and overcome every obstacle. And yet, those of us with a bit more "seasoning" realize that life is not exactly the epic quest for meaning, purpose, and impact as framed by the hero's-journey approach to vocation. Life is, frankly, much more ordinary and mundane—more about learning how to live well as a citizen of the Shire than a story of leaving kith and kin behind in order to save the world. The protagonist impulse is a notion that will resurface in the next chapter as we attempt to get much clearer on the notion of the human vocation. For now, we want to ask: Does the protagonist's impulse—the desire to live the hero's journey—actually foster more discontentment than fulfillment? Does it only increase the angst and fear around our desire to live lives of meaning and purpose? Does it further separate the haves and the have-nots in our world by celebrating shallow notions of success?

I've tried to acknowledge ways that the "calling in college" movement benefits young people at a critical juncture in their lives. But that benefit, it seems to me, fails to take a lifelong view into account. In other words, the benefits of these programs, as they are often designed, are particularly short-term

22. Reyes, *The Purpose Gap*, 33–42.
23. Reyes, *The Purpose Gap*, 33.

and narrow. They can just as easily foster discontentment, anxiety, and disappointment as they promise fulfillment. They can just as easily reinforce egocentric ways of living as they can produce citizens with concern for their neighbors. They can just as easily cosign the social hierarchy of labor to the detriment of working-class and lower-income populations. At their best, they foster a thoughtful and contemplative disposition that seeks to situate day-to-day discernment and decision-making in some larger schema (ideally the kingdom of God). At their worst, however, they can become exercises in short-sighted indulgence, foisting an expectation of personal fulfillment on one's work that it was never meant to bear.

Within calling and vocation programs, we have an opportunity to ask good and hard questions about our work and the promise and possibility of that work in the lives of our students. In other words, this is not a rejection but an invitation to consider a rejuvenation. How might the work of "calling in college" programs change were we to infuse them with these ideas? How might we create a wider breadth of opportunity, better calibrated to engage all types of young people?

## Missional Workplaces

What do you do if your work doesn't feel like a calling? What if you missed out on the chance to discern a vocation, and now you are midstream in a career that feels devoid of purpose and meaning? What if your job feels like a bs job, just the work of a paper pusher in a larger system for the production of God knows what? What if you work long hours in tough conditions solely for the purpose of making ends meet? What if the unjust systems of the world have you locked up in a workplace that exploits or abuses you? What if your work is mundane and routine—like driving sacks of feed to farmers across county lines—and you do the same thing day after day, year after year? These questions highlight the fact that much of this faith-animated vision of vocation cannot adequately respond to the lived experience of many people and communities. It cannot account for the actual work realities that most people wake up to each day. It cannot respond to the major questions brought on by industrialization, mechanization, and globalization. The language of calling is not sufficient to resist the forces of dehumanization that await workers the world over.

Still, infusing *all* work with meaning has been a central aim of Christian thought in this area for centuries. Recall Martin Luther's milkmaid, whom he assures is doing work that glorifies God. "God even milks the cows through you" is an attempt to inject meaning and purpose into work. That impulse is laudable, and it is an ultimate goal of mine in this project as well. Luther's consolation to the milkmaid is representative of the second way Christians have tended to respond to the human desire for meaning and purpose in their work—by giving individual workers a sense of spiritual mission in their work, irrespective of context or conditions, perhaps particularly in work situations apparently devoid of intrinsic meaning.

In fact, the infusion of spiritual meaning into everyday work life may be the primary contribution of the Faith and Work movement. Across the history of the movement, the primary message to every Christian worker is "God wants *you* . . . in *your job*."[24] Every Christian worker, no matter their working conditions, can see their workplace as a mission field ripe for an evangelistic harvest. The movement weaves together several themes that seek to bring the gospel to bear in the workplace. Writers emphasize the universal Christian commission to evangelize, the workplace as a sacred space where one can glorify God through their work, and work as a distinct arena whereby one can make the world a better place.[25] This is a different way to arrive at the same place: calling. If work is how we glorify God and spread the gospel, then each person is right where God wants them to be. A worker is in their position for the kingdom's sake, and faithful service to God *in that workplace* is the highest calling of that particular person. In the words of the old hymn, "Whate'er my God ordains is right."

The challenge lies in the fact that, instead of being called to a job, a person in this situation is called to spread the gospel through their job. The subtle shift in emphasis from *intrinsic meaning in* one's work to *eternal meaning through* one's work provides ways to encourage all workers, but particularly low-wage workers, in their day-to-day labor. For example, there is a significant emphasis on the kind of relationships one cultivates while on the job.[26] Carl Henry encouraged working-class folks to see that "sometimes the routine of the assembly line permits more occasional conversation with one's fellow worker than does creative work."[27] At face value, this has some merit. I, for one, would commend the notion that the workplace is a prime place where a Christian might live out, and even bear witness to, their faith and values.

But notice what else is happening in the shift to focus on relationships. It is subtly implied here that meaningful work is not universally available. There are some jobs that just don't contain the same sense of purpose. Instead

24. Henry, *Aspects of Christian Social Ethics*, 71 (emphasis original).
25. Lynn, *Saving the Protestant Ethic*, 141–43.
26. Lynn, *Saving the Protestant Ethic*, 162–63.
27. Henry, *Aspects of Christian Social Ethics*, 61.

of asking the seemingly obvious questions—Why does our theological lens prevent us from affirming the meaning and value of that job, or from directly challenging the type or conditions of that labor?—the meaning of work is relocated to interpersonal interactions.

This is the social hierarchy of labor in action. There is a higher class of workers who are blessed with work that fulfills them, work that gives expression to their innate gifts and talents. The people for whom this is true are generally also upwardly mobile. One wonders whether catering to this audience, without challenging the system that tangibly benefits them, helps the Faith and Work movement capitalize on the social and economic mobility of those ascending their various laborial ladders.[28] It is interesting to note that those who most likely resonate with the primary themes of the movement are those who already occupy positions society has already deemed valuable.

At the same time, there is a lower class of workers who do not enjoy those benefits. But even though direct vocational fulfillment is not accessible to them in their jobs, they are given the impression that they can find meaning in a personal commitment to cultivating evangelistically oriented relationships. Emphasizing "the notion that all *relationships matter* to God when all *work* may not matter" provides a kind of missional silver lining for folks who don't work the "so-called big jobs."[29] Of course, the vast majority of those for whom this is true are workers who make up labor sectors less prized in the eyes of society. These folks who are forced to find a silver lining in their labor fill low-wage, blue-collar, and service-industry jobs. Think about Henry's assembly-line worker, Doriani's stock clerk, and maybe even my feed-salesman grandfather. The regrettable end result is a theological vision for faith and work that both *commends* the aspirations of the movers and shakers and calls the more downtrodden to *contentment*. Here the hierarchy of labor is intact, buttressed by theological supports.

This should cause us to challenge some of the basic assumptions of the Faith and Work movement, because it exposes its inadequacy to deal with real-world issues faced by working- and lower-class people. Writers contributing to this movement are clearly motivated to help readers bear up under difficult circumstances; and certainly, the capacity to develop perseverance and resilience is a worthy aim. However, there is a significant difference between that aim and the inference that one ought to cultivate contentment in one's situation—even if toxic or unjust—as a way of demonstrating faithfulness to God. Too often, this view reinforces the status quo of working conditions

28. Lynn, *Saving the Protestant Ethic*, 152.
29. Lynn, *Saving the Protestant Ethic*, 164.

that dehumanize and otherwise fail to see, respect, and celebrate the fullness of human dignity. Adam Joyce says that, too often, "pious vagaries . . . were offered up as the answer to the everyday violence of economic suffering."[30] Because Faith and Work reflection on these situations—even with the best of intentions—has tended to invite the worker to look for some kind of mission-oriented silver lining in a bad work context, far too many of these threads merely try to help workers find meaning in situations that dehumanize.

Even Martin Luther is not exempt from careful examination, particularly of the unintended consequences of his ideas.[31] Positively, he seems motivated to help workers with lower social status realize a greater sense of divine importance for their labor. But, as we've seen, this sentiment is unsatisfactory for those in fundamentally bad jobs—"bullshit jobs" or jobs that debase workers—because it encourages them to accept their situations, telling themselves either "I was made for this" or "God might work through me here." What about situations where workers are being exploited or abused? Are they to submit to demeaning treatment because of this sense of divine calling? Luther himself said, "Let each one remain in his vocation, and live content with his gift."[32] It is easy to see how these sentiments could be interpreted in such a way as to "ennoble dehumanizing work in a situation where the quality of work should be improved through structural or other kinds of change."[33] Volf suggests that Luther is "*indifferent toward alienation* in work."[34] The fact that those conclusions might lead a person to think they must submit to exploitation and injustice is a major gap in this line of thinking.[35] This is the same logic used by slave masters to solidify their control over converted enslaved peoples in antebellum America, and it is the kind of thinking that leaves a hyperpersonalized view of work insufficient to deal with modern-day injustices.

Might God *work through* someone being exploited or abused in their labor? Certainly. Does God need someone to submit to their own exploitation in order to work out kingdom purposes in the world? Of course not. To suggest otherwise is to try to obscure unjust labor conditions with divine

30. Adam Joyce, "Theology for the One Percent: The Problem with the Evangelical Faith and Work Movement," *ABC Religion and Ethics*, October 21, 2019, https://www.abc.net.au/religion/theology-for-the-one-percent-the-evangelical-faith-and-work-mov/11625040.

31. See, e.g., Volf, *Work in the Spirit*, 106–9; and Dan Doriani's "The Power—and Danger—in Luther's Concept of Work," The Gospel Coalition, May 16, 2016, https://www.thegospelcoalition.org/article/the-power-and-danger-in-luthers-concept-of-work/.

32. Quoted in Volf, *Work in the Spirit*, 108.

33. Volf, *Work in the Spirit*, 108.

34. Volf, *Work in the Spirit*, 107.

35. See Doriani, "The Power—and Danger—in Luther's Concept of Work."

platitudes. Think about the story of Joseph from the book of Genesis. Could Joseph bear witness to God as a slave in Potiphar's house? Yes. And he did. Could Joseph also seek redress and new conditions? Yes. And he did. Could he assert his dignity by refusing the exploitative demands of Potiphar's wife? Yes! And he did! As we said in the previous chapter, Christian morality insists that we not affirm the notion that workers should submit to exploitative work environments; furthermore, it is never enough simply to focus on one's work relationships.

This is why we need a more capacious understanding of calling. God's call to work—to inhabit a vocation of labor that gives expression to the *imago Dei*—is not something so narrow as to be confined to one particular workplace. Certainly, we can join in the chorus of the aforementioned hymn, "Whate'er My God Ordains Is Right," without suggesting that God calls a person to cement themselves in a workplace that violates their humanity. We cannot affirm the logical implications of Luther's (and others') claims, according to which "to change one's employment is to fail to remain faithful to God's initial commandment."[36] That sense of calling is never applied to those who are actively climbing the corporate ladder. In those cases, we readily affirm God's call to move on. Equity and love demand that we apply that same sensibility to those who may not be ascending the ladder of success but who just want to wake up each day to ply their labor in work that reflects what is true of them—that their humanity is worthy of dignity and, as such, their work is dignified. In those situations, God's *call* is not something we need to tie to a specific workplace, or even a specific kind of work. In other words, "One can change jobs without coming under suspicion of unfaithfulness."[37] God calls people to labor so as to inhabit the *imago Dei*. There are many ways any particular person might do so, any number of vocational outlets for an individual human to more fully live the image of God.

Of course, this is just a brief sketch of two Faith and Work responses to the question of meaning and fulfillment in the world of work. These responses have merit within a certain range of thinking. We can also see how they demonstrate a way of thinking about work that tends to disregard working-class questions. The discourse is so thoroughly rooted in upwardly mobile, white-collar spaces that the logic behind it is ill-suited to adapt to the change in social location.

And so, we find ourselves returning to the original question that began this chapter: What makes any given job a *good* job in that existential sense?

36. Volf, *Work in the Spirit*, 108 (see 107–8).
37. Volf, *Work in the Spirit*, 116.

Is there a way to think about *good work* that can account for our more expansive commitment to the dignity of labor, one that does not ring hollow in working-class contexts? How do we think about questions of meaning, fulfillment, calling, and vocation in a way that does not privilege the already affluent and upwardly mobile? If we are willing to take a hard look at the discourse around calling and vocation, we may find a way to navigate these difficult questions.

## Flourishing, Not Fulfillment

Recalibrating our understanding of calling and vocation begins by recognizing that the quest for fulfillment in our work is misguided. The world of work is awash in the language of fulfillment, or as Miroslav Volf says, "the insatiable hunger for self-realization."[38] But human labor was never meant to bear up under the strain of the felt need for existential fulfillment. This is a stark departure from most of the discourse around calling and career, but at a theological level it is very difficult to defend that argument.

To start, there is little (to nothing) in the witness of Scripture that would suggest that fulfillment is, or ought to be, a goal of one's work. Fulfillment is, in its most basic sense, the satisfaction of longing. Seeking fulfillment is a natural and understandable response to the reality of longings common to all humanity, even if they present differently depending on the person. Human longings are symptoms of the brokenness, pain, loss, and overall absence of the good in our lives and our world. The ache for a world made right, and for everything in one's life to be right, is to be expected.

Theologically, that is an eschatological ache. It is, in my view, a reflection of our deep connection with God—even if disrupted by sin—and an intuitive, and sometimes Spirit-guided, sense that things are not as they should be. As humans, created in the image of God, we are hardwired to ache for the redemption and restoration of God in the world. This is why we *long*. Our bodies, our brains, our emotions, our psyches, know—at the most fundamental level—that the world, and our lives, should not have the brokenness and gaps they do. As humans, we *feel* the unresolved note deeply, in our souls. That is a disquieting experience. It troubles us, shakes us to our core. And it fuels a quest to fulfill those longings.

The problem here is that humans look for resolution, for fulfillment, in places that do not actually satisfy the ache. Saint Augustine's famous line from *Confessions* that "our hearts are restless until they rest in you [God]"

38. Volf, *Work in the Spirit*, 129.

is a straightforward articulation of the reality we are describing.[39] Augustine acknowledges the restlessness of heart that we all experience, the gut-level longings we all endure. And there is no place our souls can find true *rest* save for God. Resisting cliché application of this notion is not always easy, but it is important. The cosmic restorative work of God in Christ that redeems and reconciles each of us to God, to creation, to ourselves, and to one another is the only way the unresolved aches we feel will relent. Yet too often we observe humans trying to alleviate those tensions in lesser ways, ways not designed to carry that mantle. If God and God's restorative work is the only way our longings are satisfied, then putting the expectation of fulfillment on anything except God will leave our longing unfulfilled. Tragically, when we do so—particularly when we don't realize it—we come to view everything on which we have foisted the expectation of fulfillment as a disappointment. Everything leaves us wanting more than what that thing can deliver. Everything leaves us dissatisfied.

This is, concretely, why work cannot deliver on the promise of fulfillment. Work is hard, it is a struggle, it can be frustrating, it can feel futile. Studs Terkel said that "work is, by its very nature, about violence."[40] Genesis 3:17b–19 says as much, as God pronounces the implications of the fall:

> Cursed is the ground because of you;
>     through painful toil you will eat food from it
>     all the days of your life.
> It will produce thorns and thistles for you,
>     and you will eat the plants of the field.
> By the sweat of your brow
>     you will eat your food
> until you return to the ground.

Alongside the reality that work is a primary way we inhabit the image of God in the world, we must also acknowledge that sin breaks down the ideal world of work such that we experience it as something *less than*. That means there is no perfect job, no perfect workplace, no career that will satisfy our ache for fulfillment. Not in its original design, and much less in its broken state, is work suited to fulfill our longings.

And even though this idea might challenge some deeply held convictions about work, and in that sense be somewhat disappointing, I contend this

39. Augustine, *Confessions, Volume I: Books 1–8*, trans. Carolyn J.-B. Hammond, Loeb Classical Library 26 (Harvard University Press, 2014), 1.1.1.
40. Terkel, *Working*, xi.

realization is actually the path to the freedom we need to find, to the meaning that our labor *is* designed to bring us. If you've ever experienced the stress and pressure of someone's unrealistic expectations, you know firsthand how demotivating and demoralizing that can be. Inversely, when we place unrealistic expectations on our work, we are setting ourselves up for that same kind of disappointing letdown. Expecting our work to fulfill us—something it cannot do—almost guarantees we will find ourselves in one of the two positions we named at the start of this chapter: reducing work to what it provides for us or nomadically wandering from job to job in the assumption that fulfillment is simply a matter of being in the right job at the right time. Releasing that expectation—recognizing its impossibility—also releases the pressure we put on our employment to deliver existential satisfaction. Were we to orient our longings toward God (à la Augustine), it would allow us to view our work through a different frame, one it is much more suited to deliver—namely, flourishing, or our capacity to bear good fruit.

Said another way, human labor is, or should be, oriented toward the promotion of human flourishing for both the worker and the wider community. For the worker, labor should reflect the "flip side" of the dehumanizing effects of disregard, vulnerability, and the absence of creativity we discussed in the last chapter. The type and character of work would instead be a celebration of each worker's dignity and would actively resist violations of it. Using that frame as a standard provides an added way to observe opportunity for reform—continually striving to cultivate forms of work that meet the standard, that help humans become more human. For the community, human flourishing is a matter of the lived experience of individuals and communities, a way of cultivating tangible expressions of truth, goodness, and beauty that benefit society and push back against the harmful effects of sin and brokenness in the world. Work is a primary way humanity contributes to human flourishing. And contribution to human flourishing need not take on an overtly missional texture. It can have explicitly redemptive intentions, but participation in human flourishing is typically an ordinary endeavor. This is an essential idea in our recalibration of calling and vocation, but more of that in the next chapter.

Esther D. Reed argues that "too often we think of vocation as something that belongs or is given primarily to us as an individual."[41] That insight helps us see how distinguishing between personal fulfillment and human flourishing might help us resist the ego-centered protagonistic thinking we explored earlier related to the discovery of calling. Instead of vocation being a call to a

41. Reed, *Good Work*, 87–88.

hero's journey, it may just be that each of us is called to contribute toward the flourishing of some larger whole. What would change if we saw our work as a contribution to "the cumulative work of the whole human race"?[42] It may help to chasten our obsession with trying to connect the infinitely unique nature of the human person with an equally infinitely unique life journey. Instead of placing that expectation on our work, we can embrace a different perspective knowing that we do not have to blaze our own trail in the world to assert our dignity and worth. Shifting our focus from fulfillment to flourishing also exposes the way over-attention to the hero's journey normalizes and sanctions a kind of spiritual self-indulgence that often justifies blind ambition with the spiritual language of vocation. Disconnecting work from a quest for fulfillment creates space for us to acknowledge the dignity of a wider spectrum of work and more sectors of labor.

## Everyone Has a Calling—but Not Like You Think

A more pointed question is whether everyone has a unique vocation. Is everyone *called* in that sense?[43] But recalibrating our sense of vocation invites us to reconsider what we mean when we say that everyone has a calling, because we are reminded that while Scripture supports the idea that every person has a calling, it doesn't uphold the idea that calling is person specific.[44]

We noted earlier that the calling and vocation discourse can find support in the many stories of calling we find in Scripture. And for good reason, too. Scripture is rife with stories of calling, and most of the most significant characters in the biblical narrative had some demonstrative experience of calling. Adam and Eve had a particular calling. Abram experienced a direct call from God, as did Moses when he came across a bush on fire. Samuel's anointing carried a distinct vocational overtone, as did David's when Samuel discovered him while he was tending sheep in a field. The New Testament continues along similar lines: The call of the disciples, the baptism of Jesus, and the conversion and call of Paul, among many others, demonstrate a supernatural layer to the experience of calling.

Reading those stories, it is sensible to conclude that calling—in the ways we've explored in this chapter—is a normative mode of operation for God. But even though it is reasonable, I do not think it is accurate. And challenging

42. Volf, *Work in the Spirit*, 97.

43. Volf, *Work in the Spirit*, 110.

44. A very helpful overview of calling that aligns well with how I'm framing this can be found at "Calling and Vocation (Overview)," Theology of Work Project, https://www.theologyofwork.org/key-topics/vocation-overview-article/.

that misguided conclusion is essential to a more faithful conception of calling. So, I grant that stories of calling are everywhere in Scripture, but even if we have, say, one hundred stories of calling in the biblical narrative, that is but a fraction of the people whose stories are represented across the pages of Scripture.[45] It's reasonable to challenge the assumption that the comparatively miniscule number of calling narratives should be projected onto the *millions* of God's people represented across the stories of Scripture. Surely those who did not have a burning-bush experience exponentially outnumber those who did. Rather than assuming they are normative, I suggest that a more faithful read would be to take these stories of calling as aberrations from the norm. That means the overwhelming majority of God's people navigated their existence without a vision of calling and vocation as typically defined today.

That introduces some problems to the conventional logic around calling. If it's true that the overwhelming majority of people in Scripture did not have a personalized vocation, then when did personalized callings begin? Can we locate a time in history when God clearly began to reveal highly individualized vocations to people, a time when it became important to locate the intersection between our deep gladness and the world's greatest hunger? Or were the people represented in Scripture and across history simply missing out on the possibility of personal callings until the discourse on calling and vocation became widely disseminated? The self-evident answers to these questions suggest that our current conceptions of calling might not lead us down a very helpful road.

Interpreting the biblical stories of calling as normative is a direct expression of the protagonistic hermeneutic we discussed earlier. It is a straight-line way of inserting oneself into the lead role of a biblical story and inhabiting that story as if it were one's own. There are countless passages of Scripture where direct connection to the modern person may be appropriate, but that is rarely the case for these narrative texts. However, interpreting these stories of calling as aberrations to the norm opens up new possibilities for our desire to better understand our human vocation. For instance, it allows us to see stories of calling as primarily related to mission. A consistent through line of these narratives is the connection to the redemptive story that culminates in Christ and is continuing to work out through the church today. But these stories do not conform to the near-mystical way calling is framed now. God was not hiding each person's calling, asking them to discover their unique vocation. Instead, God was—in each case—calling these people to particular roles at specific times for specific reasons. And even though the calling conversation

45. See "Calling and Vocation (Overview)," Theology of Work Project, https://www.theologyofwork.org/key-topics/vocation-overview-article/.

can be unhelpfully wielded in the ministry or social-good contexts, it seems that these comparatively rare stories of calling in Scripture would more likely apply to those jobs. It's very likely that all the rest of those represented by the narrative of Scripture took up their work not on the basis of "calling" but for other, more practical reasons: talent, opportunity, family/community continuity or need, and so on. In other words, the "work" being done by the people across the biblical story is done for largely the same reasons all the work is done to make our society work today.

## The Future of Calling

Practically, we need to reconsider our approach to the discussion about, and programming related to, calling and vocation.[46] There are too many gaps in the logic and too many people excluded from its benefits to warrant an uncritical continuation. Perhaps most critically, the discourse is wedded to the social hierarchy of labor in ways that reinforce and celebrate some of its most harmful effects. Of course, there are many good elements to the conversation on calling, particularly its emphasis on contemplative discernment. However, a disposition toward contemplative discernment is more likely to produce fruitful wisdom in one's life than it is to reveal some unique conception of purpose. As appealing as it is to think that discerning one's vocation is like the unearthing of a charted course for one's life journey, it is more appropriate to think of calling and discernment as the development of a vocational compass. That is, we are more likely to err when we chart out a specific course of action toward a specific end than if we learn to discern next steps across every arena of life in directions that align with our values and those of God's kingdom. It seems to me that a person committed to that approach to daily decision-making is likely free to pursue whatever job or career they want based on their talents, personality, interests, and opportunities. And you do not need to pursue a college degree or a career requiring one to reap the rewards of that conception of calling.

Calling and vocation need not be as infinitely unique as each human to still carry serious importance for us today. On the contrary, the vocation we are called to as humans is essential to God's intentions for our world, communities, neighborhoods, and families. The next chapter explores what I contend is the core human vocation: the calling of God on each of our lives that is not hidden from us and has significant bearing on the type and character of the work we do.

46. One recent and compelling contribution to this discussion is *Called Beyond Our Selves: Vocation and the Common Good* (Oxford University Press, 2024), edited by Erin VanLaningham. I commend this text for a wider exploration and as a bridge between the concepts presented in chaps. 3 and 4 here.

# 4 CALLING IN COMMON

## How the Common Good Gives Work Meaning

Learning is work. Caring for children is work. Community action is work. Once we accept the concept of work as something meaningful—not just as the source of a buck—you don't have to worry about finding enough jobs.

—Studs Terkel[1]

My grandfather would have laughed at the suggestion that being a feed salesman was a calling. He was good at his job, proud of his work ethic, and respected by those around him. But the notion that, of all the infinitely unique people in the world, his job was also uniquely "prepared in advance for him to do," and that such a calling provided his work with a compelling sense of purpose, would not be an intellectually serious argument. It would have seemed a little pie in the sky for him to consider his work in such a way. Traveling feed sales isn't the type of work you'd point to when wanting to make a larger point about how labor and purpose intersect. There was no way that he could have applied that logic to his own life in a substantive way, no way for him to discern a personalized sense of calling. And if a vision for

1. Studs Terkel, *Working: People Talk About What They Do All Day and How They Feel About What They Do* (Pantheon, 1974), xxiii.

a particularly personal conception of calling falls apart for one person, it necessarily falls apart for every person.

So we need another way to understand the human vocation. In particular, we need to find a way to think about deep questions of meaning and purpose—in the world of work—that does not exclude massive swaths of the population. If vocation isn't unique to each person, how should we think about questions of calling and of what makes any particular job *good*? What might we say we *are* called to? In the world of work, we hold our callings in common because every person's calling is the same as any other person's—namely, fostering a community of interdependence between parts for the sake of the flourishing of the whole. In other words, our calling is the common good.

Eric Mount argues that "for work to be a vocation, it must contribute to the common good. Striving for private gain and corporate success is not enough."[2] Instead, "the good of others must be a goal toward which I am consciously striving."[3] Remembering our earlier discussion of Martin Luther King Jr., work that befits the dignity of the human person is work that serves and builds humanity. That is another way of saying that the point of work is contribution to the common good. It also nods to the reciprocal relationship between individual parts and the whole, because the dignity of specific forms of work is magnified by its contribution to the whole society. This is also how human bodies function, and it serves as a metaphor for the way the apostle Paul envisions communities working, where "parts should have equal concern for each other. If one part suffers, every part suffers with it; if one part is honored, every part rejoices with it" (1 Cor. 12:25–26). Individual parts work to help the whole flourish—and in so doing, they find health and wholeness. Interestingly, Paul notes that this vision for the interconnectedness of the body is the antidote to individual parts of the body thinking they are more or less valuable than other parts, which means that embracing a vision for the common good will help us resist the social hierarchies all around us.

This shifts our discussion of work toward its more fundamental origins, rooted in the creation mandate. The original human vocation was a call to co-creation, stewardship, and cultivation of God's creative work, a tending to the world as it came into its own fullness that required all manner of human contributions to sustain and strengthen. And while God's redemptive mission impacts every arena of life such that we cannot disconnect God's mission from

2. Eric Mount Jr., *Covenant, Community, and the Common Good: An Interpretation of Christian Ethics* (Pilgrim, 1999), 82.

3. Miroslav Volf, *Work in the Spirit: Toward a Theology of Work* (Wipf & Stock, 2001), 191.

the arena of work, some recalibrating seems to be needed, because work is an expression of our *human*, not exclusively *Christian*, vocation.

When work is too narrowly framed, Christians can co-opt the arena of work as something distinctly, or more fully, ours. But Christians are not a privileged class of workers. We are not made more in the image of God than others, so while we have a unique sense of mission as part of the body of Christ, we do not have a differentiated way of participating in the creation mandate. Instead, work is a space for every person to flourish and for each one to make a contribution to the flourishing of every other, because "work, in itself . . . is the way that we serve our communities."[4] If the work we do allows us to do that, we are right to call it good work. This is why we cannot abide comparative value judgments about the relative importance and value of different types of work. Those claims are rooted in culturally conditioned values. The same way individual parts of a body flourish when the whole body flourishes, any job can be called a "good job" when it serves the common good.

## What Is the Common Good?

If that's the case, it's important to know what we mean when we say "common good," which is no easy task. "Common good" is one of those phrases or ideas that gets tossed around a lot; it is a notion in danger of meaning anything anyone wants it to mean. Still, despite its wide use, it is a wonderfully rich idea worth our time to explore and grapple with its implications for our conversation around labor.

Even though the concept is employed in the service of many arenas outside theology, I want to commend the common good as primarily a theological concept. For instance, the common good is a natural fit in political spaces, where questions about the nature of civic life abound. But political leaders often depend on theological ideas to explain their understanding of the common good. Former Secretary of Labor Robert Reich leans on Saint John Chrysostom's view of the common good, where Chrysostom says, "This is the rule of most perfect Christianity, its most exact definition, its highest point, namely, the seeking of the common good. . . . For nothing can so make a person an imitator of Christ as caring for his neighbors."[5] This is an indication that the concept of the common good begs for a deep theological

4. Zena Hitz, "What Is Time For?," *Plough*, August 16, 2023, https://www.plough.com/en/topics/life/work/what-is-time-for.

5. Quoted in Robert Reich, *The Common Good* (Vintage, 2018), 40.

rootedness that enlivens our imagination for the possibilities of communities and provides a way of evaluating the character of society.

As a formal idea within church teaching, the common good came into view in the late nineteenth century.[6] Informally, it stretches back through the entirety of church history. The concept is engaged by some of the most significant theologians over time, including Augustine, Thomas Aquinas, and Ignatius Loyola, who "saw the common good as the good of the whole of humanity, extending to the ends of the earth."[7] Yet within the broad evangelical Protestant tradition, the common good is an underdeveloped idea. As we turn to consider a set of defining characteristics, we do so informed by the wider Christian tradition, with the aim of setting up a more robust understanding of the aims of good work.

We begin with the end in mind because the common good longs for a fully flourishing society. In short, the common good imagines a world where people have what they need to flourish, where everyone belongs and everyone is included in a broad sense of society-wide thriving. The Catholic Church teaches that the common good is the entire point of organized societies[8] and broadly defines it as "the sum total of social conditions which allow people, either as groups or as individuals, to reach their fulfillment more fully and more easily."[9] There is a kind of complexity to the common good because it is not one thing but a collection of things creating situations where everything people need to thrive is present.

And even though this makes the common good difficult to define neatly, it is clear that the common good is a dynamic balance between individual and communal flourishing.[10] To speak of the common good is to take notions of human dignity to their logical conclusions—that is, when communities

6. The term first appeared in Leo XIII's *Libertas*, June 20, 1888. See Dennis P. McCann, "The Common Good in Catholic Social Teaching: A Case Study in Modernization," in *In Search of the Common Good*, ed. Dennis P. McCann and Patrick D. Miller (T&T Clark, 2005), 122.

7. David Hollenbach, SJ, *The Common Good and Christian Ethics* (Cambridge University Press, 2002), 5–6.

8. McCann, "The Common Good in Catholic Social Teaching," 131.

9. *Catechism of the Catholic Church*, 2nd ed. (Libreria Editrice Vaticana, 1997), para. 1906, quoting Second Vatican Council, *Gaudium et Spes*, Pastoral Constitution on the Church in the Modern World, December 7, 1965, para. 26, https://www.vatican.va/content/catechism/en/part_three/section_one/chapter_two/article_2/ii_the_common_good.html. (Note: Fulfillment in this sense is not referring to the existential fulfillment I discussed in the previous chapter. Rather, this seems to be equating fulfillment with potential.)

10. McCann, "The Common Good in Catholic Social Teaching," 122, quoting *Gaudium et Spes*, para. 26, 65; Hollenbach, *The Common Good and Christian Ethics*, 189; and Pontifical Council for Justice and Peace, *Compendium of the Social Doctrine of the Church* (Libreria Editrice Vaticana, 2004), 73, para. 165.

of people who bear the *imago Dei* come together to form shared ways of life, the principle of dignity and respect must guide the norms of that life together.[11] David Hollenbach captures the dynamic this way: "Any good of a person that is a real good, therefore, is embedded in the good of the community. Conversely, any common good that is a real good is simultaneously the good of persons."[12] In other words, for something to be truly good for an individual, it must have the potential to increase goodness for the entire community, and vice versa.

To that end, we could say that the common good is a family matter. It is fundamentally relational and views individual people as a part of larger collectives, whether that be nuclear families, neighborhoods, cities, nations, or even the global population.[13] The implication here is that the common good is a shared (common) reality and is not something one can experience in isolation from others.[14] We are reminded of Paul's words according to which, as members of a body, we know that we exist not in isolation but as parts of a dynamic, interdependent network, parts that together make up a larger, hopefully healthy, whole.[15]

If the common good is a family matter, that means the common good involves everyone. This highlights one of the more significant emphases of the Catholic social tradition: the idea of contributive justice. Contributive justice suggests that because each person—irrespective of class, creed, race, gender, and so on—bears the image of God and carries the capacity for contribution, the participation of all members of a community in that community is, in fact, a matter of justice.[16] Contributive justice means that everyone gets to play, and getting to play is one way we realize what it means to be human. Michael Sandel says, "Contributive justice . . . is not neutral about human flourishing or the best way to live. . . . Theories of contributive justice teach us that we are most fully human when we contribute to the common good and earn the esteem of our fellow citizens for the contributions we make."[17] A community marked by contributive justice is one where no one is left out,

11. Pontifical Council for Justice and Peace, *Compendium*, 72, para. 164.

12. Hollenbach, *The Common Good and Christian Ethics*, 79.

13. Benedict XVI, *Caritas in Veritate*, June 29, 2009, §7, https://www.vatican.va/content/benedict-xvi/en/encyclicals/documents/hf_ben-xvi_enc_20090629_caritas-in-veritate.html.

14. McCann and Miller, *In Search of the Common Good*, 2.

15. Hollenbach, *The Common Good and Christian Ethics*, 181.

16. United States Conference of Catholic Bishops, "Economic Justice for All: Pastoral Letter on Catholic Social Teaching and the U.S. Economy" (November 1986), 77, https://www.usccb.org/resources/economic_justice_for_all_1.pdf. See also Mount, *Covenant, Community, and the Common Good*, 43; and Kim Hawtrey, "The Oxford Declaration on Christian Faith and Economics," *Transformation* 7, no. 2 (April/June 1990): 4.

17. Michael Sandel, *The Tyranny of Merit* (Picador, 2020), 212.

where everyone is invited to give their contribution. Taken further, to exclude the contributions of any one person is to harm both that individual—robbing them of the opportunity to share their gifts and talents with others—and the community, which is robbed of the gift of that individual's contribution.[18] David Hollenbach goes so far as to say, "This good is truly common *only* when all members of society *jointly* create a common life *together*."[19]

The other side of the contributive-justice coin is distributive justice, which means that the common good includes everyone. The common good recognizes "we're all in it together."[20] Just as the common good cannot be pursued or even partially realized without everyone's participation, we cannot call it the common good unless we are looking out for everyone,[21] particularly those who live on the social margins and experience the most significant threats to their flourishing. Because the common good is committed to the needs of *all* of its members,[22] it must take special care to ensure the flourishing of the vulnerable as they face the compounded dangers of deprivation and exploitation by the powerful.[23] Social ethicist Clemens Sedmak makes the point strongly, arguing that "it is contrary to the idea of the common good to leave behind or write off even a single person."[24] That means there is a difference between the common good and the greater good. The common good is not satisfied with providing a flourishing society for the greatest number of people. If flourishing is not possible for everyone, it is not possible for anyone. We have a responsibility to others outside of ourselves and those closest to us.[25] Pope Benedict XVI taught this in *Caritas in Veritate*, saying, "The more we strive to secure a common good corresponding to the real needs of our neighbours, the more effectively we love them."[26] In that sense, the common good establishes a high ethical bar for communities. It calls for the highest good for everyone, individually and together. Note that we did not say "the

18. Pontifical Council for Justice and Peace, *Compendium*, 73, para. 167.

19. Hollenbach, *The Common Good and Christian Ethics*, 71 (emphasis added).

20. Reich, *The Common Good*, 18.

21. John XXIII, *Pacem in Terris*, April 11, 1963, §56, https://www.vatican.va/content/john-xxiii/en/encyclicals/documents/hf_j-xxiii_enc_11041963_pacem.html.

22. Pontifical Council for Justice and Peace, *Compendium*, 74, para. 167.

23. "We face a choice between pursuing the good of social participation for all or accepting the evil that occurs when the strong dominate the weak or the privileged try to wall themselves off from the vulnerable." Hollenbach, *The Common Good and Christian Ethics*, 77.

24. Clemens Sedmak, *Enacting Catholic Social Tradition: The Deep Practice of Human Dignity* (Orbis Books, 2022), 70.

25. Reich, *The Common Good*, 32; and Patrick D. Miller, "'That It May Go Well with You': The Commandments and the Common Good," in McCann and Miller, *In Search of the Common Good*, 20–21.

26. Benedict XVI, *Caritas in Veritate*, §7.

highest *possible* good," as though the notion were being content with doing the best we can for people. Instead, the common good pushes the boundaries of what is possible and suggests that there is a moral standard—a "social and community dimension of the moral good"[27]—beyond what may be realizable.

That makes the common good more aspirational than achievable.[28] Theologically speaking, the common good is something we trust will come to fruition once and for all in the new heavens and the new earth. And yet, even though we place hope in that "someday," we press on toward its ends in the present day.[29] To pursue it is to exist in an ongoing state of aspiration, for the standard is too high, the bar too far beyond our reach. We seek the common good even as we fail to realize it fully. We may catch glimpses of the common good, we may foster expressions of it, we may note short bursts of society nurturing the flourishing of every neighbor, but the moral demands of the common good are simply too high to achieve through human will and effort.

Coming to terms with the fact that we can never fully realize the common good could discourage and dissuade us from action. Thankfully, though, the high moral standard of the common good is an eschatological vision. Eschatology has a long association with the study of the end times, but it is more than just that. Eschatology does engage the "future," but in a more nuanced way than dealing in mere predictions. Instead, thoughtful eschatology is often concerned with the way God's future shapes the present. Scholars have found many ways to try to describe this, but in general the Scriptures we refer to as eschatological are those that convey a future vision meant to "break into" the status quo of the current day. That interruption is meant to shake up the way of life of those who hear, to shine a light on sin and injustice, and to invite or demand repentance and faithful response. Eschatological visions tend to balance the demands for justice with a picture of a future where things have been made good and right. That hope-filled future serves to animate the imaginations and inform the actions of the hearers in their present. To say that the common good is eschatological is to say that a vision of the common good similarly animates our imaginations and informs our actions day-to-day. The common good is a vision for a moral way other than the status quo of our society. To advocate or act for the common good is to work for the things "God wills for the world."[30] It is "the ultimate telos of society."[31] God has given us the common good both "as goal and as gift," a vision of something

27. Pontifical Council for Justice and Peace, *Compendium*, 73, para. 164.
28. McCann, "The Common Good in Catholic Social Teaching," 142.
29. McCann, "The Common Good in Catholic Social Teaching," 143–45.
30. Walter Brueggemann, *Journey to the Common Good* (Westminster John Knox, 2021), ix.
31. McCann, "The Common Good in Catholic Social Teaching," 139.

we pursue and in which we delight and take hope, something that "is not simply *achieved*; it is both *sought* and *received*."[32]

Given that, it is clear that the common good is meant not to de-motivate our active engagement, but rather to deepen our resolve and active commitment to it. The eschatological vision of the common good is not passive but active. We are called to "work in active anticipation of the eschatological transformation of the world."[33] It is not static; it is simultaneously an end and the means to that end. In some ways, this entire book is an expression of this idea, but the wider tradition has much to say about the common good as both the end and means of the church in the world.[34]

The common good is an important notion in many religious and philosophical traditions. The ancient Hebrew concept of *shalom* is a striking example of this.[35] The philosophical tradition is deeply shaped by notions of the common good and its connection with the idea of "the good life." Aristotle's "entire understanding of morality was built upon this conviction that a good life is one devoted to pursuit of good purposes or ends. One of Aristotle's most significant conclusions was that a good life is oriented to goods shared with others—the common good of the larger society of which one is a part."[36] There is a similar resonance in what Indigenous peoples call the "harmony way."[37] Many Indigenous communities emphasize the interrelated nature of communities (including ties to the land) and highlight the way *harmony* between all those parts is an aspiration, a sign of health and healing.[38] Randy Woodley says that "the harmony way, is the Creator's original instruction for the way in which all societies should be ordered, and for how all life on this planet should be lived."[39] Miroslav Volf ties these threads together, saying that "human work, properly understood theologically, is related to the goal of all history, which will bring God, human beings, and the nonhuman creation

32. Jacqueline Lapsley, "Introduction," in McCann and Miller, *In Search of the Common Good*, 13; and Miller, "'That It May Go Well with You,'" 21.

33. Volf, *Work in the Spirit*, 123.

34. For examples of this in the official encyclical teachings of the Catholic Church, see Benedict XVI, *Caritas in Veritate*, §7; Leo XIII, *Rerum Novarum*, May 15, 1891, §51, http://www.vatican.va/content/leo-xiii/en/encyclicals/documents/hf_l-xiii_enc_15051891_rerum-novarum.html; and John XXIII, *Pacem in Terris*, §56.

35. I've written about shalom extensively in other places. See *Becoming a Just Church: Cultivating Communities of God's Shalom* (IVP Books, 2019); and, with José Humphreys III, *Ecosystems of Jubilee: Economic Ethics for the Neighborhood* (Zondervan, 2023) for more in-depth treatment.

36. Hollenbach, *The Common Good and Christian Ethics*, 3.

37. Randy Woodley, *Shalom and the Community of Creation* (Eerdmans, 2012), 18.

38. Woodley, *Shalom and the Community of Creation*, 67–93.

39. Woodley, *Shalom and the Community of Creation*, 18–19.

into 'shalomic' harmony."[40] The point here is that if, as you've been reading, you've resonated with the idea of the common good—perhaps thinking it is common sense—that's a good thing! Countless societies across time and space have had a deep and innate sense of the common good as a moral standard shared by the community. The common good is ancient, future, and always in our bones, and the DNA of our humanity is shaped by both the moral demands and the imaginative possibilities of the common good.

## A Scriptural Case for Common-Good Calling

Our calling is the common good. It provides substance and guidance for those navigating the waters of discernment. It shapes our views on what constitutes a good job and what makes for a meaningful life. And it is a thoroughly biblical notion. Let's return to Genesis 1:26–28:

> Then God said, "Let us make mankind in our image, in our likeness, so that they may rule over the fish in the sea and the birds in the sky, over the livestock and all the wild animals, and over all the creatures that move along the ground."
>
> So God created mankind in his own image,
> in the image of God he created them;
> male and female he created them.
>
> God blessed them and said to them, "Be fruitful and increase in number; fill the earth and subdue it. Rule over the fish in the sea and the birds in the sky and over every living creature that moves on the ground."

Our common calling is rooted in this Genesis passage. Our identity as the *imago Dei* and our vocation of building and sustaining community intersect here. Walter Brueggemann argued that "the image of God in the human person is a mandate of power and responsibility."[41] That combination of power and responsibility forms the basis of our shared calling. God invites Adam and Eve, and by extension all who come after them, to embrace the responsibility of a divinely orchestrated process of co-creation, of tending to the creation that has been entrusted to them. There is a telos to this tending, an end goal, one that Brueggemann describes as "securing the well-being of every other creation and bringing the promise of each to

40. Volf, *Work in the Spirit*, 85.
41. Brueggemann, *Genesis*, 32.

full fruition."[42] This is a good articulation of the common good. It is the goal of our engagement in the world and the normative guide that shapes the character of each individual act and actor.

Bringing "the promise of each to full fruition" implies that each part of creation has something to contribute that must be both protected and promoted for the benefit of all. Only when each part has realized and contributed its full promise can the whole most fully flourish. In this way, the human vocation is a mandate to cultivate the conditions for widespread flourishing and to amplify the unique potential of every corner of creation. Cultivating and ensuring the flourishing of each corner of creation is how human beings work to build and sustain community.

This way of describing the human vocation is mirrored in John's vision of the new heavens and the new earth in Revelation 21. The chapter as a whole is a sweeping and stunning vision of God bringing the fullness of the kingdom to bear across the cosmos. This is the culmination of the salvation story of Christ, where he is seated on the throne making everything new, doing away with all the evil, injustice, sin, and death of the world. John's revelation provides us a portrait of the new Jerusalem bedecked with jewels, splendor, and the full glory of God. However, near the end of this vision, John provides a small detail that is significant for our discussion. In verses 22–26 he writes, "I did not see a temple in the city, because the Lord God Almighty and the Lamb are its temple. The city does not need the sun or the moon to shine on it, for the glory of God gives it light, and the Lamb is its lamp. The nations will walk by its light, and the kings of the earth will bring their splendor into it. On no day will its gates ever be shut, for there will be no night there. The glory and honor of the nations will be brought into it."

Notice that amid the rich imagery of God's new Jerusalem, John mentions the splendor, glory, and honor of kings and nations. Connected to the very technical description of the city of God, complete with dimensions and descriptions of the building materials themselves, it is reasonable to assume that the splendor, glory, and honor of the kings and nations of the earth are not metaphors but are, most likely, concrete objects—meaning that the kings of the earth will contribute to the building of the eternal city of God. Volf says that human work is given special meaning in the eschatological vision of Scripture because "the results of work [are] 'building materials' in the glorified world."[43] This suggests that the creative vocation of humanity is not restricted to life on earth in this age. Rather, it is an inextricable part of our humanity,

42. Brueggemann, *Genesis*, 32.
43. Volf, *Work in the Spirit*, 96.

one that will extend into eternity. Contribution to the creative efforts of God is not a spiritual idea alone; it involves the works of our human hands, which gives work a sense of "ultimate significance."[44]

In *Culture Making*, Andy Crouch treats this idea in greater detail, emphasizing what he calls the "cultural goods" of the kings of the earth. He writes, "The new Jerusalem will be . . . a place suffused with culture, a place where culture has reached its full flourishing."[45] There is no indication that the splendor, glory, and honor of kings and nations is a notion reserved for overtly artistic works, either. The context of this passage implies that the material and capacity for the ongoing process of building up the holy city, and for all of life in the holy city ever after, is included in what John names as the contribution of the kings and nations of the earth.[46] The eternal city will not just be beautiful; it will also be built. It will include the contributions of artists and the building trades. The full scope of human labor will be employed to sustain life in the new Jerusalem, and so we see that the narrative thread of Scripture begins and ends with humanity's vocation on display.

Interestingly, the vocation of building and sustaining community shows up throughout the biblical narrative in ways that support our overall thesis about the ends of human work. In Jeremiah 29:4–7, the prophet conveys a message to the people of God, in exile in Babylon: "This is what the LORD Almighty, the God of Israel, says to all those I carried into exile from Jerusalem to Babylon: 'Build houses and settle down; plant gardens and eat what they produce. Marry and have sons and daughters; find wives for your sons and give your daughters in marriage, so that they too may have sons and daughters. Increase in number there; do not decrease. Also, seek the peace and prosperity of the city to which I have carried you into exile. Pray to the LORD for it, because if it prospers, you too will prosper.'" It stands to reason that the people of Israel, displaced from their home—which they saw as the place God carved out for them to be the people of God—would have experienced serious cognitive dissonance trying to understand the meaning and purpose of day-to-day life in Babylon. They were likely thinking, "Everything has changed. We aren't where we are supposed to be. What do we do now?" But through Jeremiah, God reminds the people that their essential vocation is unchanged.

In this text, we get one of the most straightforward articulations in all of Scripture of the call to build and sustain community toward the flourishing of the whole. We hear echoes of Genesis in the call to build houses and plant

44. Volf, *Work in the Spirit*, 94 (see 94–95).

45. Andy Crouch, *Culture Making: Rediscovering Our Creative Calling* (InterVarsity, 2023), 168; for his wider discussion see 166–71.

46. Crouch, *Culture Making*, 170–71.

gardens, the charge to have children and raise them across generations. And we see clearly how this seemingly ordinary work is aimed at the flourishing (or prospering) of the whole of the city of Babylon and is in many ways unchanged from their vocation as the people of God at home in Israel.[47] We may also get whispers of Revelation here, as the people of God are called to engage and tend to the flourishing of Babylon in ways similar to how the people will in the new Jerusalem.

What we find is that, irrespective of context or situation, the charge to humanity within the story of God remains unchanged: fostering communities where each and all can flourish. This is a vision for the common good and the role of humanity in its pursuit. We acknowledge that the fullness of the common good is not something humanity will achieve on our own; rather, the Scriptures support the eschatological vision of a cosmic work of God that individuals and communities *contribute* to as a reflection of their divinely unique "splendor, glory, and honor."

### We Are All in It Together: A Different Way of Thinking About Self-Interest

A second significant idea that we see throughout Scripture is that we are all in it together. Recalling the *included* and *involved* characteristics of the common good, Scripture consistently reminds us that we are responsible for one another's well-being. For instance, in the Jeremiah 29 text we just examined, the prophet points to the interdependent nature of human flourishing when he tells the people in verse 7 to "seek the peace and prosperity of the city . . . because if it prospers, you too will prosper." We have repeatedly said that the common good and the creation mandate point toward a sense of human vocation focused on shared flourishing. Here Jeremiah confirms this idea, suggesting that the flourishing of the whole is the goal of Israel's presence in Babylon and that the flourishing of individuals is contingent on the flourishing of the whole.

This echoes the body metaphor we've considered along the way, as well as other passages throughout Scripture. In Genesis 4:9, when God confronts Cain about the murder of his brother Abel, Cain asks the question, "Am I my brother's keeper?" Of course, the answer is implied. Yes, Cain is actively responsible for the well-being of his brother. Similarly, God commands the people in Leviticus 19:18, "Love your neighbor as yourself"—and in the Gospels, Jesus emphasizes this as the very heart of the law. Cain's killing of

47. Miller, "'That It May Go Well with You,'" 22.

Abel out of jealousy is the antithesis of loving a neighbor as oneself. The same dynamic is at play in Jesus's parable of the prodigal son, where the self-interest of the older brother prevents him from sharing a concern for the well-being of his younger brother. Interestingly, the Scriptures do not seem to suggest that self-interest is wrong, but they do warn us that self-interest can be weaponized against the well-being of others. In such cases, it is a fast track to all manner of sin and injustice. In the context of a body, corrupted self-interest is the eye saying to the hand, "I don't need you!" This prioritizes autonomy and self-sufficiency at the expense of the well-being of others. However, it seems clear that Scripture intends to reinforce the idea that preferencing self-interest in this way ultimately leads to harm for everyone involved.

Instead, the Scriptures point us toward a nuanced imagination for the role of self-interest.[48] If the well-being of Israel depends on the well-being of Babylon, if the health of the eye corresponds to the health of the entire body, and if the way and character of our love for our neighbors is to be informed by the way we love ourselves, then it stands to reason that there is a dynamic and moral relationship between self-interest and the well-being of others.[49] In *Work in the Spirit*, Miroslav Volf notes that self-interest *can* corrupt a person's capacity to pursue the common good, but it does not have to.[50] "Individual self-interest can be pursued validly, but it must be accompanied by the pursuit of the good of others. These two pursuits are not in principle mutually exclusive but complementary. . . . My own good and the good of the whole human family are both included in the shalom of the new creation."[51] It seems clear that the well-being of others is to be the guiding premise of a faithful way of life and that our own individual well-being is included in the flourishing of the larger whole. It invites the fostering of a robust communal identity and a commitment to flourishing in relationship with one another. This requires real intention. Without a concerted investment in the common good, self-interest will inevitably turn in on itself. But when we understand that pursuing the common good through our work increases our own capacity to flourish, it deepens our conviction and commitment to "consciously and directly work for others."[52]

48. Walter Brueggemann makes a compelling case that a significant result of the Egyptian slavery and exodus narratives was to reshape the imagination of the people of God away from self-interest and toward a conception of the common good. See Brueggemann, *Journey to the Common Good* (Westminster John Knox, 2021).

49. Hawtrey, "Oxford Declaration," 4.

50. Volf, *Work in the Spirit*, 188.

51. Volf, *Work in the Spirit*, 192.

52. Volf, *Work in the Spirit*, 189.

## "We" Includes Our Enemies

Taking that notion further, Scripture consistently speaks to the idea that the "we" in "we are all in it together" includes our enemies. Again, in Jeremiah 29 Israel is charged with seeking the well-being of their oppressors—certainly a radical notion. These oppressors turn out to be their neighbors, and so the call to love enemies and to love neighbors is the same command. That neighbor love is to be worked out in tangible and concrete ways in their community. This calls to mind Walter Brueggemann's description of neighbor love: He says that loving our neighbors is "the practice of neighborhood," an expression of "covenantal commitment to the common good."[53] So too do we encounter this notion in Jesus's parable of the good Samaritan, where the unexpected twist is that an ethnic other and cultural enemy turns out to be the exemplar of neighborly love.

Perhaps the most striking example of this notion is in the book of Jonah. Throughout the story, Jonah's intuition is that the Ninevites—ethnically and culturally other and enemies of Israel—are not worthy of God's redemptive intentions. He initially rejects the call to voice God's concern for Nineveh, and when he finally reroutes to the city, he delivers a half-hearted message of judgment. In the face of Nineveh's repentance, Jonah is despondent and retreats in anger and bitterness toward God, forcing God to take Jonah to task for his heartlessness. God declares his great concern for the people of the city, as well as for the whole of creation tended by Nineveh.

The implications of the story of Jonah for our understanding of the common good return us to the dynamic relationship between the *imago Dei* and the creation mandate. Jacqueline Lapsley argues that "the book of Jonah makes a bold claim: God is not parochial, but cares for the good of all, even our most reviled enemies. . . . The story suggests not only that God's mercy and justice extend beyond our parochial borders to our enemies, to animals, and to all of creation, but also that we, *in imitatione Dei*, must enlarge the boundaries of whom and what we consider 'common' in the common good."[54]

As bearers of God's image, our conception of who is included in the common good must match that of God, who has deep concern for the well-being of one of Israel's most strident enemies. Here the notion of self-interest pitted against the well-being of others takes on a communal dimension. At a larger level, communities cannot pit their interests over the interests of other communities, be they racial, ethnic, cultural, geopolitical, or otherwise. Instead,

53. Brueggemann, *Journey to the Common Good*, 30.
54. Lapsley, "Introduction," 12.

the story of Jonah—exemplary of the entire narrative of Scripture—leaves little room for any type of privileging perspective, posture, or practice. Rather, the normative standard of Scripture demands ways of being committed to the well-being of all, even of enemies or oppressors, with a recognition that unless every person and place is flourishing, no one and nowhere can truly flourish. The story of "Jonah 'invites' us to reimagine the boundaries of the common good."[55]

## Focus on the Flourishing of the Vulnerable

Given that moral standard, concern for the vulnerable should be our highest priority. This idea is commonly referred to as the *preferential option for the poor and vulnerable*. Put simply, claiming that God maintains a preference for the poor and vulnerable is a way of acknowledging that God has a particular kind of concern for individuals and groups who experience life at the margins, who live under threat of victimization, oppression, and exploitation at the hands of the more powerful and society at large. Tim Keller has coined the term "quartet of the vulnerable" to refer to Scripture's refrain of concern for widows, orphans, immigrants, and the poor.[56] We see evidence of God's overriding concern for this quartet throughout the pages of Scripture. The same way the Bible offers visions of hope and redemption that prioritize the painful experience of the poor and oppressed, the common good champions the thriving of the most vulnerable as a barometer of our commitment to the flourishing of the whole.

The preferential option for the poor highlights the zero-sum nature of the common good. The testimony of Scripture consistently points to the relationship between concern for the poor and the overall health and faithfulness of the community. Miroslav Volf rightly observes that a concern for everyone's needs necessitates such a preferential option for vulnerable and poor people(s).[57] In practice, a concern for the poor operates like a check against codifying the preferences of the status quo and the desires of those at the center of society into systems that further exclude and marginalize the vulnerable. The New Testament church had multiple ways of ensuring the well-being of the vulnerable. For example, in Acts 6:1–7 the Jesus community restructured systems to respond to the cries of vulnerable widows.

55. Lapsley, "'When Mercy Seasons Justice': Jonah and the Common Good," in McCann and Miller, *In Search of the Common Good*, 56.

56. Timothy Keller, *Generous Justice: How God's Grace Makes Us Just* (Viking, 2010), 4.

57. Volf, *Work in the Spirit*, 16.

From a wide view, we see that Scripture unpacks a vision for the common good. The human vocation of building and sustaining community is aimed at the well-being of the whole, with the flourishing of individual parts included by way of their incorporation into that larger whole. This is an expansive vision that includes everyone, crosses lines of discord and division, ensures the possibility of flourishing for those most vulnerable to threat, and reimagines self-interest not as the enemy of the common good but as existing in dynamic relationship with, and having an overriding concern for, the well-being of others. The Scriptures provide a hopeful vision of a God who is working for the well-being of all creation. That same God invites all those who bear the *imago Dei*—not just Christians—to the ongoing and eternal task of building and sustaining (not exclusively Christian) communities of shared and mutual flourishing, so that all may be active participants in a shared life together.

## Implications for a Theology of Labor

Eric Mount argues that "where work is good work, where it is a part of a covenantal vocation for the common good, it will be done by a community, in a community, and for a community."[58] The creation mandate alone supports such a claim, but Scripture's more expansive vision for the common good helps us fill out an understanding of the implications of our work in the world. As we seek to put flesh on our shared vocation as humans, the common good provides a helpful framework for evaluation and reform. Consider the following four areas of assessment.

First, *the whats of work matter*. The common good provides moral guidance on both what work we do and what our work contributes to—what I've taken to calling the type and character of our work. Given all we've considered thus far, common-good work would be characterized by one or more of the following:

- Common-good work promotes the well-being of everyone (including workers), particularly the poor and vulnerable.[59]
- Common-good work nourishes and amplifies the potential of individuals and communities.
- Common-good work contributes to healthy social and civic life for all.

58. Mount, *Covenant, Community, and the Common Good*, 84.
59. Hawtrey, "Oxford Declaration," 3.

- Common-good work builds and maintains the complex of systems that provide for the needs and aspirations of individuals, communities, and society at large.
- Common-good work solves problems that create obstacles to a shared life in common with others.
- Common-good work unlocks creative possibilities for and expressions of human flourishing.

The fact that we can articulate a set of characteristics for good work implies that there are types of work that fall short of contribution to the common good. In other words, the common good also provides a way to challenge or critique human labor that does not reflect these normative principles.

- If work detracts from, or directly harms, the well-being of anyone (including workers), it cannot be common-good work.
- If work diminishes the potential of anyone (including workers), it cannot be common-good work.
- If work fosters unhealthy relations at the interpersonal or social level, it cannot be common-good work.
- If work interrupts or inhibits the fluid functioning of social or civic systems, making it harder for people to get what they need to flourish (let alone survive), it cannot be common-good work.
- If work creates new, or amplifies existing, obstacles to healthy shared life, it cannot be common-good work.
- If work stifles human flourishing, it cannot be common-good work.

Is this list exhaustive? Likely not. I'm sure there are other ways of describing what is, or is not, common-good work. However, the primary point here is that the common good provides another normative frame (in addition to human dignity) through which we can venture moral judgments about particular forms of labor. It is important to remember that the forms of labor implicated by this moral lens are not necessarily judgments of the workers themselves. For instance, is the assembly-line worker to blame for ways their work fails to cultivate the fullness of their unique creative contribution to the larger whole? Of course not. But is the assembly-line worker complicit in a disruption of the common good if the products of that assembly line harm the well-being of others, say through the manufacturing of weapons? Possibly, yes. The common good acts as a frame that gives us space to challenge larger systems and structures of labor that create and codify job types, and entire industries, perpetuating these ends in the world.[60]

Of course, any particular job, workplace, or industry could be taken to task on one or more of these points. Consider the example of the street sweeper. Most downtown associations hire workers to walk up and down commercial districts, cleaning the sidewalks, emptying trash, tidying up the landscaping, and so on. Given our framework, this is an essential and important job. It makes a meaningful contribution to the systems of a community. But a job like this could get repetitive and seem a little like drudgery. A few things might be said here. First, we can affirm the importance of this work and still question the health of the work environment (see further down in this section). We might also ask whether part of the problem is related to other issues like wages (chapter 5) and/or worker agency (chapter 6). We might also wonder about the way this particular role has been disconnected from other aspects of the work of maintaining a city. Similar to how the division of labor creates jobs that are too repetitive, we may come to see ways jobs could be better if the scope and responsibility of the work were wider. Caretaking for a city is invaluable. Can we create jobs, or adapt existing ones, that reflect that value and celebrate the people who do them?

Remembering that the common good is always more aspirational than achievable, we use this lens as a basis for evaluation and ongoing reform. If we are committed to cultivating more and greater expressions of the common good in the world, then it helps to see these two sets of characteristics existing on a spectrum such that we can explore ways of moving specific expressions of labor toward the common good in these areas.

This is, after all, the telos of work. Here is where we most explicitly connect our vision for work to the eschatological vision of the common good. Remember Volf: "Human work, properly understood theologically, is related to the goal of all history, which will bring . . . creation into 'shalomic' harmony." He says that "a theology of work is not anthropology, but an all-encompassing eschatology."[61] Cultivating an actionable vision for the common good allows us to inform and critique our status quo with a more informed sense of God's ideal future.[62]

Second, *the ways of work matter*. The common good establishes a moral standard that extends to the way we do any type of work. Similar to how the notion of the *imago Dei* shines a light on ways we may violate the image of

60. Volf, *Work in the Spirit*, 192.
61. Volf, *Work in the Spirit*, 85.
62. Volf, *Work in the Spirit*, 120.

God in another through exploitative or degrading labor practices, our vision for work as contribution to the common good creates a filter for making normative judgments about the character of the work environments we create and foster. We may do work intended to bring large-scale societal benefit, but if that work is done in unjust or unethical ways, it is still indicted by the moral demands of the common good. So, organizations whose work is dedicated to social justice or community benefit but that demand unreasonable work hours from their staff, pay so little that staff can barely make ends meet, manipulate and demean their employees, or foster toxic workplaces cannot reflect the common good. One cannot view the ends, or goals, of work as permission to look the other way in these situations. Commitment to the common good means that these environments should reflect, even in small ways, the intended ethos of all creation—that is, the dynamic interconnection between the flourishing of the individual and the whole. This will come to bear directly when we consider labor questions related to wages and workers' rights in later chapters.

Third, *the whos of work matter*. When we consider the types of jobs that contribute to one or more of the characteristics of common-good work, we come away with a deeper appreciation for the vast spectrum of people who perform essential jobs in our society. The global pandemic of 2020 provided a moment of prophetic clarity for us when, as a society, we had to reckon with the reality of our dependence on a complex system of different types of labor. It forced us to recalibrate the way we bestow value on particular jobs by showing us that essential work is not always compensated accordingly. It invited us to see that the delivery worker and the doctor both perform jobs that we need in order to function as a society, not just during a pandemic but also in the normal workings of day-to-day life. A list of jobs that matter from the vantage point of the common good will be stunningly more inclusive than a list organized around the social hierarchy of labor, common conceptions of calling, or cultural values for impact or return on investment.

The same way a robust embrace of human dignity challenges bias in labor, the common good calls us to see, appreciate, and value (tangibly even) the contributions toward shared flourishing made by all manner of people doing all manner of jobs. This is why King can say, correctly, that the sanitation worker's labor has value—because their work plays a vital role in the building and sustaining of the community. The common good calls us to recognize the necessary role each specific form of labor plays and how the people doing those jobs reflect our shared human vocation.

So, it turns out, selling feed to hog farmers really could be considered good work. It may have had some qualities of being a cog in a vast agricultural machine, but at a local and relational level my grandfather provided an essential service to women and men who knew his name, just as he knew theirs. It allowed a specific local economy to continue to function and contributed to the essential food system of the area. Certainly, there were larger globalizing economic forces that were rapidly changing the nature of his work from the mid-1940s through the latter half of the twentieth century. But putting aside factors outside his control, his work made a contribution to the building and sustaining of the community. Perhaps not everyone recognized it as such, but that is not the fault of the man or the job.

Fourth, *the whys of work matter*. This brings us back around to our common calling. If work is primarily aimed at contribution to the common good, this will likely challenge dramatically what we emphasize as the *why* of work. This is not at odds with the innate desire we all have for our work to matter. It is also not at odds with the good desire each of us has for a good life. It does reframe the perspective by which we articulate what it means to do good work and have a good life. Work is designed to be a primary way we participate in and contribute to human flourishing, as well as to the ultimate realization of God's intentions for creation. In just the same way work is inextricably tied to our humanity because it allows us to more fully reflect the image of God, work also helps us embrace our humanity more fully, as it takes seriously the human vocation of building and sustaining community. There is a vast spectrum of ways one might do this, as countless job types fit that bill in one way or another, and we should readily affirm the idea that "human beings are created by God as persons endowed with gifts which God calls them to exercise freely."[63] In other words, any job that allows a person to shoulder responsibilities as part of a local community, and of the human family overall, is a job that reflects the moral standards set out by the common good. This is where work sources its intrinsic meaning and purpose. The significance of our work, individually and as the human family, is found in its "eschatological significance."[64]

Because that is true, the common good tempers the protagonistic thinking we discussed in the last chapter. The common good reminds us that the point of work is much less about advancement or achievement and significantly more about positive, generative, and increasing contribution to the well-being of others and the whole. We do not have to be the protagonist of the story for our work to matter; we do not have to be the star of the show. Instead, the common good reminds us that our work matters precisely because we

63. Hawtrey, "Oxford Declaration," 4.
64. Volf, *Work in the Spirit*, 90.

are not the protagonist, precisely because we are not the star of the show. True, everyone is irreducibly unique, which means each person's participation and contributions are slightly different from those of others. But rather than taking that as an invitation to self-centeredness, we do well to embrace that notion as an invitation to discern ways, and develop capacities, to contribute the means and ends of our labor toward the common good. The same way an eye doesn't exist for its own sake, the common good reminds us that our work is not primarily for us, but for the larger whole, recognizing that only when the whole flourishes can an individual thrive. All labor has value and worth when it contributes to the overall functioning of the whole and amplifies the capacity of each to make their particular contribution. The way we do that will be incredibly varied and, usually, incredibly ordinary. This is an alternative to our conventional conceptions of calling and one way we begin to dismantle the social hierarchy of labor.

A shared human vocation—committed to the common good, celebrating the image of God *wherever* it is found—radically redefines the way we think about "good work." In this way, we find a theological imagination for work that is capable of grappling with the labor question in substantive ways. It does not deal in abstractions unable to prioritize the lived experience of the working class. Instead, this theological vision for work informs the way we understand labor issues and shapes the character and aims of our response as people of faith. Applying this vision for labor to specific labor questions is the task to which we now turn in part 2.

# PART 2

# PUTTING A THEOLOGY OF LABOR TO WORK

# 5 RIGHTEOUS WAGES

## Fostering Worker Well-Being

To earn one's bread by the sweat of one's brow has always been the lot of mankind. At least, ever since Eden's slothful couple was served with an eviction notice. The scriptural precept was never doubted, not out loud. No matter how demeaning the task, no matter how it dulls the senses and breaks the spirit, one must work. Or else.

—Studs Terkel[1]

My grandfather's profession was a strange combination. Part agricultural worker and part traveling salesman, he worked long hours for low wages doing manual labor year-round. My grandmother worked in small, consolidated, and rural public schools her entire career and kept part-time school-system work until very late in life. While she didn't make much money, and didn't benefit from any collectively bargained wages or benefits, she earned more than my grandfather. As I reflect on this, the fact that a small-town public-school teacher's salary surpassed my grandfather's earning power really puts his economic fortunes in perspective. My grandparents lived in a time and place where wives merely working outside the home was rare, and wives outearning their husbands was nearly unheard of.

1. Studs Terkel, *Working: People Talk About What They Do All Day and How They Feel About What They Do* (Pantheon, 1974), xii.

That introduced a kind of friction into their marriage. I think the economic tension in their house was probably heightened because their situation upended cultural norms. But it also highlighted one of the more challenging aspects to any discussion of wages—namely, the way they act as an indicator of the relative worth of one's labor. Under the surface of their barb trading was an entire complex of social values that assign more, or less, value to jobs based on what a job pays.

This is a perfect example of how the social hierarchy of labor wages war against human dignity and the common good. My grandparents had every reason to see life as a shared journey. Relational solidarity should have been an obvious characteristic of their marriage. Yet the disparity in their wages—and the implicit messages of relative value and worth that disparity communicated—created fault lines of relational discord. My grandfather—like those Memphis sanitation workers—was asserting his dignity in a space where it was questioned by the cultural messaging attached to their disparate income levels.

At a micro level, the conflict and tension that intermittently threatened to blow the roof off that little brick ranch on Southview Court highlight how the issue of wages will force us to reckon with a deeply culturally ingrained value system. That system can have a devastating psychological effect on people's personal sense of worth. It is not just that high-paying jobs are prized and aspired to; it's tragically simple to observe, on the other hand, ways that lower-income work is weaponized to demean and devalue workers in those jobs. Ignoring the impact of cultural values on wages and the reciprocal influence compensation has on the social hierarchy disregards commitments to dignity and the common good. It does not take long to recognize that a theological imagination for labor must be able to engage the question of wages in a substantive way. That can be a dicey proposition because wages are also *the* flashpoint for controversy, contention, critique, and unrest in discussions of labor justice—no other labor topic captures the central issues of debate more than what workers are paid. This issue reminds us that violations of human dignity and antagonism toward the common good manifest themselves in concrete injustice toward populations on the margins and the lower rungs of the social hierarchy.

We should champion the notion that the toxic relationship between wages and the social hierarchy of labor is not the only option available to us. We should challenge those connections and foster an imagination for a new, and nuanced, perspective on the wage question, one that celebrates dignity and contributions to the common good. Our theological commitments should move us to consider what John Ryan called the "ethical value of labor."[2] Ryan recognized over a century ago what we must still admit today: We face a moral crossroads when it comes to wages. The financial realities of so many Americans raise the question of whether those of us animated by theological convictions around justice will use our prophetic voices in service of those who experience life on a razor's edge of financial calamity. Dan Graff and Clemens Sedmak make plain the signs of the times:

> From Baltimore to Bangladesh and beyond, far too many people across the globe struggle with making ends meet on a weekly basis. Living hand to mouth, too many households must rely on multiple wage earners (sometimes working multiple jobs), and even those who do get by are only one work accident, job loss, or family illness removed from economic disaster. In short, too many of the world's people are compelled to participate in what we might call a "just hope" economy, where they literally must hope (and pray) that they and their loved ones will avoid a variety of worst-case scenarios each working day.[3]

A world of growing economic inequality should give us pause. And the disparity between the haves and have-nots is only accelerating. Consider these trends. In 1973, the wage gap between the bottom 90 percent of the population and the top 10 percent (minus the very top 1 percent) was around $65,000. In 2022, that gap had risen to over $142,000. On average, wages for the bottom 90 percent had risen (in real dollars) by only a little over $10,000, while top-earning wages increased by almost $86,000.[4] In 2020, the top 20 percent of the working population controlled 55 percent of pretax income earned, and by 2022 the top 10 percent of the population controlled 73 percent of the nation's wealth.[5]

Also, from 1973 to 2013 the average hourly worker's wages rose 9 percent even though, during roughly that same period of time, production grew 74 percent. Middle-class hourly wages rose 6 percent, low-wage workers saw their pay *decrease* 5 percent, while the top wage earners saw a 41 percent increase. In 1973, the federal minimum wage was $1.60. In 2018, that would have been equivalent to a wage of $9.85. Today, the federal minimum wage is

2. John A. Ryan, *Distributive Justice: The Right and Wrong of Our Present Distribution of Wealth* (Macmillan, 1916), 279.

3. Dan Graff and Clemens Sedmak, "From a Just Hope to a Just Wage Economy," unpublished paper in response to the Vatican-sponsored project "The Future of Work, Labor After *Laudato Si*," 2024.

4. Economic Policy Institute, *State of Working America Data Library*, "Wages for Top 1.0%, 0.1% and Bottom 90%," 2024. See real-time wage-data charts at https://data.epi.org/#wages.

5. A. Sherman, D. Trisi, and J. Cureton, *A Guide to Statistics on Historical Trends in Income Inequality*, Center on Budget and Policy Priorities, December 11, 2024, https://www.cbpp.org/research/poverty-and-inequality/a-guide-to-statistics-on-historical-trends-in-income-inequality.

$7.25 (unchanged since 2009)—a net reduction in spending power of $2.60 over the past fifty years.[6] Had the minimum wage increased with the rate of production, it would be over $18 today, instead of a meager $7.25.[7] The federal poverty line for a family of four (in 2023) was the equivalent of $14.87 per hour.[8] That means the federal minimum wage—even in a two-earner household—produces only poverty.

It is also important to recognize that economic precarity is not a problem just for those at or below the poverty line. For example, real wages—a measurement that considers the impact of inflation—grew only 36¢ for most workers between 1973 and 2005. That lack of growth seems even more stark when you consider that real wages doubled in every income level between 1943 and 1973.[9] In other words, it is more difficult to make a wage that pays the bills today than it has been at any time since World War II.

This is to say nothing of the way the wage gap manifests itself across sectors of the population. In 2023 men on average made 19.6 percent more than women, and White workers made 24.5 percent more than Black workers and 28.9 percent more than Hispanic workers. The wages of college-educated workers were 47 percent higher than those of workers with only a high school diploma (whose wages were 23.9 percent higher than those of workers without a high school diploma).[10] It is cause for concern when wage disparities map onto the standard categories of inequality in society. From a Christian perspective, good work should have the capacity to respond generatively to these ongoing disparities.[11]

## Wages: Minimum, Living, and Just

Concern for human dignity and the common good challenges those inequitable economic realities. There is a moral demand to provide workers, as Ryan

6. Economic Policy Institute, *State of Working America Data Library*, "Minimum Wage." See real-time minimum-wage data at https://data.epi.org/#wages.

7. Lawrence Mishel, Elise Gould, and Josh Bivens, "Wage Stagnation in Nine Charts," Economic Policy Institute, January 6, 2015, https://www.epi.org/publication/charting-wage-stagnation/.

8. Economic Policy Institute, *State of Working America Data Library*, "Poverty Level Wages." See real-time wage-data charts at https://data.epi.org/#wages.

9. Chuck Collins and Mary Wright, *The Moral Measure of the Economy* (Orbis Books, 2007), 60.

10. Economic Policy Institute, *State of Working America Data Library*, "Gender Wage Gap," "Black-White Wage Gap," "Hispanic-White Wage Gap," "College Wage Premium," "Non-High School Wage Penalty." See real-time wage-disparities charts at https://data.epi.org/#wages.

11. Eric Mount Jr., *Covenant, Community, and the Common Good: An Interpretation of Christian Ethics* (Pilgrim, 1999), 84.

argued, "the economic opportunity to live decently, to live as human beings in the image and likeness of God."[12]

What kind of wage allows a person to "live decently"? Our minds might initially return to the minimum wage. Instituted in the 1930s, the federal minimum wage—as well as much of the economic policy created during the Great Depression—was aimed at providing a social safety net to help individuals and families avoid cataclysmic economic disaster. As we've already seen, however, the minimum wage, while creating a wage *floor*, has not helped low-wage workers avoid severe economic hardship, as it essentially ensures a worker and their family lives at or below the poverty line. That shouldn't surprise us, because as the name suggests, wages that meet only a *minimum* standard are unlikely to produce anything resembling the opportunity to live decently. Neither can the concept of minimum stand up under the scrutiny of any normative framework.

It makes sense, then, that the discourse around wage justice does not center on the minimum wage—aside from the clear charge of the minimum wage's insufficiency. Instead, worker advocates more often refer to a "living wage" as a way of articulating something closer to a moral standard. The Global Living Wage Coalition argues that a living wage must be "sufficient to afford a decent standard of living for the worker and her or his family."[13]

But what is a decent life, exactly? Chuck Collins and Mary Wright argue that "workers should earn at least a 'living wage,' enough to have a decent life and support a flourishing family life."[14] Here "decent" wages correlate with thriving families. This seems to be a standard conception in theological circles. In *Distributive Justice*, John Ryan treats the topic of a living wage, and a decent life, at length. He says that a decent life is "food, clothing, and housing sufficient in quantity and quality to maintain the worker in normal heath, in elementary comfort, and in an environment suitable to the protection of morality and religion; sufficient provision for the future to bring elementary contentment, and security against sickness, accident, and invalidity; and sufficient opportunities of recreation, social intercourse, education, and church-membership to conserve health and strength and to render possible the exercise of the higher faculties."[15]

There is no way to read Ryan and come away thinking that a moral wage standard could be anything resembling a so-called minimum, or just enough to

12. John A. Ryan, *Social Doctrine in Action* (Harper & Brothers, 1941), 1.

13. See "What Is a Living Wage?," Global Living Wage Coalition, https://www.globallivingwage.org/about/what-is-a-living-wage/.

14. Collins and Wright, *Moral Measure of the Economy*, 92.

15. Ryan, *Distributive Justice*, 273.

get by. A decent life demands more than a merely adequate wage. Wages should promote decency of life for a worker (and their family) and not leave them exposed to a life of indecency. A living wage is one that accounts for the comprehensive nature of personhood and derives from holistic considerations of what helps individuals and families thrive. For a wage to truly be a living wage, it must create what Christine Firer Hinze calls the "sustaining conditions needed for full human development."[16] In that sense, a living wage could be called a *just wage*.

There is, though, a degree of complexity and relativity that makes wage determinations resistant to concrete standards or minimums. We need a way of framing the conversation that allows us to take complex factors into account as wage considerations are made in real time. Perhaps the best example of such a frame is the Just Wage Initiative, a scholar-practitioner research project spearheaded through the Higgins Labor Program at the University of Notre Dame.[17] The multidisciplinary project brings academics together with practitioners and leaders from various labor sectors, convening an ongoing dialogue on a framework for just wages. Similar to Ryan's description (above) of a decent life, the Just Wage Initiative has identified a number of factors that, through critical analysis, reveal the relative justness of any given wage. The initiative centers normative dimensions of the wage question as a primary filter through which concrete determinations about wages can be made.[18] The Just Wage Tool evaluates ways that wages do or don't contribute to the holistic flourishing of individuals and families and, as such, deals with much more than just the number on the paycheck.[19] Instead, a just wage must have a just effect in the lives of workers. In other words, *the moral standard for wages is not a number but an outcome.*

## A Righteous Wage: A New Starting Point for an Ongoing Conversation

Before we explore different outcomes that wages should produce in the lives of workers, a survey of the Scriptures provides nuance that informs a distinctly

16. Christine Firer Hinze, *Radical Sufficiency: Work, Livelihood, and a US Catholic Economic Ethic* (Georgetown University Press, 2021), 34.

17. To learn more, see "A Just Wage Tool," Institute for Social Concerns, https://socialconcerns.nd.edu/just-wage-tool/.

18. We will consider two of these factors—worker agency and assets—in chapter 7.

19. The Just Wage Initiative proposes seven criteria that make up a just wage, suggesting that all wages should enable a decent life, enable asset building, provide basic social security for the worker and their household, extend from nondiscriminatory structures, not promote excessive compensation, reflect participation by workers, and consider performance, qualification, and type of work. You can engage the tool directly and read more about each criterion at https://socialconcerns.nd.edu/just-wage-tool/.

Christian view of these issues. In particular, as often as Scripture centers the lived experience of the poor, the wage conversation is directed at the wage *giver*. More than mere semantics, Scripture makes a direct connection between wages and religious fidelity. That means wages should be a central concern for people of faith because paying a righteous wage is a matter of faithfulness not only to one another but also to God.

In Scripture, God sets a moral wage standard that first implicates the faithfulness of the wage giver. In that sense, wages are as much a matter of righteousness as they are a matter of justice. The effect of wages on the wage earner—outcomes that define the experience of the poor and vulnerable—serves as evidence of the wage giver's fidelity to God. We might say that exhibit A in the examination of the wealthy class is the lived experience of the working poor. Insofar as there is such a thing as a *just wage received*, Scripture invites us to embrace the complementary notion of a *righteous wage given*.

Deuteronomy 24:14–15 expresses this idea: "Do not take advantage of a hired worker who is poor and needy, whether that worker is a fellow Israelite or a foreigner residing in one of your towns. Pay them their wages each day before sunset, because they are poor and are counting on it. Otherwise they may cry to the LORD against you, and you will be guilty of sin." I will make three observations about this text.

First, we should notice that the plight of the poor is evidence against the actions of the rich. These verses evoke a courtroom scene suggesting poor workers will "cry out" against owners, resulting in a guilty verdict. The idea that the cries of the poor cast doubt on the faithfulness of the wealthy class emerges in the New Testament as well, in what is perhaps the primary text for a distinctly Christian treatment of wages. In James 5:1–5 we read the following:

> Now listen, you rich people, weep and wail because of the misery that is coming on you. Your wealth has rotted, and moths have eaten your clothes. Your gold and silver are corroded. Their corrosion will testify against you and eat your flesh like fire. You have hoarded wealth in the last days. Look! The wages you failed to pay the workers who mowed your fields are crying out against you. The cries of the harvesters have reached the ears of the Lord Almighty. You have lived on earth in luxury and self-indulgence. You have fattened yourselves in the day of slaughter.

Again, the context is the courtroom of religious fidelity, and the rich are on trial for economic negligence toward the poor. Their accumulated wealth is testifying against them because they are gains ill-gotten, profits that should have been given to the working class and poor, who are crying out for deliverance from God. Notice that wage injustice perpetrated against their workers is the only evidence needed to deliver a guilty verdict. Had the rich paid the wages due, they would be considered righteous in the eyes of God. As it is, they are guilty, having prepared their very selves for "the day of slaughter."

Second, we should note that the Deuteronomy text nods to the way wages *can* be used manipulatively—weaponized against workers—and that the practice of wage exploitation is explicitly condemned by God as a sign of direct religious infidelity. That the text has to address economic exploitation ("Do not take advantage of a hired worker who is poor and needy") suggests such exploitation was common enough to warrant the warning. This text explicitly declares wage exploitation to be sin. The same is true in texts like Leviticus 19:13 and Jeremiah 22:13, which prohibit practices that defraud and withhold wages.[20] Taken together, these texts imply that owners and elites were using wages as tools of manipulation. Withholding wages, delaying payments, defrauding workers—these are all actions aimed at coercing production from vulnerable peoples under the promise of financial remuneration. Whether this was done ostensibly as worker incentivization ("Show me good work tomorrow and you'll get paid!") or an outright threat ("Come back tomorrow or else!") is irrelevant. The Scriptures leave no room for such activity, calling all of it exploitation.

This is why the prophet Isaiah can level such an extreme charge of religious unfaithfulness against the wealthy owner class in Isaiah 58:1–3:

> Shout it aloud, do not hold back.
> Raise your voice like a trumpet.
> Declare to my people their rebellion
> and to the descendants of Jacob their sins.
> For day after day they seek me out;
> they seem eager to know my ways,
> as if they were a nation that does what is right
> and has not forsaken the commands of its God.
> They ask me for just decisions
> and seem eager for God to come near them.
> "Why have we fasted," they say,
> "and you have not seen it?
> Why have we humbled ourselves,
> and you have not noticed?"
>
> Yet on the day of your fasting, you do as you please
> and exploit all your workers.

20. Miroslav Volf, *Work in the Spirit: Toward a Theology of Work* (Wipf & Stock, 2001), 164.

Isaiah 58 is a textbook example of the connection between the quality and character of religious practice and economic injustice. The people are surprised that their overt religious practices are not eliciting any response from God. They are unable to entice God to act in line with their desires. This is a stark contrast to the way God responds to the cries of the poor against the rich. Here, God is seemingly deaf to the concerns of the rich. Yet it is not God who cannot hear but the people who cannot see their hypocrisy. We are not given specifics regarding the exact nature of that exploitation, but it is hard to imagine the exploitation of workers that does not involve wages in some way. The first piece of evidence proffered in prosecution of their infidelity is the exploitation of workers. In the eyes of God, the exploitation of workers undermines their religious practice and renders them rebellious, guilty of sin, and worthy of judgment.

The judgment motif is employed in other places as well. Jeremiah 22:13 says, "Woe to him who builds his palace by unrighteousness, his upper rooms by injustice, making his own people work for nothing, not paying them for their labor." In Malachi 3, the prophet envisions a final judgment against the wicked as an expression of God's righteous character. Malachi lists those who are in the crosshairs of God's judgment in verse 5: "So I will come to put you on trial. I will be quick to testify against sorcerers, adulterers and perjurers, against those who defraud laborers of their wages, who oppress the widows and the fatherless, and deprive the foreigners among you of justice." Of the many ways a person might find themselves guilty of religious infidelity, God is quick to name wage injustice as primary evidence of guilt.

Third, and critically, the Deuteronomy text points us to the reality that paying right wages is an obligation. The law commands the owner class to "pay them *their* wages" (emphasis added). Who are *they*? The poor and needy, the working class. What is *theirs*? The wages themselves. The wages do not belong to the rich; they belong to the workers. Jesus lends support to this idea in Luke 10:7 when he tells his disciples that "the worker deserves his wages." Similarly, the apostle Paul says in Romans 4:4, "Now to the one who works, wages are not credited as a gift but as an obligation." Obviously, in this case Paul is using wage earning to make a more overtly spiritual point. He is utilizing the moral standard and obligatory nature of wages as a metaphor. However, if wages were not *owed* to workers, a concrete *obligation* for employers, Paul's larger spiritual argument would not hold up. The veracity of his spiritual claim depends on the validity of his assumption about ordinary wages.

The obligation of wage payment resists any view that sees the employment of workers—particularly the working poor—as an act of benevolence. It may seem obvious to say that the payment of wages is an act not of charity but of duty, yet we do not always recognize this in practice. The obligation of right wages also pushes back against manipulative appeals to brand or business loyalty as a means of excusing wage injustice. Business owners do not get to count right wages as signs of extravagant holiness; rather, wages are a baseline way of demonstrating religious faithfulness—the first piece of evidence regarding the character of their lives before God.

Admittedly, this is straightforwardly spiritual language, and a great many wage givers give little to no thought to a religiously motivated moral standard for wages. However, this explicitly theological conclusion can guide theologically animated convictions regarding wages and our engagement with questions of economic justice in general. It provides an initial lens through which to view the relative righteousness of wages. This challenges not only the wage itself, and how it is employed, but also the spirit and character by which the wage giver pays the wage. That the wage question implicates the character, not just the actions, of the wage giver is a helpful point of connection to the next consideration in our exploration of righteous wages.

## Wages and the *Imago Dei*

There is no worker/owner divide when it comes to the image of God. Just as a worker demonstrates something of God to the world in their work, so too an owner discloses something of God's character in their work. We should expect to learn something of God by watching any person bear God's image well and truly. This has bearing on our discussion of wages, as the wage given a worker is a reflection of the extent to which an owner is inhabiting the image of a God that Scripture consistently describes as showing *unintuitive generosity*.

The biblical text is rife with evidence of God's generosity. Starting with the very opening chapters of Scripture, we read a creation narrative full of God's immense generosity. God gives humanity a garden of earthly abundance. Later we see God's promised land for the people described as a place "flowing with milk and honey" (Exod. 3:8). There is a deep connection between the abundance of God and the generous way God gives gifts to humanity out of that abundance, so much so that we could rightly describe generosity as *enacted abundance*. From the start, the biblical text sets up the reality of abundance and complementary acts of generosity as the foil against the lies of scarcity and the sins of selfishness and hoarding. The narrative of Scripture—think of the manna in the wilderness, the widow's oil, the feeding of the five thousand, and so on—intends to demonstrate the importance of a worldview steadfastly committed to living in light of God's abundant generosity.

Jesus remarks on the generosity of the Father as well in Matthew 7:9–11: "Which of you, if your son asks for bread, will give him a stone? Or if he asks for a fish, will give him a snake? If you, then, though you are evil, know how to give good gifts to your children, how much more will your Father in heaven give good gifts to those who ask him!" Jesus reminds us that God is a giver of good gifts. Jesus then connects the character of God to his expectations of God's people. He continues in verse 12: "So in everything, do to others what you would have them do to you, for this sums up the Law and the Prophets." In its context, the "golden rule" does not have a generalized application. Instead, Jesus is directly connecting the generous gift-giving character of God to the command to mimic that character in the way we treat others. In other words, the command is *specifically* connected to God's generosity.

Jesus also says that this notion sums up the entire message of the Old Testament. We've been looking at many Old Testament texts dealing with wages, and Jesus says all of those laws—and more—are pointing to God's grand vision for the way humans are to live life together. When we understand that wage laws point to God's full intentions for the human community—the common good—it helps us draw normative conclusions from those many passages without falling prey to uncritical proof texting.

God's generosity is also unintuitive. Consider the parable of the workers in the vineyard from Matthew 20: The owner of a vineyard hires workers at various points during the day. At the end of the day, the owner calls the workers together to pay them, starting with those he hired last. Naturally, those who had worked the entire day expected to receive more than those workers who had done less, so they were understandably upset when the wages were equal across the board. The parable continues the exchange between the workers and the owner:

> "These who were hired last worked only one hour," they [the workers] said, "and you have made them equal to us who have borne the burden of the work and the heat of the day."
>
> But he answered one of them, "I am not being unfair to you, friend. Didn't you agree to work for a denarius? Take your pay and go. I want to give the one who was hired last the same as I gave you. Don't I have the right to do what I want with my own money? Or are you envious because I am generous?" (vv. 12–15)

Parables are meant to be windows into the nature of God and the character of God's kingdom. Once we see clearly what the window intends to reveal to us, we are better able to draw conclusions about God's perspective on any number of topics. Recognizing that there is always an overtly spiritual dimension to parables, there is some care required in teasing out implications for real-world scenarios. A focus on how the parables reveal God's character, and attempting to understand how that shapes social realities, helps us avoid unhelpful hermeneutical leaps. So even though this parable is not directly about righteous wages, we do not need to make a direct application to the question of a just wage in order to gain insight that informs our wage discussion.

Jesus tips his hand at one point of the parable—that the unintuitive generosity of the vineyard owner mirrors the unintuitive generosity of God. I don't believe there is a need to read the offended workers as the villains of this story. They are certainly envious and upset, but that seems to be the natural or assumed response given the paradoxical amount of payment.[21] Rather, Jesus is pointing to the surprising way the kingdom of God upends social norms and common practice. God pulls the rug out from under a world divided into *firsts* and *lasts*, instead forming a community of mutuality, a community of folks who all—in equal measure—get to delight in God's abundance. What's more, we encounter a vineyard owner who seems to prioritize his right to act generously. It is the prerogative of the owner to act as he does. He acknowledges his right to do whatever he wishes with his money, and so he is free to choose generosity.

Some have argued that the relatively meager wage cuts against the notion that this parable underscores God's generosity. They point to the fact that these day laborers were hired for the expected rate for a day laborer at the time. That would have been a subsistence wage, not one likely to be seen as generous.[22] But since the story rises and falls on the act of higher-than-expected compensation, the parable does seem to be making some point about God related to that unexpected twist. That the workers hired last receive a full day's wage for short hours worked is at least an oblique reference to God's prerogative and disposition toward generosity—giving more than what would be expected. The owner of the vineyard did not equate the wage given directly to hours worked. He gave everyone the expected daily wage. The workers hired last would almost assuredly not have been at another job site prior to being selected to work the vineyard. Instead, they likely sat around all day waiting for work to provide for their needs. If the owner were to cut the wage to reflect the hours worked—lowering it to a fraction of a daily wage, which was the explicit expectation in the relevant rabbinic literature at the

21. Klyne Snodgrass, *Stories with Intent: A Comprehensive Guide to the Parables of Jesus* (Eerdmans, 2008), 375–77.

22. Snodgrass, *Stories with Intent*, 369–70, 375.

time—those workers would have been left in their already dire circumstances.[23] The unintuitive compensation from the owner jars us into asking different questions about the nature of how God gives.

Because we bear God's image, God's generosity becomes our responsibility. We are, as bearers of God's image, obligated to do in the world as God does in the world. We don't get kudos; we are counted faithful. Wages aren't a sign of charity; they are an expression of the link between God's character and ours. When we find ourselves in the position of giver, what is the character of that giving? When we are giving wages, what message are we conveying? Wage giving is, in the world of work, a primary way we can give expression to God's abundance. Beyond that, God intends that we learn to want to enact abundance in the world. In the same way the vineyard owner was free to give more than expected, so we are free for God's way of giving. In the end, the more we inhabit the image of God, the more abundance we should see in the world.

Seeing wages that give expression to God's abundance as a concrete obligation undermines the accepted ways that wages ascribe value to work in at least two ways. First, it allows us to champion the pervasive dignity of people irrespective of their labors. At the end of the day, the vineyard owner was creating a community of equity. It did not matter the amount or type of work; each was worthy to receive. This challenges the way societal values influence economic activity and govern wage structures, a starting point for a decidedly Christian response to wage disparity.

It also exposes the way conventional wisdom masks the vices of miserliness and stinginess. A full embrace of divine generosity is rooted in a worldview of abundance, a way of being that sees "plenty" as a reality to be shared.[24] The full baskets of leftovers after Jesus fed the five thousand are actionably instructive, and the life of the church described in Acts 2 is inviting us to live out a belief that in God there is always enough to go around. If humans are created to give expression to God's character, then the generosity of God is not an extraneous consideration. More than being an example of benefaction, enacting abundance is a way of demonstrating the wage giver's belief and trust in God.

To that end, one wonders how a distinctly Christian perspective might shape the public debate about raising the standards of minimum and living wages. A perspective committed to giving expression to the character of God

23. Snodgrass, *Stories with Intent*, 375.

24. David H. Jensen, *Responsive Labor: A Theology of Work* (Westminster John Knox, 2006), 103.

might look for a different, more creative way forward. As before, this overt spiritual language is not aimed at establishing a pseudo-spiritual approach to economic policy. Instead, it aims to influence the way people of faith wrestle with the wage question.

### Wages for Well-Being: Common-Good Compensation

Righteous wages create the conditions for the common good. They help us reimagine the purpose of compensation as the promotion of flourishing for individuals and communities. That reminds us that we are after more than a number; we are after wages that produce particular *outcomes*. A commitment to the pursuit of the common good in society invites us to champion what we might call "wages for well-being."

Decency demands that wage considerations extend beyond the specific number on a paycheck to an evaluation of what that number enables a worker to do for themselves and others. This means wages have a catalytic quality, where compensation is judged according to the ripple effects it creates in the lives of workers and their families.

John Ryan argued for a living wage in the following way: "The intrinsic worth and sacredness of personality imply something more than security of life and limb and the material means of bare existence. The man who is not provided with the requisites of normal health, efficiency, and contentment lives a maimed life, not a reasonable one. . . . Man's personal dignity demands . . . the opportunity of pursuing self-perfection through the harmonious development of all his faculties."[25] Note that Ryan roots this argument in the appeal to "man's personal dignity," reinforcing the direct connections of the image of God to wage considerations.[26] But we also highlight that Ryan extends his argument to say that a wage is not sufficient should it provide only for "security of life and limb." In other words, the minimum wage (a life-and-limb wage, we might say) is not a morally defensible standard. Instead, wages must provide for health, contentment, and the opportunity to pursue things that contribute to the development of a worker.[27] In a notion that has been echoed even up to the present day, Ryan argues that workers should be paid such that they have the capacity and margin to use and hone their gifts, skills, talents, and passions.[28] When wages support these holistic considerations, they can

25. Ryan, *Distributive Justice*, 273.
26. Hinze, *Radical Sufficiency*, 34.
27. Mount, *Covenant, Community, and the Common Good*, 97–98.
28. See "A Just Wage Tool," criterion 1, https://socialconcerns.nd.edu/criterion-1/.

create the conditions for widespread human flourishing. Righteous wages for individuals help foster the well-being of all—the common good—which in turn creates the conditions for individual flourishing.

Let's consider two texts, Zechariah 8:3–12 and Micah 4:2–4, both of which add to our understanding of the way wages are impacted by, and contribute to, the common good. First, Zechariah 8 imagines economic well-being at the community level:

> This is what the Lord says: "I will return to Zion and dwell in Jerusalem. Then Jerusalem will be called the Faithful City, and the mountain of the Lord Almighty will be called the Holy Mountain."
>
> This is what the Lord Almighty says: "Once again men and women of ripe old age will sit in the streets of Jerusalem, each of them with cane in hand because of their age. The city streets will be filled with boys and girls playing there." . . .
>
> "This is also what the prophets said who were present when the foundation was laid for the house of the Lord Almighty. *Before that time there were no wages for people or hire for animals. No one could go about their business safely because of their enemies*, since I had turned everyone against their neighbor. But now I will not deal with the remnant of this people as I did in the past," declares the Lord Almighty.
>
> The seed will grow well, the vine will yield its fruit, the ground will produce its crops, and the heavens will drop their dew. I will give all these things as an inheritance to the remnant of this people. (vv. 3–5, 9–12; emphasis added)

Zechariah 8 is a prototypical Old Testament text that offers the people of God a hope-filled vision of God's intended future. The eschatological texture of the passage imagines a society of wholeness and healing. As is usually the case, the text opens with God's promise to "return" to the people. Periods of exile are often framed as separations from God, ostensibly because of the people's distance from Jerusalem and temple itself; but in these passages, God promises to come back to the people, reminding them that they are not abandoned to destruction, because the hope of restoration lies in the promise of God's return.

This is certainly true of Zechariah 8. The text describes a comprehensive renewal of Israel's fortunes, but what is striking about the language of Zechariah 8 is the distinctly concrete and ordinary scope of God's restorative intentions. Notice the language of health and human vitality connected to the promise of long life. Similarly, the community will be one of peace, safety, and security as children will be free to run, laugh, and play in the streets. Later, the prophet describes "fasts" transforming into "feasts," a promise to replace sadness and lament with happiness and celebration.

Central to this restored vision of life in Jerusalem is a description of economic life. To begin, the overall economic conditions will be fruitful. Zechariah declares God's promise that "the seed will grow well, the vine will yield its fruit, the ground will produce its crops, and the heavens will drop their dew" (v. 12). Life in an agricultural society depends on reliable environmental activity as the basis for economic vitality. In other words, farmers need rain to feed their families! That makes the promise of rain an economic gift. In this society of God's intentions, Israel will labor in cooperation with the earth to create real economic possibility.

Unsurprisingly, this is a picture of agricultural and economic abundance. This is, after all, a hallmark of who God is and what God shares with humanity. That abundance creates a social and economic outlook that fosters a new kind of community life. The current status quo is characterized by adversarial economic relationships. It says that no one can conduct safe business, because everyone is in conflict with their neighbor. The fabric of the community is fractured; it is not experiencing the tangible effects of God's abundance. The inference drawn is that the restorative intentions of God include addressing this frayed social fabric. The future-to-come will not pit neighbor against neighbor; instead, it will draw them into restored relationships, which will restore their ability to conduct safe and fruitful business. The holistic scope of God's restorative work will produce a healthy, generative economic life.

As the entire community experiences healing, economic conditions create possibilities for individuals as well. Near the center of Zechariah's vision is the admission that the fractured status quo included widespread unemployment. The text says, "before that time there were no wages for people or hire for animals" (v. 10). The community was experiencing destitution that took a financial toll on everyone. There were no jobs to hire out, even for the animals used to power the agricultural economic system. But the promise of restoration for the whole community contains the promise of wages for individual workers—the promise of a growing labor market. Zechariah highlights the connection between opportunity for workers and community well-being. This vision for a restored Jerusalem means well-being for its residents. In a community experiencing something of a common good, there is always opportunity at the individual level. The pursuit of the common good has a generative effect, the ripple effects of well-being.

Similarly, Micah 4:2–4 suggests that economic well-being at the community level includes a real opportunity for "the good life" for individuals. In one of the prophet's best-known eschatological promises, he pictures a day when all the nations of the earth will convene and say, "Come, let us go up to the mountain of the LORD, to the temple of the God of Jacob. He will teach us his ways, so that we may walk in his paths." Micah then declares what God will do in response:

> The law will go out from Zion,
> the word of the LORD from Jerusalem.
> He will judge between many peoples
> and will settle disputes for strong nations far and wide.
> They will beat their swords into plowshares
> and their spears into pruning hooks.
> Nation will not take up sword against nation,
> nor will they train for war anymore.
> Everyone will sit under their own vine
> and under their own fig tree,
> and no one will make them afraid,
> for the LORD Almighty has spoken.

As in Zechariah, the prophet Micah conveys God's promise of a world made right. Micah envisions a day when God will put down violence in favor of a world of peace—evidenced by fruitful agricultural practices replacing the destruction of war. In the middle of this vision of communal flourishing is a stunning line: "Everyone will sit under their own vine and under their own fig tree, and no one will make them afraid," proclaiming God's intentions to create a future where positive economic conditions foster an abiding sense of *existential shalom*.

Micah pictures a day when every person will not only own their own vine and fig tree but also have the opportunity and margin to actually "sit under" them—free of fear, worry, and anxiety. Micah affirms the idea that there is an intangible quality of life and that the absence of such is a detriment to well-being. God's promise of a world made right includes the promise of economically enabled psychological peace. Of course, anyone at every income level is in danger of being controlled by economic anxiety, regardless of whether economic struggle is realistic or probable. But Micah envisions a day when no one will live in fear of having their livelihood taken from them by economic predation.

That fear, though, is an ever-present reality in the lives of today's working poor and those on the economic margins of society. A good friend of mine often shared stories of having grown up in poverty. She always said that being poor was a full-time job. She meant that the work required to navigate the systems and structures of society, just to make ends meet as an under- or unemployed family, created a nearly untenable schedule of appointments, meetings, and responsibilities. The common trope of the poor being lazy is often not the case; the work required to make ends meet through the mechanics of our social systems leaves little time in which a person might work their way to more stable economic footing. There is certainly no time to sit, and no vine or fig tree of their own under which to do so.

Like my friend, there are huge swaths of the population in the United States who taste nothing of Micah's redemptive promise. The demands of a life that hovers around the poverty line are simply too much to afford a person either the time or the mental health by which to actually sit without fear and find any real sense of existential shalom, any "at-peace-ness" that might override money stress and allow the anxieties of life to relent.

For anyone who doesn't possess that kind of margin, existential shalom remains elusive. For many, resting from work does nothing to resolve the conditions of their economic vulnerability; in fact, it may make it worse. They do not possess the economic margin to resist lurking economic pressure and worry. Rest by itself may recharge a person's capacity for work, but it does not solve these issues. The kind of shalom we are after—a set of conditions that help foster a deep psychological abiding—demands more than just time off. The world as it should be, the world where the common good is commonplace, the world God will bring to bear one day, is one where everyone is free from economic stress and can enjoy the freedom afforded those who do not exist in a constant state of economic threat. Micah's vision implies that this intangible sense of economic well-being is part of the redemptive vision of God.

Both of these texts offer the reader a vision of God's preferred future. Economic well-being is intertwined with all the ways God's redemptive intentions will take root in the world. Our pursuit of the common good is always informed by that eschatological vision of the future. Righteous wages can promote the common good when they foster well-being for workers and their families. Wages for well-being are two for one. They are a demonstration of righteousness (for the wage giver) via the cultivation of justice (for the wage earner and the community).

## So, What's the Number?

Admittedly, we've not gotten any closer to hard numbers for righteous and just wages. The minimum wage, and in many places the more recently instituted living wage, at least deal in concrete declarations. However, as we close out this discussion, I want to offer some caution as it relates to a fixation on deciphering an exact number that constitutes a righteous/just wage. If that is the front-burner question, at the end of all we've explored across these pages, we may be tipping our hand. At the beginning of the chapter, I suggested that focusing on the right minimum wage attempts to determine just how little we can pay someone with a clear conscience. The same is true here; we've just changed the label from *minimum* to *righteous*. We have not moved from trying to identify the bare minimum one can pay workers to meet some moral standard. This strays from the guiding sense of God's abundance and the invitation to allow wages to exhibit a desire to see well-being for workers and their families and promote the common good in our communities.

Miroslav Volf introduces a helpful thought exercise when he describes "ethical minimums" and "ethical maximums." An ethical minimum does not employ the same logic as a minimum wage, where the question is, How little can we pay someone? Instead, an *ethical* minimum provides a lens by which Christians can offer critique to unjust wage structures. Ethical maximums introduce an aspirational vision toward which Christians can enact approaches to compensation that seek the common good more explicitly. Volf is quick to name the moral demands on the Christian, saying, "All responsible Christian behavior has to satisfy the ethical minimum and . . . move toward the ethical maximum. The ethical minimum is the *criterion* for structuring the world of work, the ethical maximum the necessary *regulative ideal*."[29]

Guided by this notion, what would change about the way our system of labor runs if we stopped asking what we *have to* pay and started asking what we *can* pay? What if the world of work was obsessed with providing wages that enable the well-being of each person? That's a world focused not on a number but on an outcome.

29. Volf, *Work in the Spirit*, 82–83.

# 6 IS SOLIDARITY POSSIBLE?

## Reimagining Relationships Between Workers and Owners

The drones are no longer invisible. . . . They're in the office as well as the warehouse. . . . Bob Cratchit may still be hanging on, . . . but Scrooge has been replaced by a conglomerate. Hardly a chance for Christmas spirit here. Who knows Bob's name in this outfit?

—Studs Terkel[1]

The battle over just and righteous wages is just one layer of the fraught relationship between the owner class and working people. The many ways the working class experiences vulnerability in, and because of, their labor situation contribute to a nearly universal and thoroughly historical rift between owners and workers. So much so that when people hear the claim "God is passionately pro-worker," they often assume that must mean God is also *anti-owner*. Thankfully, God doesn't operate in such a narrow binary. Still, that rift is real and characterizes the owner/worker relationship even when the worker is not working class. Consider the constant labor unrest in professional sports. Athletes and owners are in an ever-present state of "at odds" that fill pages of banner copy across every sports news outlet in the world. There is an ever-widening gulf of distrust between owners and workers of all stripes

1. Studs Terkel, *Working: People Talk About What They Do All Day and How They Feel About What They Do* (Pantheon, 1974), xiv.

that is consistently accelerated by the many disparities between the two and the perpetual sense that the relationship is a zero-sum game.[2]

Whether we are talking about wages, benefits, working conditions, job security, the implications of automation, the number of hours in a work week, the merits of remote work, or any other issue that stokes conflict between owners and workers, we are ultimately talking about power. In particular, we are talking about *power disparity*. Consider any example of workers'-rights issues across history, and chances are the issue comes down to conflict between the power-full and the power-less. It is a question of how power is used, for whose benefit, and toward whose detriment.

Making progress on any labor problem requires a renegotiation of power, as is the case with so many justice questions. It is hard to think of a justice issue that is not ultimately about the misuse of power by one person/group toward, or over, another. The work of justice throughout this nation's history is a litany of power negotiations, away from structures that exploit and oppress and, ideally, toward structures that liberate and allow for flourishing. Those stories typically center on those without power asking for or demanding change in situations where power differentials result in dehumanization, exploitation, and oppression. But because the power-full have a vested interest in the status quo, these disruptions almost always create a battle between sides. As Frederick Douglass framed it in 1857, "if there is no struggle, there is no progress."[3] Douglass continues, putting a finer point on this idea: "The struggle may be a moral one, or it may be a physical one, and it may be both moral and physical, but it must be a struggle. Power concedes nothing without a demand. It never did and it never will. Find out just what any people will quietly submit to and you have found out the exact measure of injustice and wrong which will be imposed upon them, and these will continue until they are resisted with either words or blows, or with both. The limits of tyrants are prescribed by the endurance of those whom they oppress."[4]

Silent submission to oppression allows the power-full to maintain a status quo that benefits them. This requires the power-less to resist injustice lest it continue unchanged. But that resistance also requires reciprocation. Without a confrontation demanding social change, the power-full are unlikely to change; but unless they actually change or enact change, there can be no meaningful,

2. David H. Jensen, *Responsive Labor: A Theology of Work* (Westminster John Knox, 2006), 103.

3. Frederick Douglass, "West India Emancipation," August 4, 1857, in *Two Speeches by Frederick Douglass* (Rochester, NY, 1857), 22.

4. Douglass, "West India Emancipation," 22.

sustained progress for the power-less. In the end, justice always requires a renegotiation of power.

Thinking about this imbalance of power helps us make sense of the labor struggle. When wages are insufficient, owners have a power advantage over workers. When conditions are dangerous, owners have a power advantage. When job security is consistently in question, again: advantage ownership. Owners hold the cards, leaving workers looking for ways to find relief, make progress, and secure a better situation. A renegotiation of power is needed.

At a basic level, this is why labor unions exist. Since the late eighteenth century, unions in the United States have helped workers build a countervailing power base to shield individual workers from economic vulnerability and protect them from exploitation and mistreatment. Individually, workers have no reasonable expectation for this. They can, however, come together and put pressure on a system committed to maintaining an unjust status quo. A labor union intends to represent workers as a collective force, able to make stronger demands in the face of unjust situations. Unions give exploitable or vulnerable workers a realistic way to resist wrongs the powerful permit or intend to impose on them. They allow workers a path to bring balance to the scales of power that too often tip in favor of ownership. In the long and fraught history between owners and the rank and file, unions give many millions of "Davids" a chance against "Goliaths" like Rockefeller, Carnegie, Gould, Vanderbilt, Astor, Ford, Shultz, and Bezos.

So, how should Christians make sense of this issue of power in the context of labor, the often conflict-filled relationship between owners and workers, between the Scrooges and the Cratchits? Despite its delicacy, we can develop a theological lens to help us navigate the rifts and conflicts present between workers and owners. We can discern the common good in situations where power is being weaponized against more vulnerable groups. A posture shift will be required, though.

## The Church and Worker-Justice Movements

Despite their attraction to the David and Goliath story, evangelicals are increasingly skeptical of, and even antagonistic toward, the worker side of the labor struggle. Studies show that evangelicals oppose unions more than most other religious groups do.[5] There are a few reasons for this, as we saw in chapter 1.

5. See Tobin Grant, "Polling Evangelicals: Not Pro-Union, but Split Over Unions Versus Government," *Christianity Today*, March 4, 2011, https://www.christianitytoday.com/2011/03/pollunions/.

The first reason is political. As evangelicals gravitated toward the Republican Party after World War II, the increasing divide between evangelicals and Democratic politics fueled an anti-labor stance. Political data confirms that evangelical politicians are "consistently" and "uniquely" opposed to the labor agenda when compared to adherents of other religious traditions.[6]

A second reason is shaped by religious practice. Evangelicals are decidedly individualistic in their understanding of the practice of religion.[7] That hyper-personalized Protestant disposition toward salvation and piety carries with it a deep-seated skepticism toward collectivism of any kind. A brief review of popular treatments of the question of the compatibility of the Christian faith and union membership reveals that conservative evangelical streams of American Christianity are deeply suspicious of unions on theological grounds. They argue that one cannot be a member of a union because of Christianity's demand for full allegiance to Christ.

A third reason is socioeconomic. As the Faith and Work movement became the primary way evangelicals talked about work, it comes as no surprise to observe the many ways the movement centers the questions of those higher up the socioeconomic order. Labor unrest and drives for unionization are direct assaults on the financial positions of many evangelicals, which makes the movement unlikely to sympathize with worker concerns.

However, there have been Christians who have taken decidedly pro-labor stances. Within the broader tradition, there have been many faith-filled labor movements supporting workers and campaigns for worker justice. Dorothy Day founded the Catholic Worker movement, which focused on labor and other economic issues and supported workers in their pursuit of fair labor practices in many ways—providing food, supporting picket lines, and speaking at rallies and other labor events.[8] Other examples of ecumenical, faith-filled labor movements include Interfaith Worker Justice, a nonprofit most notably engaged with the "Fight for $15" movement in the United States.[9] And, of course, we remember that the Hispanic and Black church traditions have many examples of explicitly faith-animated movements concerned with labor justice.

But I've observed what the data bears out—that opposition to movements for worker justice (including recent examples like the fight for a higher

6. John McTague and Shanna Pearson-Merkowitz, "'The Worker Deserves His Wages'? Religion and Support for Organized Labor in the U.S. Senate," *Politics and Religion* 16 (2023): 175.

7. McTague and Pearson-Merkowitz, "The Worker Deserves His Wages," 175.

8. Dorothy Day, "House of Hospitality: Foreword," January 1, 1939, https://catholicworker.org/435-2/.

9. See "Interfaith Worker Justice," Influence Watch, https://www.influencewatch.org/non-profit/interfaith-worker-justice/.

minimum wage) draws the ire of evangelicals in an outsized way. And they often object on moral grounds, where it seems that maintaining an anti-labor position is a sign of theological purity—a demonstration of Christian orthodoxy. But is that right?

## God Is Passionately Pro-Worker

Arguing that the cause of worker justice is not supported by Scripture is factually incorrect. That argument fails to see that Scripture is not only *not silent* on the issue but that Scripture is actually ardently *pro-worker*. That makes opposition to workers'-rights questions on theological grounds a fundamental error.

At the same time, Scripture doesn't provide moral permission for every action, tactic, outcome, and motivation of worker-justice movements (unions, etc.). And being biblically pro-worker does not require supporting a particular political party or agenda. We can affirm the intention and possibility of the mechanisms of worker justice—and even support various expressions of that work—and still maintain an ability to discern when human, and therefore broken, institutions fall short of what they might be.

Still, the idea of poor and working-class people seeking redress for injustice is a fundamentally biblical notion. We previously explored Deuteronomy 24:15, which says, "Pay them their wages each day before sunset, because they are poor and are counting on it. Otherwise they may cry to the Lord against you, and you will be guilty of sin." Again, the sins of the owner class cause workers to cry out to God, who hears their cries and pronounces judgment on owners. The exact same idea is present in James 5:4 (also considered earlier), where James writes, "Look! The wages you failed to pay the workers who mowed your fields are crying out against you. The cries of the harvesters have reached the ears of the Lord Almighty."

These two worker-specific passages mirror a larger scriptural notion that when the oppressed experience injustice, their recourse is to cry out to God. For example, consider this passage from Psalm 10:14–18:

> But you, God, see the trouble of the afflicted;
> you consider their grief and take it in hand.
> The victims commit themselves to you;
> you are the helper of the fatherless.
> Break the arm of the wicked man;
> call the evildoer to account for his wickedness
> that would not otherwise be found out.

> The LORD is King for ever and ever;
> the nations will perish from his land.
> You, LORD, hear the desire of the afflicted;
> you encourage them, and you listen to their cry,
> defending the fatherless and the oppressed,
> so that mere earthly mortals
> will never again strike terror.

These are three examples of how the Scriptures thoroughly affirm the experience of the oppressed—oftentimes of workers in particular. They consistently reinforce the pride of place God maintains for the powerless and afflicted—those at the mercy of the powerfully unjust. In each case, God is the champion for the oppressed over against those doing the oppressing. We see that the violated know that they can cry out to God, that God will hear those cries, and that God will side with them and will attend to their plight.

Perhaps the most significant example of this is the exodus. The epic saga of Israel's liberation from Egypt is an incredible story of God's faithfulness to the people in a moment of extreme exploitation and oppression. Notably, the exodus story begins with labor negotiations in the face of worker exploitation.[10] The final straw (pun intended) was a dangerously unreasonable demand from Pharaoh, insisting that the Israelites produce more bricks with less material than was possible. That incident incites the very familiar story of Moses taking God's demands before Pharaoh, the many plagues (public demonstrations?), the stunning journey out of Egypt, and the long years of wandering in the wilderness as they travel to the promised land. God's call of Moses in Exodus 3 is another example of the now-familiar pattern of exploited workers crying out to a God who hears with the intent to intervene. God says, "I have indeed seen the misery of my people in Egypt. I have heard them crying out because of their slave drivers, and I am concerned about their suffering" (v. 7). The wide-ranging theological and practical importance of this story only enhances the importance of the specific context of the passage where God is again revealed to be passionately pro-worker.[11]

Pharaoh is a type for the owner class—exacting, manipulative, oppressive; an "extractor."[12] By contrast, God cares about the plight of the poor / working class in ways that the wealthy / owner class does not. In that sense, God is

10. Miroslav Volf argues that this is a central expression of alienation in work. See Volf, *Work in the Spirit: Toward a Theology of Work* (Wipf & Stock, 2001), 164.

11. Kim Hawtrey, "The Oxford Declaration on Christian Faith and Economics," *Transformation* 7, no. 2 (April/June 1990): 4.

12. Walter Brueggemann, *Tenacious Solidarity: Biblical Provocations on Race, Religion, Climate, and the Economy* (Fortress, 2018), 39.

the foil to Pharaoh and, more broadly, the owner class throughout Scripture. Because the pharaohs of the world turn deaf ears to the pleas of the people they have power over, God gives the poor / working class a way to bypass the wealthy / owner class and come directly to him. Oppressed people are always free to bring their grievances to God because their oppressors refuse to listen. As we know, God does much more than simply lend an ear. God responds with redemptive intent.

What's more, Scripture presumes that the owner class is *actually exploiting* the poor and working classes. These are not hypothetical situations; these passages are in the Bible to end and prevent injustice. While the rift between owners and workers is regrettable, the text suggests that more often than not the rift is widened by the unjust or unkind actions of owners. This makes Christian skepticism regarding the cause of the worker today misplaced.

Is this a universally true phenomenon? Are owners always doing the wrong thing and workers always doing the right? Of course not. And we can affirm the idea that God is pro-worker without being anti-owner even in cases where God sides against owners. Pharaoh had opportunity after opportunity to repent and show mercy. The escalation of the plagues in some ways reads as an example of God's long-suffering patience with hard-necked perpetrators of injustice. These circumstantial judgments do not mean that God takes a categorically antagonistic posture toward owners as a group. Clearly, though, Scripture affirms an overarching reality that the divide between owner and worker or power-full and power-less exists because of injustice toward "the least" by "the most."

## God as the Exemplar Person-in-Power

What accounts for God's pro-worker posture? Beyond the obvious, though wonderfully true, reality of God's universal love and care for all of humanity, there is more we can say about God's overriding concern for the lived experience of exploited workers. For example, of the many incredible things we can say about God, we know that God is a compassionate, generous, and kind "person-in-power." And as a compassionate, generous, and kind person-in-power, God fosters a particular kind of relationship with humanity, overtly committed to flourishing and freedom. Whether we know it or not, every single person, and all of humanity together, is in relationship with the all-powerful God of the universe. God is the ultimate person-in-power, and humanity lives in relation to that power. That makes the experience of being human fully dependent on whether God is a "good-faith actor." Thankfully,

God is the kind of person-in-power who cares, hears, and responds to the experience of his people.[13]

Beyond that, God has extended that very gift—of having a means to engage with him—to every person across history. This is why we have spiritual practices like prayer and fasting. These practices give every person a means of communicating with God and trusting God to respond with compassion, generosity, and kindness. Of course, we practice prayer and fasting for many reasons. But as we develop a theological lens to view this issue of power between the power-full and power-less, I'm keen to highlight the way these two practices—usually coupled together—act as communication channels that cross the divide between persons-in-power and persons below.[14]

Seen through that lens, prayer and fasting are God-given means for *self-advocacy*. Some care in description is useful here. Howard Thurman called prayer—and fasting fits the same description—an "act of barnstorming the gates of heaven," a way of going before God "wanting something for ourselves."[15] These practices allow us to draw attention to our plight and the plight of others and invite God to respond. But even though prayer and fasting are ways of bringing what we need or want to God, we don't use them as methods of manipulation, and we don't predetermine the manner of God's response.[16] God does not need to be informed, nor does God need to be pressured to act—as some commonly misinterpret the parable of the unjust judge in Luke 18.[17] Instead, we pray and fast believing God already knows. Just like the father in Jesus's parable of the prodigal son in Luke 15, we believe that even as we move toward God, God has already begun to move toward us. Prayer and fasting are means of self-advocacy before an already-responding God.

This models the standard for human relationships between persons-in-power and persons below. The ideal relationship is one where, as situations demand it, a power-less person can bring their concerns to the person-in-power. The person-in-power is called to imitate the movement of God—toward the cries of the power-less with redemptive intent. On the other hand, the exploitation

13. Most of the time, "God's people" is a specific designation for Israel (in the Old Testament) and the church (in the New Testament). I'm using this language to denote a more cosmic-level reality that "the earth is the Lord's and everything in it, the world, and all who live in it" (Ps. 24:1). At that level, God's relationship with all of humanity is the same. Differences in the way God relates to Israel or the church do not have enough bearing to treat for the purposes of this chapter.

14. Scot McKnight, *Fasting* (Thomas Nelson, 2009), 38.

15. Howard Thurman, "Concerning Prayer: Prayer and Pressure," in *Sermons on the Parables*, ed. David B. Gowler and Kipton E. Jensen (Orbis Books, 2018), 147.

16. McKnight, *Fasting*, xxi–xxii.

17. Thurman, "Concerning Prayer," 148.

of the power-less corrupts God's intention for this relationship and amplifies God's concern for what exploited peoples are experiencing. When the power-less are exploited, their dignity is violated. And when the power-full exploit, they are acting outside of the *imago Dei*, which violates *their* dignity. There is a deep, doubled sadness that accompanies these expressions of injustice.

The person-in-power—held to the standard of the well-being of the power-less—bears the weight of responsibility in these situations. Just like humanity's relationship with God, the experience of the power-less depends on whether the person-in-power is a good-faith actor. So, the powerful person's response is accountable to the moral standards set by God's example. In the context of labor, the onus for repair of the rift between owners and workers rests with ownership. Repair means responding to the plight of the working class with compassion, generosity, and kindness. This is a moral standard that leaves little room for skepticism and antagonism toward workers. Instead, it invites the owner class to enact a particular kind of solidarity with their workers, one that requires movement toward the cries and experience of the power-less with redemptive intent and restorative action. We could call this "self-implicating solidarity."

## Self-Implicating Solidarity

Solidarity, as Pope John Paul II said, "is not a feeling of vague compassion or shallow distress at the misfortunes of so many people. . . . It is a firm and persevering determination to commit oneself to the common good; that is to say to the good of all and of each individual, because we are all really responsible for all."[18] It's easy to see how this definition of solidarity is characteristic of God's actions toward us.

For example, one of the most common descriptors of God's character is the Hebrew word *hesed*. Though the Old Testament uses the term well over two hundred times—usually in reference to God's character and actions—it is, famously, one of those words that does not translate cleanly from Hebrew to English. And, importantly, the word has multiple emphases. First, the word clearly connotes something of a permanent love. God's *hesed* is a long-term loving commitment, joining God to humanity in a deep and abiding relation. Second, that commitment is expressed as a kind of promise. Without taking a deep dive into the world of ancient Hebrew covenantal theology, the idea of covenant can be summed up as a permanent state of devotion from

18. John Paul II, *Sollicitude Rei Socialis*, December 30, 1987, §38, http://www.vatican.va/content/john-paul-ii/en/encyclicals/documents/hf_jp-ii_enc_30121987_sollicitudo-rei-socialis.html.

one party to another. God's *hesed*, demonstrated in making a covenant with Israel, is also public. The covenantal "liturgy" described in the pages of the Old Testament—specifically in Genesis 15—required a public testimony. The ceremony, similar to other covenantal acts like marriage, was on display for others to see. There is a kind of relational power generated by an act observed and witnessed by others. That power is amplified when one considers the relative disparity of the social position of each party. In the case of God's *hesed*, it is a public demonstration of an all-powerful God entering into a relationship with a party that simply cannot reciprocate. That God establishes this covenant with humanity in a uniquely one-sided way—a dramatic act of *self-implication*—is evidence of humanity's relative inability to do anything but accept and receive this relationship, recognizing God is establishing the relationship this way for the sake of the more vulnerable party.[19]

The interpretive challenge here is clear. The word carries such varied notions of God's character and actions that every choice feels like an oversimplification. Old Testament scholar Walter Brueggemann offers a compelling alternative translation of *hesed* when he suggests that the word means "tenacious solidarity," which takes the wide richness of the word into account and orients our attention toward God's willingness to implicate himself in the establishment of the relationship.[20]

Self-implicating solidarity is undoubtedly best evidenced in the life and work of Jesus. Christ's incarnation, for example, shows the extent to which God will go to ensure human flourishing, revealing a God "definitively for and with us."[21] As Rachel Douglass says, "the incarnation is God's practice of solidarity."[22] Crossing lines of power, position, and privilege, Jesus joins the life of God to ours. If people colloquially think of solidarity as "being in it together," then the incarnation is perhaps the clearest expression of divine solidarity, as it reveals Immanuel—God with us.

We should not, though, compartmentalize our vision of God's solidarity to peaceable scenes of mangers and magi. It is important to realize that solidarity is not a passive concept. Rather, it requires "elements of conflict

19. If you study the practice of covenant making and read the scriptural account of God's covenant (in particular the Abrahamic covenant in Gen. 15) with the people of Israel, you will note that God takes on "both sides" of the promise of faithfulness. It is a unique expression of this practice that scholars suggest means that God is taking on the full responsibility for the sanctity of the relationship.

20. Brueggemann, *Tenacious Solidarity*, 354.

21. Mary Jo Iozzio, *Disability Ethics and Preferential Justice: A Catholic Perspective* (Georgetown University Press, 2023), 69.

22. Rachel M. Douglass, "Solidarity and the Incarnation: A Dialogue with Denise Ackermann and Allan Boesak," *Stellenbosch Theological Journal* 5, no. 3 (2019): 278.

and cohesion."[23] Self-implicating solidarity resists soft or superficial calls for community. True and meaningful solidarity confronts situations where the status quo of society collides with God's intentions. The earth-shattering idea that God would join his life to ours reminds us that self-implicating solidarity always involves conflict with "the way things are." At the same time, solidarity doesn't perpetuate toxic divisions that give rise to injustice; it fosters a different kind of community. That balance of conflict and cohesion is an apt way to refer to the work of Christ—particularly on the cross—because in this ultimate act of solidarity with us Jesus defeats the powers and principalities (Col. 2:15) *and* establishes a new kind of family (Eph. 2:15) that is capable of overcoming lines of difference in service to a new humanity being stitched together in him. Jesus's radical work of self-implicating solidarity creates the conditions for human solidarity to be expressed in a new and powerful way. The solidarity required to foster justice in the labor context is more possible because of God's redemptive action in the world.

And lest we allow ourselves to think of divine solidarity in too abstract or transcendent terms, the life of Christ also returns our attention to the way that self-implicating solidarity centers the concrete experience of the exploited and oppressed. The cosmic significance of Christ's solidarity with all of humanity is balanced by his deep sense of compassion and interpersonal connection with "the least," as evidenced in Matthew 25:31–46. In this famous text about the sheep and the goats, Jesus identifies with the poor and vulnerable to such an extent that he inhabits their lived experience. He is implicated by their experience because their struggle is his struggle. Consider this excerpt from Matthew 25:34–40:

> Then the King will say to those on his right, "Come, you who are blessed by my Father; take your inheritance, the kingdom prepared for you since the creation of the world. For I was hungry and you gave me something to eat, I was thirsty and you gave me something to drink, I was a stranger and you invited me in, I needed clothes and you clothed me, I was sick and you looked after me, I was in prison and you came to visit me."
>
> Then the righteous will answer him, "Lord, when did we see you hungry and feed you, or thirsty and give you something to drink? When did we see you a stranger and invite you in, or needing clothes and clothe you? When did we see you sick or in prison and go to visit you?"
>
> The King will reply, "Truly I tell you, whatever you did for one of the least of these brothers and sisters of mine, you did for me."

23. Leah Hunt-Hendrix and Astra Taylor, *Solidarity: The Past, Present, and Future of a World-Changing Idea* (Pantheon, 2024), 14.

Matthew 25:31–46 creates a conceptual bridge between the character and work of God in Christ and the invitation to emulate God in our day-to-day life. Jesus's vision of the sheep and the goats is primarily a picture of God's judgment—a divine sorting, of sorts. The basis of that judgment is whether or not people lived the way Jesus did: with an abiding sense of solidarity with those on the margins. As followers of Jesus, "if we are to be in communion with God and God's body, we must be in communion with these people too."[24] Because of Jesus's life and work on our behalf, self-implicating solidarity is meant to be our way of life as well.

Paul outlines the same idea in Philippians 2:5–11. In his soaring treatment of the character of Christ evidenced by his incarnation among us, he intends to highlight the specific way Jesus opts out of the "upward mobility" his position and privilege afford him. Notice how Paul, when he says that Jesus "made himself nothing by taking the very nature of a servant, being made in human likeness" (v. 7), seems to link the incarnation with the kind of "downward" movement characteristic of self-implicating solidarity. So when Paul opens this passage with the charge "In your relationships with one another, have the same mindset as Christ Jesus" (v. 5), it strengthens the argument that the narrative of Scripture invites a posture of relational solidarity that implicates each person. Anytime God interacts with any person(s), it represents God's determined commitment to human flourishing. Self-implicating solidarity sets the standard for the relationship between persons-in-power and persons below.

## Implications for Labor and Worker-Justice Movements

Seeking to practice self-implicating solidarity with others—particularly the exploited and oppressed—is a normative expectation for Christian people. In the context of labor, self-implicating solidarity helps us imagine new ways of responding to the rifts between owners and workers and gives us new eyes to discern the common good in situations where power is being used to the detriment of others. Adam Joyce argues that "the relationships of power that create the inequality and instability that scar American life can only be overturned through a mass movement based in and built by solidarity."[25] How might people of faith imitate the character and action of God in these fraught labor situations and move toward the power-less with redemptive intent and restorative action?

24. Douglass, "Solidarity and the Incarnation," 279.

25. Adam Joyce, "Theology for the One Percent: The Problem with the Evangelical Faith and Work Movement," *ABC Religion and Ethics*, October 21, 2019, https://www.abc.net.au/religion/theology-for-the-one-percent-the-evangelical-faith-and-work-mov/11625040.

First, a decidedly Christian disposition toward the working class would be receptive, ingenuous, and compassionate. The previously mentioned suspicion and antagonism toward working-class concerns is wildly out of place considering the wide testimony of Scripture. Too often, working-class concerns are dismissed or maligned in ways that demonstrate a closed posture and an unwillingness to take the experience of workers seriously. This is out of step with the action of God in the world.

This has a particular bearing on Christian posture toward the direct actions workers take to incite a renegotiation of power. Of course, here we are talking about tactics like protests, labor strikes, and other strategies aimed at putting pressure on the status quo. It is helpful to note that, because prayer and fasting are God-given means of taking potentially drastic action in response to our plight, or the plight of others, tactics that add stress to a tense labor situation are not automatically something to reject. Instead, we remember that the exodus story begins with protest. Moses's interactions with Pharaoh, and the subsequent plagues, are examples of the radical measures needed at times to get the full attention of the owner class. What's more, it is important to remember that God participated in, and even directed, that work for the sake of the power-less Israelites. The exodus account reveals the occasional necessity of these strategies in order to bring about justice and liberation.[26]

Typically, though, Christians—particularly evangelicals—have chosen to frame these tactics as unholy rebellion. Rather than seeing protest and/or strike as possibly a way of emulating Christ's reaction to the temple money changers (Matt. 21:12–17), our national story has seen many Christians side with the wealthy owner class. This is true even in cases of clear and blatant injustice and oppression (slavery and civil rights, among many others). This track record of taking the side of unjust ownership should chasten any instinct we may have to label workers'-rights tactics as sinful, indulgent, entitled, or any of the other many labels that get thrown about thoughtlessly. Instead, we ought to imagine ways of enacting God's posture toward workers and practice ways of being receptive, open-handed, and passionate about their concerns.

Second, self-implicating solidarity suggests that Christians should be willing to share in, and shoulder, the burdens of the working class and exploited workers. This is a straightforwardly Christocentric notion, but it also nods to the origins of the idea of solidarity in the Western world. The formal notion of solidarity took shape in the sixth century, when civil codes established something referred to as "obligation-in-common," essentially a code that

26. Brueggemann, *Tenacious Solidarity*, 44–46.

saw economic debt as something that a community held together.[27] Bearing another's debt as one's own seems as clear a way to embody the life of Christ in the world as possible, and our faith "does make demands on people to accept economic responsibility for others."[28] That is why those aforementioned faith-filled movements for worker justice are such powerful witnesses to the way of God in the world. They are concrete expressions of solidarity willing to pay a price to see a more equitable distribution of power. God does not leave us to fend for ourselves. God's redemptive designs move him toward us for the purpose of taking on our experience and our struggle. How might Christians emulate that example in the world when it comes to the struggles faced by workers?

Third, self-implicating solidarity on the part of owners *begins* with introspection, repentance, and kindness. As we've said, there is no denying the fact that Scripture takes a concerned posture toward the wealthy owner class. We've also noted that this posture is not anti-owner but anti-exploitation. The great tragedy of these texts is the fairly universal reality of the mistreatment of the poor by the owner class. It is for this that God takes the owner class to task and calls them to account. In the face of that witness, defensiveness, what-about-ism, demonization, and fostering an economically combative relationship toward workers is categorically out of place.

This call to introspection and kindness has historical merit as well. Throughout the history of the United States, we have seen horrific examples of the owner class playing the role of Pharaoh. The March 1911 Triangle Shirtwaist Fire in New York City claimed the lives of nearly 150 workers—mostly young women. These women faced brutal working conditions, and the demand for production was so high that the company locked exits to the building so they could not leave. As a result, when the fire raged, they could not escape, and many of these young women died by jumping out of the building to escape the flames. Just a few years after the Triangle fire, striking workers in the Colorado coal mines faced the National Guard and militias sent to quell labor tensions between workers and ownership (in this case, John D. Rockefeller Jr.). The violence was extreme, as machine guns were turned on workers, killing many. In the aftermath, the National Guard set fire to the worker encampment, killing more than a dozen women and children.[29] The Ludlow Massacre, as it

27. Hunt-Hendrix and Taylor, *Solidarity*, 6.

28. Volf, *Work in the Spirit*, 194.

29. "Machine Guns Spit Death in Labor Battle," *The Seattle Star*, April 21, 1914, https://www.loc.gov/resource/sn87093407/1914-04-21/ed-1/; and "Ludlow Massacre: Topics in Chronicling America," Library of Congress, https://guides.loc.gov/chronicling-america-ludlow-massacre.

came to be known, is one of scores of examples of violent tactics used against workers in the mining industry that continue into recent decades. These examples are not anomalies. Workplace conditions were commonly dangerous at the turn of the twentieth century, claiming the lives of, on average, one hundred workers per day.[30] And ownership violently suppressing the cries of their workers is not just a historical issue. I've seen firsthand the modern-day sweatshop-worker experience, where the demand for production drives down the willingness to recognize the dignity of workers. Migrant farm workers face similar challenges, as the disregard of farm owners is evidenced by all manner of unsafe and exploitative work situations.[31] Self-assumed innocence is not a credible starting position for owner and wealthy classes in the United States.

Conflict between owners and workers stems from and contributes to the view that the other is the enemy, or at the very least the competitor. But viewing the working class as an obstacle to or opponent of the success of industry will cripple the owner class's capacity and willingness to practice self-implicating solidarity. This is far too often the reality. A radical revolution of the culture of labor is required—beginning with the owner class. Reengineering industry toward authentic and comprehensive collaboration between owners and workers is essential if we are to see anything of equitable distribution of power and the curbing of worker exploitation. Doing so will embrace a cooperative mindset and reject an economic worldview that divides people into what Wendell Berry calls "a class of winners and a class of losers."[32] Viewing the owner/worker relationship through the winner-and-loser frame turns toxic competition into, at a minimum, a value-neutral proposition, if not an ideal. Competition as social value has a significant impact on our economic life and the life of our society. As Berry says, "The defenders of the ideal of competition have never known what to do with and for the losers. The losers simply accumulate in human dumps, like stores of industrial waste. . . . A loser, by definition, is somebody whom nobody knows what to do with. There is no limit to the damage and the suffering implicit in this willingness that losers should exist as a normal economic cost."[33]

The "winners" in an economic context dominated by competition continue to accumulate and concentrate wealth and power. As they do so, the class of

30. See "Triangle Shirtwaist Fire," AFL-CIO, https://aflcio.org/about/history/labor-history-events/triangle-shirtwaist-fire.

31. See, e.g., 2024 Farmworker Survey, Migrant Justice, https://migrantjustice.net/sites/default/files/2024-Farmworker-Survey-Results_1.pdf.

32. Wendell Berry, "Economy and Pleasure," in *The Art of Commonplace: The Agrarian Essays of Wendell Berry*, ed. Norman Wirzba (Counterpoint, 2002), 208.

33. Berry, "Economy and Pleasure," 208–9.

losers grows ever larger. The "loser" class of people exists to produce wealth for the winners; they are reduced, as Berry says, to "economic 'units,' or integers of production."[34] Taken to its logical end, a competitive economic life will ultimately turn everyone against one another.[35]

Maintaining this system would be radically out of step with the way God acts in the world. God, who moves toward the exploited and oppressed, who hears their cries and stands in judgment of any who might mistreat them, seeks to join with them through acts of compassion, generosity, and kindness. There is nothing in a society of winners vs. losers that fosters those virtues toward those labeled "losers." God invites us into a different posture, into a different way of being, toward different ends.

34. Berry, "Economy and Pleasure," 208 (see 208–9).
35. Berry, "Economy and Pleasure," 208–9. See also Jensen, *Responsive Labor*, 100.

# 7 AGENCY AND ASSETS

## Becoming Exploitation Resistant

> I find some delight in my job. . . . I'm able to set my own pace, my own standards, and determine for myself the substance of each program. Some days are more sunny than others, . . . but it is, for better or worse, in my hands.
>
> —Studs Terkel[1]

Perhaps the most significant takeaway from our reflections thus far is the extent of God's concern for the working class. God's pro-worker posture is reinforced again and again across the Scriptures. That posture informs the way we think about wages—a mechanism for the well-being of workers and a barometer of faithfulness for owners. It challenges antagonism toward worker self-advocacy and invites an optimistic receptivity to bringing balance to power structures. What's more, the Scriptures show us that while God's decided position is that the most direct responsibility for worker well-being rests with ownership, the flourishing of workers is everyone's concern.

And the more vulnerable a worker is to exploitation, the less they can flourish. When conditions or circumstances are such that people are not just in an economically precarious position but are also left exposed as targets of economic extraction and injustice, their capacity for thriving diminishes

1. Studs Terkel, *Working: People Talk About What They Do All Day and How They Feel About What They Do* (Pantheon, 1974), xvi.

rapidly. When economic flourishing goes up, exploitation goes down. To care about the economic well-being of the working class requires a commitment to eliminating economic exploitation, which in many ways has come to "pass as good business."[2] There is a sense in which the labor question is really a question about building resistance against worker exploitation. Righteous wages help that, as does a shifting balance of power. The more we reflect on how the Scriptures inform a faith-animated disposition toward laborers, the moral urgency of an exploitation-resistant working class becomes even more clear. This is not just an urgent question for the moment. Eliminating economic exploitation is an ongoing pursuit. Ensuring that the working class (and every class "under" them) is increasingly exploitation resistant should be a natural result of a working theology of labor over the long haul. The long-term effects and adequacy of our application of these ideas will be evaluated not just on whether the owner class is exploiting the working class (a near-term result) but also on the capacity of working-class folks to successfully resist their own exploitation over time.

To that end, two ideas—worker agency and asset building—are important for several reasons. First, increasing both worker agency and asset-building capacity helps build a more exploitation-resistant workforce. Second, it increases the possible fruitfulness of relations between owners and workers. And third, they are concrete ways of enacting our commitments to human dignity and the common good related to the labor question. Importantly, worker agency and asset building are also thoroughly biblical notions that provide crucial theological support to this work.

## Worker Agency: The First Step in Eliminating Exploitation

One of the questions I would have loved to ask my grandfather is what it felt like doing his job every day. I want to know whether he felt like a pawn in some larger game or, because he was a traveling salesman, whether he felt that his job afforded him autonomy and authority to make his own decisions, establish his own routines, and so on. What aspects of his work did he have control over, and where did he feel disempowered? I can imagine all manner of ways his work could have felt liberating, and just as many that could have made him feel small. It seems to me that those in his line of work would have been ripe for being taken advantage of, as he had little to no decision-making power in setting his economic terms and conditions. The disconnect between

2. Dom Rembert Sorg, OSB, *Holy Work: Towards a Benedictine Theology of Manual Labor* (Pio Decimo, 1953), 15.

his labor and his company's power structures likely had a major influence on his daily experience.

He seems like a perfect case study of the tenuous situation many working-class folks face. My grandfather's daily reality matched the classic definition of a worker as one who does not own the means of production and therefore must sell their labor for a wage. This left him exposed to unkind economic forces. In one sense, my grandfather had dignified work and was able to carve out some (perhaps small) sense of flourishing for himself and his family. In another, there would have been a consistent economic precarity that he had little control or influence over. He was at the mercy of his employers. Would they be benevolent? Would they be manipulative? Even in good working situations, workers are still exposed to the constant threat of exploitation because their labor and livelihoods rest in someone else's hands. As we've said, the economic well-being of workers is far too dependent on the whims of owners. This is not only a relational imbalance; it is also a structural imbalance, as power and capital are concentrated in the owner class. The system is designed in such a way that workers are too often disconnected from the things that would help them resist exploitation and experience something other than constant economic vulnerability.[3]

This is, in the first place, a question of agency. Agency—the capacity and freedom to self-determine—helps workers resist exploitation in a fundamental way. The more autonomy I have over the labor my body produces, the less I am at the mercy of someone else's decision-making. This is not only a blue-collar concern, of course. It is something every worker faces. Over the course of the many jobs I have worked, I've experienced nearly every amount of worker agency I imagine possible. I've been self-employed, been a senior leader, supervised a large team, felt the press and pressure of being middle management, and sold my labor for a wage as an hourly worker. Thankfully, I've never worked in situations with objectively unsafe working conditions, even though many millions do. But I have had other unfortunate experiences that are common to many workers—such as overbearing managerial oversight, micromanagement, and demeaning work policies that attempt to exert control over employees. The policies governing employee freedom in the workplace are often infantilizing, and workers face forms of monitoring that can easily venture into invasion of privacy.[4] I also worked

3. Kim Hawtrey, "The Oxford Declaration on Christian Faith and Economics," *Transformation* 7, no. 2 (April/June 1990): 7.

4. J. Hariharan, and H. Noorda, "Imprisoned at Work: The Impact of Employee Monitoring on Physical Privacy and Individual Liberty," *Modern Law Review* 88 (2025): 333–65, https://doi.org/10.1111/1468-2230.12922.

in the restaurant industry, where employees often have few choices other than to purchase food from their employer. When taken to an extreme, that is a straightforward expression of worker exploitation.[5] In another job, I worked on the manufacturing floor, performing the same repetitive tasks over and over again. In many ways, that job was the most difficult I ever had, primarily because I failed to understand the general lack of interest in the promotion of worker agency. I naively thought that ideas would always be welcome and offered them freely. They were . . . not received. A trivial example, to be sure, but it felt like the kind of job Carl Henry had in mind when he critiqued the way assembly-line work dulls the creative possibility of workers over time. I imagine that almost every blue-collar worker knows the experience of having one's agency disregarded, ignored, suppressed, or taken away. Nothing renders a worker to cog-in-machine status as quickly as the removal of or resistance to their initiative, creativity, and problem-solving skills.

The removal or suppression of worker agency is an abuse of power and a corruption of God's intent for the relationship between owners and workers. Beginning again with the narratives of Genesis 1 and 2 helps us consider the foundational biblical argument for the co-creative intentions of God. Consider these two excerpts from the creation narrative:

> God blessed them and said to them, "Be fruitful and increase in number; fill the earth and subdue it. Rule over the fish in the sea and the birds in the sky and over every living creature that moves on the ground." (Gen. 1:28)

> Now the LORD God had formed out of the ground all the wild animals and all the birds in the sky. He brought them to the man to see what he would name them; and whatever the man called each living creature, that was its name. So the man gave names to all the livestock, the birds in the sky and all the wild animals. (Gen. 2:19–20a)

Collaboration is built into the God-ordained system of labor. God, the exemplar person-in-power, designs creation's function in a way that demands collaborative participation from everyone who works to tend what God has made. Eden is a coworking space where God will work out the creation mandate together with Adam and Eve, who bear God's image. It is not only Adam and Eve's but every image bearer's role and responsibility to work alongside one another and with God in this way.

5. Tina Vasquez, "US Farms Are Forcing Workers to Buy Inedible, Expensive Meals," *The Guardian*, October 2, 2024.

Consider a few striking characteristics of this system of labor. First, God confers an area of responsibility to humanity. God mandates subduing and ruling over all of creation. This is a straightforward delegation of authority. The person-in-power gives away authority, providing humanity its own "freedom of action."[6] There is real autonomy here that emphasizes humanity's role in the system rather than merely providing them a checklist to accomplish. Recalling Wendell Berry from the last chapter, this structure commends a cooperative relationship between persons-in-power and persons below rather than the competitiveness and combativeness that so often characterizes these relationships.[7]

That delegation of authority is perhaps best expressed in the real decision-making power God extends to Adam. The naming of the animals—not just a Sunday school story—is significant. By naming them, Adam does for the animals what God did for him. This is a wonderful example of the interplay between God and humanity—God is openhanded with authority, and Adam is giving expression to the image of God. God's willingness to hand over decision-making authority is not a way of "cheerleading," throwing Adam a bone to keep him motivated in his work. It is a declaration of the value and worth of Adam's contribution to the work God set in motion. In giving Adam real responsibility and authority, God is affirming Adam's innate dignity and recognizing the contribution Adam has to offer.

God is not confusing ultimate authority and responsibility either. God is not blurring lines. Instead, there is a commitment to a way of working that is instructive for us today. The idea that God would entrust "the creature" with the "power and authority to rule" would have been a radical notion across religious traditions throughout history, and it is just as countercultural today in the arena of labor.[8] It "presents an inverted view of humanness. This man and woman are not the chattel and servants of God, but the agents of God to whom much is given and from whom much is expected."[9] The relationship between persons-in-power and persons below as defined in Genesis stands as a prophetic witness against much of what we see in our world today. Workers in God's creation are not a means to the owners' ends but stewards and active agents in collaboration with God.

6. Walter Brueggemann, *Genesis*, Interpretation: A Bible Commentary for Teaching and Preaching (John Knox, 1982), 28.

7. See Wendell Berry, "Economy and Pleasure," in *The Art of Commonplace: The Agrarian Essays of Wendell Berry*, ed. Norman Wirzba (Counterpoint, 2002); and also David H. Jensen, *Responsive Labor: A Theology of Work* (Westminster John Knox, 2006), 100.

8. "The key to good work is not the abolition of workplace distinctions, but whether management, labor, and stockholders understand their labors are interrelated and shared or conflicted and hoarded." Jensen, *Responsive Labor*, 102.

9. Brueggemann, *Genesis*, 33.

The commitment to give away decision-making power and ownership of process is known as "subsidiarity." Subsidiarity is the practice of ensuring that authority and autonomy get pushed far "down the ladder" and that decision-making should be done as close to the ground as possible. Subsidiarity finds a source in this creation story as God extends authority and ownership to on-the-ground laborers. While God makes many decisions for humanity, a nontrivial area of responsibility is also conferred to them. A commitment to subsidiarity takes the vocation of humanity seriously.[10] In other words, conferring agency and authority to workers is a mandate of the mandate.

God also entrusts the assets of creation to humanity. The charge to steward the earth toward the flourishing of all creation requires humanity to have a real sense of ownership over creation. It is as if God is saying, "All this is yours. Do with it as you choose." The fact that God allowed humanity to make a mess of creation is not an argument against worker agency. Instead, it reveals the extent of God's commitment to giving agency over the assets of his creation to humanity. Just as in the case of decision-making authority, there is no question about *ultimate* ownership of creation. God *could* take away the agency and authority extended to humanity at any time. But he doesn't. God charges Adam and Eve to enact ownership in a way that reflects the intentions of the ultimate owner, in a way that helps them inhabit the *imago Dei*.

So, how might one structure a workplace to give workers agency? Minimally, this would look like increasing participation; delegating responsibility, decision-making, authority, and ownership of processes as close to the factory floor as possible.[11] Maximally, this could mean considering cooperative models of ownership, exemplified by companies like Mondragon or Equal Exchange.[12]

If not owning the means of production contributes to the economic vulnerability of working-class folks, then these insights invite us to look for ways to reimagine who owns the assets of production and who owns the labor of the workers themselves.[13] This is often a fraught fault line. But when owners maintain a stranglehold on assets, it concentrates power and can solidify the fractures between owners and workers.[14] Pope John Paul II cautioned against viewing assets as being "possessed against labour," a posture that inevitably

10. Pontifical Council for Justice and Peace, *Compendium of Social Doctrine of the Church* (Libreria Editrice Vaticana, 2004), 185, para. 81.

11. Hawtrey, "Oxford Declaration," 4; and Jensen, *Responsive Labor*, 100–104. See also "A Just Wage Tool," Institute for Social Concerns, criterion 6, https://socialconcerns.nd.edu/criterion-6/.

12. See their websites, https://www.mondragon-corporation.com/en/; and https://shop.equalexchange.coop/.

13. Jensen, *Responsive Labor*, 99–104.

14. See Jensen, *Responsive Labor*, 100.

corrupts the possibility of a collaborative labor relationship, devolving into competition and conflict. Rightly seen, assets are meant to work for the benefit, or service, of those who labor.[15]

Cooperatively owned companies are difficult propositions and are often written off as idealistic. But even though it may be true that these models do not fit well within the conventional structures of American capitalism, the feasibility of particular models does not make the important questions at hand irrelevant. The moral demands around agency require straightforward engagement. We can't avoid the responsibility of bringing balance to power and equity in labor because "whether these various proposals can or cannot be applied concretely, it is clear that recognition of the proper position of labour and the worker in the production process demands various adaptations in the sphere of the right to ownership of the means of production."[16]

Worker well-being requires increasing worker agency.[17] Even though this discussion might not be prescriptive in precisely the same way the commandment "Do not murder" is, God's disposition and action toward the power-less people under his purview suggests that there is something normative in this narrative. The creation story creates a template for a much more cooperative model of labor than we typically see today. If we take seriously the way human relations are meant to mirror relations within God (the Trinity) and with God (person-in-power and persons below), there's little room to challenge the moral implications of questions related to the distribution of agency within a company.[18] Doing so proactively is a way of demonstrating a commitment to God's intentions for labor and to fostering labor contexts that are resistant to the exploitation of workers.

## Resisting Exploitation and Increasing Flourishing Through Asset Ownership

The second of the seven criteria for what makes any given wage just or unjust, according to the Just Wage Research Lab, is that a just wage must enable asset building. The research team expounds on that criterion: "A just wage offers disposable income, enabling savings and property ownership; provides benefits in the form of educational enrichment, professional development

15. John Paul II, *Laborem Exercens*, September 14, 1981, §14, https://www.vatican.va/content/john-paul-ii/en/encyclicals/documents/hf_jp-ii_enc_14091981_laborem-exercens.html.
16. John Paul II, *Laborem Exercens*, §14.
17. Miroslav Volf, *Work in the Spirit: Toward a Theology of Work* (Wipf & Stock, 2001), 176.
18. Jensen, *Responsive Labor*, 100.

and skills enhancement; and promotes opportunities for advancement and income growth. Further, a just wage structure facilitates personal and community development."[19]

Immediately, we notice a holistic framing of this notion of assets. Certainly, the capacity for (and effects of) building a portfolio of tangible assets is present here. Beyond that, the lab highlights intangible assets—education, enrichment, leisure—as essential to a just wage. No doubt a nod to the idea of a decent life, asset ownership has both economic and existential qualities.[20] In that sense, asset ownership works at two levels at once, with concrete and psychic effect.

In the first place, there are many practical economic reasons for ensuring the asset-building capabilities of workers. Asset ownership has been shown to increase economic gains in a variety of ways. It can generate investment revenue, increase work and income productivity, and decrease costs typically required for survival in low-income situations. Asset ownership also allows workers and their families to withstand moments of economic misfortune that may come about through crisis events (divorce, disaster, disability, etc.). Assets provide the possibility of cash flow in difficult economic seasons, so they play a significant role in helping people resist exploitation from predatory loans. Because working-class families often are the first to feel the effects of an economic downturn—through factory layoffs, for example—asset ownership provides an economic base that allows people to better navigate periods of income uncertainty as well. Assets also form the foundation of any sound retirement strategy, enabling people to provide for themselves and others into old age.[21] More broadly, expanding asset ownership helps reduce social inequality by shrinking wealth gaps.[22] All of these effects work against exploitation of folks lower on the socioeconomic ladder and actively promote economic flourishing for workers and families.

To that end, persons-in-power concerned with the well-being of their workers should ask themselves how their approach to wages and compensation contributes to, or detracts from, a worker's ability to build their own assets. This is not just sound economic strategy; the wider aperture of Scripture

19. "A Just Wage Tool," https://socialconcerns.nd.edu/higgins/just-wage-tool/.

20. "A Just Wage Tool," criterion 2, https://socialconcerns.nd.edu/criterion-2/.

21. Robert Lerman and Signe-Mary McKernan, "The Effects of Holding Assets on Social and Economic Outcomes of Families: A Review of Theory and Evidence," The Urban Institute, November 2008, https://aspe.hhs.gov/reports/effects-holding-assets-social-economic-outcomes-families-review-theory-evidence-0#_Toc165715577.

22. "The reasons for encouraging ownership are diverse: it lessens the gap between the rich and poor, it promotes a legitimate sense of pride in one's labors, and a sense of fellowship and common bond with one's neighbors in the land." Jensen, *Responsive Labor*, 114.

demonstrates concern about the concentration of assets and advocates for asset equilibrium. Over the last 150 years, official teaching from the Catholic Church has continually highlighted the critical nature of wages that support asset building in one way or another.[23] What is often referred to as a "just distribution of goods" is a primary means for promoting the well-being of all, but in particular those who might fit the classification of working class.

In the Scriptures, we encounter the Year of Jubilee—a safeguard or remedy to the assumed exploitation of economically vulnerable peoples in ancient Israel. As outlined in Leviticus 25:8–10, every fifty years (roughly two generations) land that had been lost over time would be returned to its familial origins. Over time, assets would slowly consolidate into the hands of a relative few and increase the numbers of the asset-less population. The loss of land—even today, the primary and most important asset for nearly every person—leaves one less capable of resisting the exploitative intentions of others. Debts and economic enslavement were pervasive, as was economic injustice.[24] God designed the Year of Jubilee to restore the economic fortunes of those on the lower rungs of society, those most likely doing the dirty jobs, those least likely to garner society's acclaim. It is interesting to see how the prophetic promises of asset restoration in the future overlap with the concrete structures of a society operating as God intends. In other words, eschatological promises are not merely a future reality; God fully intends for those promises to find at least partial fulfillment in real time. The just distribution of assets is a normative expectation meant to ensure economic resilience in more vulnerable corners of the community.

In the New Testament, we find a similar emphasis on the community of faith ensuring the economic resilience of all its members. Consider the well-known description of the early church in Acts 4:32–37:

> All the believers were one in heart and mind. No one claimed that any of their possessions was their own, but they shared everything they had. With great power the apostles continued to testify to the resurrection of the Lord Jesus. And God's grace was so powerfully at work in them all that there were no needy persons among them. For from time to time those who owned land or houses

23. Leo XIII, *Rerum Novarum*, May 15, 1891, §5, http://www.vatican.va/content/leo-xiii/en/encyclicals/documents/hf_l-xiii_enc_15051891_rerum-novarum.html; Pius XI, *Quadragesimo Anno*, May 15, 1931, §§60–61, http://www.vatican.va/content/pius-xi/en/encyclicals/documents/hf_p-xi_enc_19310515_quadragesimo-anno.html; John XXIII, *Mater et Magistra*, May 15, 1961, §112, http://www.vatican.va/content/john-xxiii/en/encyclicals/documents/hf_j-xxiii_enc_15051961_mater.html; John Paul II, *Centesimus Annus*, May 1, 1991, §15, http://www.vatican.va/content/john-paul-ii/en/encyclicals/documents/hf_jp-ii_enc_01051991_centesimus-annus.html.

24. Jensen, *Responsive Labor*, 24.

> sold them, brought the money from the sales and put it at the apostles' feet, and it was distributed to anyone who had need.
>
> Joseph, a Levite from Cyprus, whom the apostles called Barnabas (which means "son of encouragement"), sold a field he owned and brought the money and put it at the apostles' feet.

This text highlights many ways the early church sought to enact the gospel in concrete terms. Unfortunately, these passages are often idealized in ways that are less than helpful, stirring disagreement primarily because the notion of a common purse and common possessions is such a stark departure from the conventional ways we think about money and other assets today. But the seemingly straightforward interpretation that the early church lived communally and rejected private property (as some radical religious sects do today) is not as clear when set against the Old Testament narratives. The Year of Jubilee provided structural security for asset ownership for the vulnerable. The prophets looked toward a day when every person would own assets that could help foster existential shalom. The notion that the early church sought full communality is discordant with those ideas. So, perhaps counterintuitively, it may be more helpful to understand that these texts are not about no one having possessions but, rather, about everyone having the assets they need to resist calamity. In Acts, that is, the church is actively seeking to bring about the prophetic promise of the Old Testament.

In our modern world, the concentration of assets is a front-burner concern. In particular, as property ownership increasingly consolidates into the hands of the wealthy—often nonlocal investors—in many communities, the working class (and other economically vulnerable groups) find themselves with fewer affordable housing options. This asset concentration drives up property values—which makes buying property increasingly appealing to investors and excludes many working-class families from home ownership in their local communities. We see more and more examples of workers resorting to drastic and dangerous measures to secure a place to sleep at night. This is true even for full-time employed workers in fields traditionally considered stable: teachers, police officers, public works employees, and so on.[25] Experts refer to workers in this situation as Asset-Limited, Income-Constrained, and Employed (ALICE). ALICE is a way of designating the percentage of the population who earn more than the federal poverty limit but who are unable to afford the

25. Addie Morfoot, "Nantucket's Workers Are Living on the Margins," *New York Times*, July 11, 2025, https://www.nytimes.com/2025/07/11/realestate/nantucket-affordable-housing-homeless.html.

essentials in the communities in which they live and work. The numbers of workers and families who meet those criteria are surprising. For instance, in 2022, 24 percent of households in the state of Wisconsin were ALICE. This is in addition to the 11 percent who lived below the poverty line.[26] All told, this means one-third of that state's population lives in a constant state of economic vulnerability that, I'm arguing, we have a moral obligation to address. The concentration of wealth that leads to these economic conditions for workers and families is the exact thing that the Year of Jubilee was meant to redress and that the early church was working to eradicate from their community.

The early church was creating a little economy in the midst of society's larger economy, and in this little economy everyone contributed to and received from the flourishing of the larger whole. In this way, the church was working out the common good in real time by practicing economic solidarity. Remember the origins of the term "solidarity," where community members shared debts as "obligation-in-common."[27] These early Christians were giving expression to a positive inflection of solidarity—where, instead of holding economic vulnerabilities in common (debts), they held economic abundance (assets) in common, reflecting their belief in the unintuitive generosity of God. When Joseph the Levite sells property, it is not because it is wrong to own private property but because Joseph is contributing assets to the community to ensure the flourishing of each one and everyone together. Joseph is participating in the common good.[28] If he didn't hold private assets, his ability to make that contribution would be diminished.

Consider the alternative example in the following verses of Acts 5:1–4:

> Now a man named Ananias, together with his wife Sapphira, also sold a piece of property. With his wife's full knowledge he kept back part of the money for himself, but brought the rest and put it at the apostles' feet.
>
> Then Peter said, "Ananias, how is it that Satan has so filled your heart that you have lied to the Holy Spirit and have kept for yourself some of the money you received for the land? Didn't it belong to you before it was sold? And after it was sold, wasn't the money at your disposal? What made you think of doing such a thing? You have not lied just to human beings but to God."

Peter acknowledges Ananias and Sapphira's freedom of discretion to do with their assets as they pleased, so we know that private asset ownership is

26. See "Meet ALICE," https://liveunitedbr.org/alice/.

27. Leah Hunt-Hendrix and Astra Taylor, *Solidarity: The Past, Present, and Future of a World-Changing Idea* (Pantheon, 2024), 6.

28. "Private property serves the common good . . . in the sense that it connects good work to the land." Jensen, *Responsive Labor*, 113.

commonplace and conventional in the early church. Their sin was not ownership but deception and a less-than-full-throated commitment to the common good of the community. The contrast seems to be a lust for money against trusting the abundance of a community holding assets in common. Ananias and Sapphira's economic deception—to keep for themselves over against the well-being of the community—is strikingly similar to the way the vice of upward mobility fosters competitive, if not combative, economic relationships between people today. We should take note that the most intense scene of God's judgment in the New Testament narrative is reserved for this kind of avarice.

And because asset ownership helps people resist their own exploitation, assets also produce a particular non-tangible effect that we've called existential shalom.[29] Returning to Micah 4:2–5, where we encountered this idea of existential shalom to begin with, we take note of the connection between assets and this expression of shalom:

> Many nations will come and say,
>
> "Come, let us go up to the mountain of the Lord,
> to the temple of the God of Jacob.
> He will teach us his ways,
> so that we may walk in his paths."
> The law will go out from Zion,
> the word of the Lord from Jerusalem.
> He will judge between many peoples
> and will settle disputes for strong nations far and wide.
> They will beat their swords into plowshares
> and their spears into pruning hooks.
> Nation will not take up sword against nation,
> nor will they train for war anymore.
> Everyone will sit under their own vine
> and under their own fig tree,
> and no one will make them afraid,
> for the Lord Almighty has spoken.
> All the nations may walk
> in the name of their gods,
> but we will walk in the name of the Lord
> our God for ever and ever.

29. "The reasons for encouraging ownership are diverse: it lessens the gap between the rich and poor, it promotes a legitimate sense of pride in one's labors, and a sense of fellowship and common bond with one's neighbors in the land." Jensen, *Responsive Labor*, 114.

Remember that Micah's vision of God's shalom-filled future includes the line, "Everyone will sit under their own vine and under their own fig tree, and no one will make them afraid" (v. 4). Notice the context in which "everyone" will experience this existential shalom. They are sitting under their own vine and fig tree. Instead of living on the land of others, tending to other's fig groves, Micah envisions a day when society's assets are distributed evenly, to everyone. Rather than the concentration of assets in the hands of a few, the assets are owned by all people. This text makes an explicit connection between asset ownership and the kind of existential shalom that God intends.

The same can be said for Isaiah's vision of the new heavens and the new earth in Isaiah 65:17–23:

> See, I will create
> new heavens and a new earth.
> The former things will not be remembered,
> nor will they come to mind.
> But be glad and rejoice forever
> in what I will create,
> for I will create Jerusalem to be a delight
> and its people a joy.
> I will rejoice over Jerusalem
> and take delight in my people;
> the sound of weeping and of crying
> will be heard in it no more.
>
> Never again will there be in it
> an infant who lives but a few days,
> or an old man who does not live out his years;
> the one who dies at a hundred
> will be thought a mere child;
> the one who fails to reach a hundred
> will be considered accursed.
> They will build houses and dwell in them;
> they will plant vineyards and eat their fruit.
> No longer will they build houses and others live in them,
> or plant and others eat.
> For as the days of a tree,
> so will be the days of my people;
> my chosen ones will long enjoy
> the work of their hands.
> They will not labor in vain,
> nor will they bear children doomed to misfortune;

for they will be a people blessed by the Lord,
  they and their descendants with them.

In the middle of a sweeping vision of God's restoration of all of creation is a couplet of compelling lines that deal directly with the topic we are considering now—assets as resistance to exploitation. See what Isaiah says in verses 21–22:

They will build houses and dwell in them;
  they will plant vineyards and eat their fruit.
No longer will they build houses and others live in them,
  or plant and others eat.

Isaiah is drawing attention to the same reality faced by working-class folks today—workers disconnected from the ends of their labor. They work for someone else's gain. The worker cultivates the economic return of the owner's asset, which leaves them in their economically vulnerable position. Notice that workers who labor for an owner's gain are contextually connected to infants and the elderly. All three groups are vulnerable to calamity, violence, and the exploitation of others. But Isaiah declares God's intention to do away with the threats faced by all three, naming an end to each one's vulnerabilities and bringing the experience of the shalom of the new heavens and the new earth.[30]

This text in particular highlights how asset ownership is not an argument against the exploitation of workers; it is a remedy for it. The subtext of these passages is the reality of the exploitation of workers who must sell their labor to some other owner. If it were not commonplace, the promise to remedy the plight of the exploited would be irrelevant. Instead, we are to assume that God's promise to bring equity to *who owns what* is welcome precisely because of pervasive exploitation taking place in this ancient society. The just distribution of assets puts a stop to this. Asset ownership allows economically vulnerable people to resist the exploitative intentions of others.

In both of these texts, the just distribution of assets is a defining characteristic of God's preferred future. When the people of God hear these promises—pledges toward a day when they and everyone they know will labor not for some other owner's gain but instead for the sake of their own flourishing—it produces an animating hope that guides and sustains the people through hardship.

This is not an isolated spiritual reality. It has a real-world effect, as research shows that asset ownership—particularly home ownership—tends to have

30. Volf, *Work in the Spirit*, 164.

"a positive effect on expectations and confidence about the future; influence people to make specific plans with regard to work and family; induce more prudent and protective personal behaviors; and lead to greater social connectedness with relatives, neighbors, and organizations."[31] Assets reduce stress and worry, increase happiness and personal self-sufficiency, and provide a greater sense of optimism about what the future holds.[32] Theologically, we call that "hope," a foretaste of the existential shalom cultivated through concrete asset ownership in the present.

Existential shalom, economic resilience, and an increased capacity to resist exploitation are all results of asset ownership, which lends a degree of moral urgency to the just distribution of assets in society—in particular with an eye toward those who lack the things we named above. Certainly, a priority on asset ownership can be corrupted by a lust for tangible things (homes, land, etc.), but the angst, precarity, and exploitative possibilities that come when one owns no assets is, as we've seen, a theological problem as much as it is an economic one. This is why the Catholic Church has, for over a century, consistently affirmed the right to property ownership as essential for a Christian vision of justice.

The lack of existential shalom is evident in the lives of those without "their own vine and their own fig tree." These are people for whom Micah 4 and Isaiah 65—and yes, even the Year of Jubilee—offer a salve to stave off the angst that is part and parcel of a life lived on the lower rungs of the social hierarchy of labor. Scripture's balm is not abstract; it is eschatological, structural, and social. Without concrete expression, the prophets' promises ring hollow. Without that prophetic vision for God's intentions, we run the risk of narrowing the redemptive possibilities of a just distribution of assets. When they are brought together, however, asset ownership is imbued with a deep spiritual significance where one's own vine and fig tree become a signpost of the existential shalom that God desires for each one and of the economic resilience required for well-being.

31. Lerman and McKernan, "The Effects of Holding Assets."
32. Lerman and McKernan, "The Effects of Holding Assets."

# 8 DISABILITY, ARTIFICIAL INTELLIGENCE, AND UNCOMPENSATED WORK

## Modern Challenges to Human Dignity and the Common Good

Ought not there be an increment, earned though not yet received, from one's daily work—an acknowledgment of man's being?

—Studs Terkel[1]

Over the past three chapters, we've moved through some of the more essential issues facing the working class. The moral demands of justice, particularly the kind of justice described in Scripture, invite our full attention to the connections between wages, power, agency, and assets. This bundle of issues forms the central nucleus of the labor question. Taking them seriously—that is, providing wages for well-being, bringing balance to the scales of power, and working to increase workers' agency and the accessibility of asset ownership—are tangible ways of putting a theology of labor into practice. While there are additional topics a theology of labor could address, it must address these directly or it is insufficient. Imagine how different the lives of workers would be if people of faith took these seriously as an expression of our shared convictions about human dignity and the common good.

Still, it's impossible to treat every possible angle of the labor question in a project of this scope. I have chosen three major topics that will allow us to

1. Studs Terkel, *Working: People Talk About What They Do All Day and How They Feel About What They Do* (Pantheon, 1974), xiii.

explore ways this working theology might respond to new or relevant questions over time. These three topics—artificial intelligence (AI), disability, and uncompensated labor—are compelling in at least two different ways. First, they each challenge some of the basic assumptions we've been teasing out in this project. If we assume all labor has dignity, what about jobs easily replaceable by AI? If work is a primary way we give expression to the *imago Dei*, what does that mean for people with disabilities? Since the primary focus of this discussion has been on waged labor, doesn't that exacerbate the social denigration of unpaid, and often exploited, labor? These questions test the strength of the overall argument. Is it sturdy enough to deal well with these critical topics? Are there weaknesses that ought to be addressed? Second, each of these topics provides concrete opportunities to enact the basic premises of this working theology of labor. Here we will find more ways—ways that challenge the basic logic of the social hierarchy of labor—to bring our voice to the public square, stand alongside the marginalized and overlooked, and live consistent with the values of Scripture. These are not the only three topics that provide these opportunities. Today, and over time, we should expect our ever-changing world to provoke new questions continuously. This means we must learn how to embrace uncertainty and how to discern goodness and truth by examining new questions using the lens of Scripture and the framework we are developing.

## Artificial Intelligence

As I waded deeper into this project, I came to realize the necessity of exploring the question of AI and its relationship to labor. The discourse around the promise and problem of AI can make your head spin, but in this arena we are in serious need of wisdom, which is in short supply these days. The rapidity of AI's evolution is bewildering. Across sectors, the influence of AI on our relationship to labor is, and will be, seismic. Naturally, there are many who praise its potential for efficiency and economic benefit. Others take a more despairing posture, worrying about the dangers posed by AI to our lives, our economy, and the environment. In a certain sense, no one is wrong. AI will make society more efficient, and the economic return for those who tap its potential will be immense. And at the same time, AI will eliminate the livelihoods of millions of people, increase the gap between the rich and the poor, and, as we are already seeing, pose a monumental threat to the environment. Discerning a disposition toward AI requires more than balancing pros and cons. Christian wisdom invites us to ask thoughtful questions about the relationship between AI and labor.

Every technological revolution radically redefines the relationship between people and labor. The Industrial Revolution created the possibility of exponential increases in economic output and also redefined the way people interacted with the economy, creating a new kind of working class. It rendered many jobs obsolete, and many of the jobs created by industry were low-skill, low-wage work. The Industrial Revolution enriched the wealthy and owner class and fostered ongoing economic precarity for the masses. The same has been true in the evolution of the energy industry. The more companies pivot to embrace cleaner forms of energy, the more vulnerable workers in the coal and oil industries become. The energy transition calls the value and worth of fossil-fuel jobs into question in a way that leaves those workers in limbo. We see similar results in the globalization of economies. Jobs that used to sustain families and communities domestically are outsourced internationally to increase efficiency and economic return. As the global supply chain becomes more agile, we rely less on the geographically local to make our economies work. Globalization makes our economic lives more affordable but also more abstract. These innovations remove the need for the worker next to us.

AI is having, and will continue to have, similar effects as any other technological innovation that replaces the need for human labor. Overwhelmingly, the aims of AI are to eliminate the need for workers in the first place. Only now, those jobs will not just be working class. Instead, AI is coming for *every* bs job. Entry-level workers should expect consistent fragility in the market for their services. Companies are instigating what they call "AI first" policies to test before hiring whether a particular role might be better served by a computer than a human. Companies are racing to develop "virtual workers" that can replace lower-level corporate jobs for small fractions of the cost of employing a person. It's estimated that AI could eliminate 50 percent of entry-level white-collar jobs within five years.[2] In the same way that the Industrial Revolution eliminated the need for huge swaths of the preindustrial workforce, the AI revolution will do so without respect to one's education, expertise, or economic class. AI is likely to automate, and so eliminate, human labor to an extent never seen before. For example, while innovation in personal computing killed around 3.5 million jobs (a massive number), projections suggest that AI could render the tangible contributions of over three hundred million

2. Kevin Roose, "For Some Recent Graduates, the A.I. Job Apocalypse May Already Be Here," *New York Times*, May 30, 2025, https://www.nytimes.com/2025/05/30/technology/ai-jobs-college-graduates.html.

workers irrelevant, inefficient, and unnecessary.[3] To put this in perspective, that is nearly twice the entire working population of the United States. AI makes it possible for industry leaders to radically reduce costs, but at the expense of the elimination of their workforce. If your job can be done by a computer, chances are it will be in the not-so-distant future. In short, industry will increasingly have less need for workers.[4]

AI is revealing a truth about our collective posture toward workers. We have reduced many of them to tools for economic return. Miroslav Volf observes that the Industrial Revolution rendered the worker irrelevant by replacing them with a machine. With a tool in their hand, the worker is still in charge of their production. The tool is the means by which that production is done.[5] The machine turns the worker into the tool, into an instrument of production. When we view workers *themselves* as tools, or means, of economic return, we instrumentalize them. We reduce the possibility and potential of any given worker, or any given workforce, for production. This happens on the assembly line (attaching this part to that part) and the office cubicle (cut and paste this data into that document). So, rather than seeing labor as a tool, or means, for human contribution and dignity, workers themselves have become "labor inputs" to serve the larger ends of production.[6]

The jobs that reduce humans to tools of economic return will be some of the first to go. The rapid elimination of those jobs will force us to reckon with the vast array of bs jobs we've created. AI will kill the jobs that turn our lives into "soul-sucking drudgery," the jobs that make us question what the point of work even is, the jobs we find to be without meaning, and the jobs that degrade and dehumanize us.[7] So, on the one hand, if AI were to force us to interrogate the forms of labor that do not honor the dignity of workers, it might not be all bad. After all, humans were not meant to be "accessories" of economic systems. That does not give due honor to the image of God in us.[8]

But we also need to be honest about and responsive to the existential impact AI will have on workers rendered replaceable. Realizing you can be replaced by a machine is the exact opposite of having your work be a celebration of your dignity. Instead of a space to work out our human vocation, a job reminds us of the ominous forecast of our own replaceability. "Perhaps

3. Emma Goldberg, "Will A.I. Kill Meaningless Jobs?," *New York Times*, August 3, 2024, https://www.nytimes.com/2024/08/03/business/ai-replacing-jobs.html.

4. Roose, "For Some Recent Graduates."

5. Miroslav Volf, *Work in the Spirit: Toward a Theology of Work* (Wipf & Stock, 2001), 33.

6. Kim Hawtrey, "The Oxford Declaration on Christian Faith and Economics," *Transformation* 7, no. 2 (April/June 1990): 4.

7. Goldberg, "Will A.I. Kill Meaningless Jobs?"; and Hawtrey, "Oxford Declaration," 2.

8. Hawtrey, "Oxford Declaration," 3.

it is this specter that most haunts working men and women: the planned obsolescence of people . . . , this fear of no longer being needed in a world of needless things that most clearly spells out the unnaturalness, the surreality of much that is called work today."[9] It might cause, or force, a person to ask different questions about their labor and vocational pursuits—opening them up to the good reflective processes described in chapter 3. But that possibility seems less than likely for the many who find themselves fighting to eke out a livelihood in a rapidly evolving economic landscape.[10] This is ultimately a pastoral concern. Who will celebrate and respond to the *imago Dei* in a world intent on questioning the necessity and value of so many image bearers? We will have to question the way we create space for the human person to inhabit the *imago Dei* to begin with.

So, we will need to get serious about creating *good* jobs. AI will magnify the moral imperative to see job creation as a theological enterprise. It will force us to create forms of labor that do not reduce people to tools, or means, of production. Those jobs won't be able to withstand AI's trajectory of automation anyway. More importantly, doing so will help Christians push back against the conventional logic of technological innovation. The possibilities of technology can bend toward or away from human dignity, making the difference between possibility and permissibility an important distinction. As the writers of the Oxford Declaration observed decades ago, "we must not allow technological development to follow its own inner logic, but must direct it to serve moral ends."[11] Because AI cannot reason out real moral demands, forms of labor marked by compelling visions of dignity and the common good are the most likely to be AI proof anyway. If we simply create stopgap, or shallow, jobs for those displaced by AI, we will only reset the cycle whereby innovation will (eventually) eliminate those jobs, illuminating how little we've learned about the connection between labor and dignity and forcing us to deal with an entirely new generation of displaced and disillusioned workers. So, rather than asking how we might "AI proof" a job, we would do better to ask, and invite others to ask, how we can create jobs for workers in service of human dignity and the common good.

"But," one might say, "doesn't innovation create new jobs too?" That is true. The clean-energy industry, for instance, generates all manner of new labor forms. Similarly, our increasingly global world creates a need for new forms of skilled labor across a host of sectors. And AI will lead to new, emerging

9. Terkel, *Working*, xviii.
10. Goldberg, "Will A.I. Kill Meaningless Jobs?"
11. Hawtrey, "Oxford Declaration," 2.

forms of work in a number of fields. "It's an old story: Technology has offset job losses with job creation throughout history. Horse drawn carriages were replaced by cars, which created jobs. . . . Personal computing eliminated some 3.5 million jobs, and then created an enormous industry and spurred many others."[12] Emma Goldberg rightly notes that none of the jobs created by technological innovation could have been imagined a century earlier. The possibility of job creation may be well and good, but Goldberg highlights the specific problem with falling back on the trope that innovation creates more than it destroys. It should be obvious—but perhaps it is not—that the jobs created by AI will almost certainly not be filled by the same people displaced by AI.

The notion that "innovation kills jobs but creates new ones" is morally neutral only if we consider humanity in the aggregate. In other words, only by lumping everyone together can we call a situation where job destruction and job creation coexist morally neutral. In this case, the end result may be "even." But this doesn't celebrate human dignity. For anyone to be excluded or discarded fails to achieve the moral standards of dignity and the common good. In the aggregate, human dignity can only be demeaned.

Disaggregating humanity allows us to see what the premise clouds: that the jobs to be created through innovation are for abstract (faceless) future persons. The jobs destroyed imperil the economic lives of flesh-and-blood persons in our midst. The question here is not whether to innovate but what we will do to respond to the three hundred million actual humans vocationally displaced by AI without appealing to abstracted future populations. What does the humanity of those people insist on in response?

AI will hold a mirror up to our values. It will expose many forms of labor that do not celebrate human dignity as they could, and ought. At the same time, the more that we champion labor as a dynamic expression of the image of God in a person, the more people of faith will inhabit a prophetic witness in a world hell-bent on eliminating the need for workers in the name of economic margins. As Christians celebrate the value of any form of labor that contributes to the common good, our imaginations will stir toward the creation of jobs that simply could not be replaced by a machine or a large language model.

## Disability

At one of my former workplaces, we had an employee named Peter.[13] Peter was a beloved member of the work community, having done a variety of

12. Goldberg, "Will A.I. Kill Meaningless Jobs?"
13. Not his real name.

things over his time at our unit. And Peter lived with a disability. Very few of the things Peter did around the office would have been described as essential when evaluating his contributions alongside values like efficiency, return on investment, and impact (narrowly defined). And yet, it seems to me that Peter made more of an impact (of a different sort) than any other worker in the history of that institution. Even years after his departure, people still told stories about him and the mark he made on the lives of our staff and those we served. Most days, he would still call the office—from across the country—to check in on how people were doing. He was a true exemplar of care, compassion, love, and community in a way that no other person in the place could match.

What if Peter had not come to work with us? The community would have been robbed of his contributions, and he of an opportunity to participate in a shared work life. That organization created space for Peter—but, to me, mere inclusion feels like the baseline of fidelity to human dignity. The possibility of every person, traditionally or differently abled, demands a wider and more expansive imagination for what it means to say that work is a primary way we inhabit the image of God and contribute to the common good.

Peter's story opens this project up to an important concern. That is, what do we do about the many people who don't, or can't, hold a job (as we conventionally think about jobs)? More specifically, do people with disabilities fit in this framework? Because, at face value, it appears that differently abled people might challenge the basic premises of this project. Many people who live with disabilities aren't integrated well into the world of work as we know it. Often chronically unemployed, their lived experience makes it difficult to perform the tasks many jobs require.[14] But if work is a God-designed avenue for inhabiting the *imago Dei*, does that mean someone who can't work bears the image of God in a less vibrant way? Ennobling the labor of the working class to the exclusion of those with disabilities would be a tragic outcome of a working theology of labor.

It's my view that people with disabilities only undermine this theological framework based on the logic of the social hierarchy of labor. The values of the social hierarchy—impact, return on investment, careerism, and so on—exclude anyone who does not fit into traditional labor molds that overvalue a particular form of productivity.[15] That is why the working class is demeaned and ostracized by those who buy into the aspirations of the social hierarchy. So too are people living with disabilities. They often do not fit naturally into

14. Dustin Galer, "Disabled Capitalists: Exploring the Intersections of Disability and Identity Formation in the World of Work," *Disability Studies Quarterly* 32, no. 3 (2012).

15. Galer, "Disabled Capitalists."

the systems that produce upwardly mobile, impact-driven workers. Like many blue-collar communities, the disability community is on the outside looking in on the modern world of work.

But centering the labor question on the reality of the *imago Dei* positions us to resist the long-standing dehumanization of people with disabilities. Tragically, too many people across history frame disability as a sign of some fundamental moral flaw. This is true across philosophical and religious traditions as well as civil and political society. Even though the Scriptures don't defend the idea, there is plenty of evidence that conventional wisdom at the time thought disability was punishment for "spiritual impurity," some sin in a person's life.[16] In John 9:2 the disciples ask Jesus, "Who sinned, this man or his parents, that he was born blind?" A person's disability has long been cause for judgment, and those judgments shore up a long and ugly "history of maltreatment."[17] Disability gave permission for incredible acts of neglect and violence. Child abandonment, infanticide by exposure, and mutilation were common. Social ostracization was accepted practice. Rather than accommodations that we find normal today, disabilities have historically given rise to extreme neglect and deprivation. Aristotle argued that the deaf, for example, shouldn't be educated because it would siphon energy and resources away from those who can hear.[18] This history of exclusion and abuse took on more formal expressions in the Middle Ages. In Europe, supportive guilds for people with disabilities became common, but so too did the so-called "idiot cages" and the "ship of fools." In these cases, people with disabilities were not just sequestered away from the rest of society but were put on display for the amusement of others. These common carnival-style practices exploited those with disabilities and framed them as sideshows, or people to be afraid of.[19]

These early examples of sequestering and exploiting people with disabilities would help fuel the eugenics movement of the nineteenth and twentieth centuries. As society moved toward more formal, and oftentimes forcible, forms of institutionalization, doctors keen to study the scientific causes of particular disabilities ushered in an era that saw people with disabilities abused in horrific ways. Forced sterilization is one example of violent mistreatment directed at people with disabilities. Even though the eugenics movement is

16. Jane S. Deland, "Images of God Through the Lens of Disability," *Journal of Religion, Disability, and Health* 3, no. 2 (1999): 54–55.

17. Mary Jo Iozzio, *Disability Ethics and Preferential Justice: A Catholic Perspective* (Georgetown University Press, 2023), 11.

18. Iozzio, *Disability Ethics*, 13–14.

19. Iozzio, *Disability Ethics*, 15.

socially rejected today—given its history and association with dictatorial regimes over the last one hundred years—it is still "in the water." The basic ideological fundamentals of eugenics are at play in much of "reproductive medicine and the selective abortion of fetuses."[20] In other words, forced sterilization and selective abortions are conceptually linked by the idea that a disability can be, and perhaps should be, removed from society's gene pool. The message to people experiencing life with a disability is clear: It would be better for the "rest of us" if you were not here.

This is just a brief sketch of the alienation, exploitation, abuse, and injustice experienced by people with disabilities—all of which stands in direct contradiction to the fundamental Christian premise that every human person is made in the image and likeness of God. Any theological construct that does not insist on the immorality of beliefs and practices that malign people with disabilities denies them "the full inheritance of the *imago Dei*."[21] This is all the more significant when we consider the fact that the resurrected Jesus "embodied both impaired hands and feet and pierced side and the imago Dei," which rejects the notion that disability is somehow a consequence for sin.[22] Along the way, though, our exploration of a more expansive vision for the image of God aids us in pushing back against these violations of dignity.

Of course, at the most fundamental level, being made in the image and likeness of God entitles a person to the celebration of the fullness of their humanity. The alienation that marks violations of human dignity is morally wrong. The sequestering of people with disabilities, something Nancy Eiesland calls "segregationist charity," exposes them to further violations—to exploitation and abuse—simply because they are not well woven into the fabric of social and communal life.[23] In the world of labor, it is not uncommon to see attempts to provide work for people with disabilities having an alienating effect. Providing work for a person living with a disability but, in so doing, increasing that person's alienation and possible vulnerability is a net disservice, not a solution to the problems we are facing.

One response to this reality is the niche market for goods produced by people with disabilities that drive profitable social-good businesses. Many of these businesses work very hard to create a loving and inclusive community for individuals and to create ways for people with disabilities to experience

20. Iozzio, *Disability Ethics*, 16.

21. Iozzio, *Disability Ethics*, 51.

22. Nancy Eiesland, *The Disabled God: Toward a Liberatory Theology of Disability* (Abingdon, 1994), 99, 101.

23. Eiesland, *The Disabled God*, 93.

a traditional employment-centered sense of purpose and direction. Still, this is a sequestered solution, one that distances people with disabilities from participation in shared economic life. To be clear, this is not an indictment of these businesses. Instead, the mere presence of this industry is an indictment of society's lack of imagination and willingness to create economic lives that include—in a more integrated way—the contributions of people with disabilities. In fact, celebrating the businesses that include folks in a sequestered way—and even buying their products—without interrogating the reasons for the necessity of such businesses reveals a stunning lack of awareness or an equally jolting measure of hypocrisy on the part of society. We should point to businesses designed specifically for the disability community as attempts to champion participation. But our working theology of labor should also challenge us to think more widely and beyond models that put the burden for inclusion back on people with disabilities, and their advocates, rather than examining the reasons why typical economic systems actively exclude them. When society must create entirely new economic arenas to include a historically excluded population, we ought to consider the ways our economic practices create the conditions for exclusion.

Exclusion, of course, destroys the common good because it limits the scope of who gets to participate—rendering whatever good there may be *not common*. Common-good participation is not sequestered, alienated, or disconnected from community relationships. Instead, the common good insists on an inclusion befitting the image of God in each person. It recognizes each person's right to participate, but also our shared need of each person's contribution. We are less than we could be when we sequester and exclude any population of people from sharing their gifts with the whole. Challenging the alienation of people with disabilities comes through a commitment to imagining ways for their liberated participation.[24] This will demand the reform of economic practices. We cannot be content with creating sequestered spaces, as these spaces do not challenge the forms of abuse and violations of human dignity that are so common today and across history. We cannot abide "cages." Those must be unlocked, and we must change the way we structure our economic lives so that each person is liberated to participate and offer their contributions.

What we will find, if we have eyes to see, is that people with disabilities will bring person-specific gifts and contributions to our lives, including our economic lives. Those contributions will be as uniquely wonderful as every other. The Catholic Church has long recognized this and teaches that people

24. Iozzio, *Disability Ethics*, 53.

with disabilities should be free to participate in communities "according to their possibilities."[25] Notice the focus is not on their "abilities" but on their "possibilities." It strikes me that this is a more spacious way of anticipating and welcoming the contributions of people with disabilities. There is something to be received from each person and this community of persons. Contribution is not always as concrete as the discussion around work can make it seem. The simple presence of a person is a contribution that manifests light and life. Making a contribution—of any sort—to a community has both tangible and positive psychological effects,[26] fostering a sense of existential shalom. This should come as no surprise to those who are committed to honoring the image of God in the world. Trinitarian inflections of the *imago Dei* remind us of the beauty and necessity of a plurality of contributions within communities of people who reflect God's image. The diversity of God—as Father, Son, and Spirit—should inspire a culture of anticipatory possibility, not one that skeptically limits the contributions of others.[27] Instead of a focus on what a particular person can't do, it seems to me that our expanding vision for the image of God insists that we cultivate a curiosity for what a person *might* do, give, or contribute. To place limits—whether in our minds or in practice—on the gifts any given person might offer a community is not reflective of an expansive understanding of a trinitarian God.

One of the reasons that we seem to possess such a narrow limitation for the inclusion or integration of people with disabilities in our labor systems is that our economic lives reflect a profound aberration from God's intentions for our shared life together. People with disabilities have difficulty finding ways of participating in our economic life because that life is guided by the values and structures of independence. So, jobs are conventionally designed for individuals to produce, create, and perform certain tasks or functions on their own. Job descriptions—and so hiring managers—prize self-starters and those "capable" of independent work. At one level, sure, that makes sense. But the explicit value for independent workers is symptomatic of an entire world of work that sees the capacity for independent work as a sign of "developmental maturity, if not the very humanity, of a person *as a human being*."[28] This tracks with the way the social hierarchy of labor assigns value and worth to different types of work and workers.

25. Pontifical Council for Justice and Peace, *Compendium of the Social Doctrine of the Church* (Libreria Editrice Vaticana, 2004), 148.

26. Galer, "Disabled Capitalists."

27. Iozzio, *Disability Ethics*, 52–54.

28. Iozzio, *Disability Ethics*, 18.

This is not a world positioned to welcome the contributions of the disability community because independence is not always a possibility for them. In most cases, a disability renders someone reliant on other people in a different way than the traditionally abled. They are unable to participate in the structures of independence in the same way as others. Instead, communities of people with disabilities are profoundly interdependent. These communities stand apart from those hypercommitted to independence. However, in much the same way the apostle Paul decried the "eye" that declares no need for the "hand," people devoted to radical independence—in labor and life—do not have a deep enough appreciation for God's designed way for us to participate in shared life. The traditionally abled have wandered off course, having built Babel-like labor structures in an attempt to shore up their independence. Interdependence—the ideal—is "a necessary condition for life."[29]

People with disabilities are perhaps much more likely to be exemplars of God's intent in this regard. For this community, solidarity—what Eiesland calls "holding our bodies together"—is self-implicating because it is very much an embodied reality.[30] This kind of solidarity recognizes the "precarious position of living a difficult life and affirming our bodies as whole, good, and beautiful. . . . Respect for our own bodies is an act of resistance and liberation."[31] Holding our bodies together as a simultaneous act of celebration and struggle fills out our understanding of how we might live in solidarity together across working classes as well. If the goal is to imagine forms of work that truly celebrate a value for interdependence, people with disabilities point us in interesting new directions.

In his book *Wondrously Wounded*, Brian Brock describes the injustice and disregard for people with disabilities as a "habitual disdain for God's good gifts."[32] I find this particularly challenging, and all the more so when I see the relative ease with which one might take a theology of labor and ply it toward the exclusion of people with disabilities. The social hierarchy of labor casts a long shadow and presents real challenges for living into a wider vision for the dignity and worth of all people. But this is where we must resist simplistic capitulation to typical social values—refusing to bow to the sacred cow that is return on investment—and insist on a more faithful frame, one capable of making space for possibility, receiving the contributions and celebrating the full humanity of people with disabilities.

29. Eiesland, *The Disabled God*, 103.

30. Eiesland, *The Disabled God*, 94 (see 94–97).

31. Eiesland, *The Disabled God*, 95–96.

32. Brian Brock, *Wondrously Wounded: Theology, Disability, and the Body of Christ* (Baylor University Press, 2019), 8.

## Uncompensated Labor

This book is overwhelmingly centered on the wage economy. And for good reason, of course. The many ways that waged-labor systems abuse and exploit economically and socially vulnerable people is worthy of long-form treatment. At the same time, there is also a real danger in this focus, one that mirrors broader society. That is, the waged economy very often serves to devalue the worth and dignity of non-waged labor. For people of faith, this is a particular concern because of the great value and importance we commonly place on labor that is traditionally uncompensated: living generously in a neighborhood, raising children, serving the needs of the less fortunate, and so on. A working theology of labor presents us with an opportunity to better examine our posture toward unpaid work because, in challenging the social hierarchy's effect on working-class labor, we also uncover ways the hierarchy's values actively discriminate against unpaid labor.

Perhaps the most obvious reason society demeans unpaid labor is that it does not fit the conventional model where the value of work is directly connected to its economic return. Unpaid labor does not generate economic return—at least not as conventionally conceived—so that labor literally does not hold value. This is an extension of the same logic used to argue for the relative value of particular waged jobs over others. In fact, it is the natural end of that line of thinking. The ultimately unimportant work, as seen from the top perch of the social hierarchy, is work that does not generate concrete economic value.

Of course, there are several theological problems here that invite reflection. To start, delegitimizing unpaid labor rejects and demeans many ways people live out their calling to contribute to the common good. Because so much of day-to-day life is unpaid labor—cooking, cleaning, gardening, art making, child rearing, and so on—we cannot affirm the dignity of this work unless we are resolute in our conviction that all work that contributes to the common good has value and worth. When we see all labor this way, "ordinary materials and practices of life are charged with the holy."[33] John Calvin said it this way: "No task will be so sordid and base, provided you obey your calling in it, that it will not shine and be reckoned very precious in God's sight."[34] Christian faith allows people to take delight in common labors, even the most mundane, as contributive toward a flourishing shared life with family,

33. David H. Jensen, *Responsive Labor: A Theology of Work* (Westminster John Knox, 2006), ix.

34. John Calvin, *Calvin's Institutes: Abridged Edition*, ed. Donald K. McKim (Westminster John Knox, 2001), 3.10.6.

neighbors, and the wider community. This view enlivens the prayer of the psalmist in Psalm 90:17:

> May the favor of the Lord our God rest on us;
> establish the work of our hands for us—
> yes, establish the work of our hands.

Rather than seeing this prayer reserved for large-scale work with the potential dramatic impact, a wider view of the value and worth of all labor allows everyone to join in prayer alongside this psalmist, whether they be a sixteenth-century milkmaid, a feed salesman in the 1950s, a sanitation worker in 1968, or a stay-at-home parent in the twenty-first century. A Christian view of work will resist the impulses of the social hierarchy of labor by refusing to reduce human labor to "commodities of exchange."[35] I believe this was Martin Luther's ultimate aim in much of his writing on work and the notion of vocation. He said as much, arguing that "when a father goes ahead and washes diapers or performs some other mean task for a child . . . God, with all his angels and creatures, is smiling—not because that father is washing diapers, but because he is doing so in Christian faith." As David Jensen notes, "in this regard, *all* labor for others, no matter how small or insignificant, are vocations."[36]

Further, seeing paid work as the only "real work" creates the conditions for exploitation to thrive. Overvaluing paid work hides unpaid work and leaves those who shoulder that labor vulnerable to all manner of abuses. This is often most true of women.[37] Because unpaid work is not considered "breadwinning," women historically have had little say in many economic and other decisions that affect them a great deal.[38] Women who do work in the waged economy, in addition to typically being paid less for the same work as men, are also often responsible for up to almost thirty hours per week of unpaid household labor. This is significantly more than men typically do and is entirely unaccounted for in ways that take a drastic but often unseen economic, physical, and emotional toll on women.[39] Our social disregard for unpaid labor—undervalued because of its lack of economic return—exacerbates social vulnerabilities and contributes to the abuse of unpaid workers.

35. Jensen, *Responsive Labor*, 3.
36. Jensen, *Responsive Labor*, 34, quoting Martin Luther, "The Estate of Marriage," in *Works*, vol. 45, ed. Walther I. Brandt (Fortress, 1962), 40.
37. Jensen, *Responsive Labor*, 2.
38. Volf, *Work in the Spirit*, 8.
39. Volf, *Work in the Spirit*, 8–9.

Connected to this, the waged economy invites further hiding of illicit enterprises. Because the waged economy—despite its track record of abuse—has some safeguards in place, there are some limits on worker abuse and mistreatment. In the United States, there is a semblance of a spotlight aiming to hold owners accountable for the just and equitable treatment of their employees. But just as the waged economy hides abuse in unpaid domestic labor, it also creates a hidden economy that hyperexploits workers who are often unpaid. Here, I am thinking of exploitation-abundant contexts such as sweatshops, human trafficking, the sex industry, and so on. The hidden nature of these industries masks many grave injustices.

There is an opportunity for Christians committed to the dignity of labor and the common good to bring unpaid labor into the light for examination. In situations where unpaid labor is essential, making significant contributions to the common good but devalued because of its low return on investment, a theology of labor invites robust celebration and a prophetic recognition of the dignity of that work. In situations where unpaid and underpaid labor is exploitative, a theology of labor insists on vigorous challenge, critique, and the pursuit of reform to enable the exploited the experience of that same kind of liberative participation we discussed above. The exploited are entitled to make their full, free, and unique contribution to the common good and are worthy of being celebrated—not demeaned—as they participate in good and different ways in a common economic life together with others.

What's more, the economic pressures of life in modern society make it increasingly difficult to manage the amount of unpaid work required to sustain life, families, and communities. The single-earner household model is more and more unrealistic. On the other hand, the rapid rise in dual-earner households widens other problems. When two-income households become the social norm, single-person/parent households are under immense financial strain.[40] Naturally, the more time that one person, or one parent, must devote to wage-earning labor, the less margin there is for the unpaid labor required for the flourishing of a household. This includes things we often refer to as "chores," but it also includes the similarly necessary requirements of rest, recreation, and leisure. These unpaid activities are essential for thriving communities.[41] People find scores of shortcuts and efficiencies to accomplish essential tasks but often do so in ways that rob work of its possible meaning. So, we microwave meals instead of preparing them. We occupy our children

40. Christine Firer Hinze, *Radical Sufficiency: Work, Livelihood, and a US Catholic Economic Ethic* (Georgetown University Press, 2021), 277.
41. Hinze, *Radical Sufficiency*, 263.

instead of raising them. We institutionalize community improvement and donate to those institutions instead of helping our neighbors. We buy new instead of repairing. We consume media instead of making art.

At the same time, I wonder whether the pressure that squeezes the value from uncompensated labor is a contributing factor to the incredible rise in the commercialization of traditional forms of unpaid work. Consider the explosive growth of the "homemaking" industry. Massive brands and destination markets that people view as pilgrimage-like experiences demonstrate the wide appeal of investing immense time and money into arenas of traditionally unpaid work. Those brands create a unique kind of glamour associated with "trad life" labor. These influencers peddle a shiny version of work that has been considered ordinary, mundane, and dirty for literally thousands of years. Is that because they, by monetizing traditional household labor, are killing two birds with one stone? Perhaps. Is it because this capitalizes on impulses people doing traditionally unpaid labor might feel—wanting a deeper sense of fulfillment and satisfaction in the overlooked and undervalued work they do day-to-day? Almost certainly.

Motivations aside, this groundswell of glamorizing and monetizing traditionally unpaid work is at least possibly a response to the fact that this labor is historically demeaned and devalued. But I'll suggest that trying to make this work more meaningful—more valuable in the eyes of society—is ultimately as theologically empty as the quest for fulfillment discussed in chapter 3. Instead of celebrating the intrinsic value and worth of all labor that contributes to the common good and insisting that society do the same, monetizing ordinary common labor can be a concession to the value system of the social hierarchy of labor, attempting to inject worth into devalued work on the hierarchy's terms.

The other day I was having a conversation with my sons about a common friend of ours who is an aspiring mechanic. He works at an auto shop and spends many evening and weekend hours fixing cars on the side in his garage. Recently, he purchased a luxury performance car in need of serious repair and rebuild. He meticulously scoured for the necessary parts, teaching himself new knowledge and skills as he brought this car back to life. He was proud of the final result. He was ready to find a kindred car enthusiast to buy it. Unfortunately, he was able to sell the car for only slightly more than the amount of money he put into it, making his labor essentially unpaid. The discussion with my sons centered on the question "Was this worth it?" On the one hand, as an aspiring working-class entrepreneur, there may be some holes in the model if he is looking to build out a business. But on the other hand, the passion, enjoyment, and personal development that the project afforded him might suggest that it was totally worth it, as long as economic return on investment was not the operating value system. We live in a society where it is difficult to find someone who has developed passion and skill in some traditionally unpaid arena who is not being encouraged to monetize that skill, revealing the unspoken belief that the only work that matters is work you get paid to do. Unpaid work is still less valuable than paid labor.

There seems to be a reclaiming needed here. Theologically, we are well positioned to celebrate many forms of labor that are unpaid, that live outside the waged economy. We do not have to inject that work with superficial forms of meaning and value. Instead, because the work is a contribution to the common good, we can recognize it as an assertion of dignity. Every meal prepared, garden planted, fence mended, neighbor helped, and child taught is some person's way of saying "I am a woman! I am a man! I am the *imago Dei*!"

As the title of this book, *A Working Theology of Labor*, suggests, I never intended to solve every problem the labor question poses. These three topics are great examples, though, of ways we might apply a thoughtful and faithful theological perspective on labor to new labor issues as they inevitably arise. Any theological frame worth its salt will be able to engage the process of discerning faithful next steps in uncharted territory. Since my goal has been to create space for a renewed conversation about theology and labor, I expect and hope that when new labor questions arise, new theological ground can be charted by others using some of the resources developed in this book.

So, what questions have come to you as you've read? If you were writing the next chapter of this book, what would the topic be? We need to keep working. . . .

# CONCLUSION

## Good Work and the Good Life

It is for our species, it would seem, to go on to other matters. Human matters.

—Studs Terkel[1]

The other day, I shared this project with an old friend whom I hadn't seen in over a decade, and his immediate question was, "Why'd you write it?" That got me thinking: What *was* my goal in writing this book? I've mentioned several reasons along the way. I think that Christians, especially those with an evangelical (or adjacent) heritage, have largely failed to see the moral urgency of the labor question. As evidenced by the relative silence on the issue from writers and theologians, the plight of the working class is too often ignored by church folks. That should be remedied. And while this isn't a comprehensive or flawless treatment, I hope it provokes sustained attention.

The economic question is the heart of God's vision for justice. The broad Christian effort for justice and a more equitable and beautiful world sometimes gets fragmented along issue lines. We work at cross purposes when that happens, and we typically fail to see the economic factors pulling the strings above the curtain. A dedicated and serious engagement with economic realities—sustained attention to the labor question—helps us love our

1. Studs Terkel, *Working: People Talk About What They Do All Day and How They Feel About What They Do* (Pantheon, 1974), xxii.

neighbors and give the world glimpses of the grand and beautiful future God desires for each of us.

I also observe ways that the working class is disrespected by the rest of society and how the church not only gives permission for such disrespect but often actively feeds into the values and aspirations that create and support the social hierarchy of labor. I do not believe that Jesus approves, or condones, a way of moving through the world that explicitly favors CEOs and corporate movers and shakers while demeaning stock clerks and sanitation workers. The idolatrous way we bestow worth on the wealthy and look down on those whose labor ensures our society functions is straightforwardly sinful. One highly regrettable result of the Faith and Work movement has been the cosigning of such social shame on those who work in jobs we deem beneath us, an opinion we've shined up with shoddy theology.

I believe we've done this, at least in part, because we see upward mobility as a God-ordained good worthy of our aspirations and energy. It is not just the prosperity gospel crowd that confuses economic success with God's blessing. Our shared social passion for upward mobility is a root cause of the social hierarchy of labor and the blatant and abusive injustices that stem from it.

And upward mobility is not just inflicting damage on others; it is eating away the health of our souls. The siren song of upward mobility is that the good life is right around the corner. The next pay raise, the next acquisition, the next step-up home, the next social signifier of wealth. And yet the perpetuality of "the next" leaves the acolytes of upward mobility forever unsatisfied. Society acts out economic addictions, rendering us incapable of contentment. Our current realities—job, family, assets, 401(k)—are not good enough; the good life is something for which we are constantly reaching. And if the good life is always just out of reach, that means none of us are living good lives. And we know it. Instead of existential shalom, far too many of us labor through our lives with an abiding sense of existential disappointment, a feeling that everything we do and everything we've done is basically meaningless.

## Ecclesiastes and the Meaninglessness of *Everything*

That is, likely, one reason why we don't spend too much time reflecting on the book of Ecclesiastes. When "the Teacher" cries out that everything is meaningless and that everything we do is just like chasing after the wind, we feel it in our soul in a way we'd prefer not to pay attention to. It isn't that the book depresses us; it's that it hits too close to the home of our already-existing depressions.

But what if that's not what the Teacher is telling us? What if he doesn't mean that nothing has meaning but instead intends to help us see that *everything* is meaningless? Let's consider a few famous excerpts:

> The words of the Teacher, son of David, king in Jerusalem:
>
> "Meaningless! Meaningless!"
> says the Teacher.
> "Utterly meaningless!
> Everything is meaningless."
>
> What do people gain from all their labors
> at which they toil under the sun?
> Generations come and generations go,
> but the earth remains forever. (1:1–4)

> So I hated life, because the work that is done under the sun was grievous to me. All of it is meaningless, a chasing after the wind. I hated all the things I had toiled for under the sun, because I must leave them to the one who comes after me. And who knows whether that person will be wise or foolish? Yet they will have control over all the fruit of my toil into which I have poured my effort and skill under the sun. This too is meaningless. So my heart began to despair over all my toilsome labor under the sun. For a person may labor with wisdom, knowledge and skill, and then they must leave all they own to another who has not toiled for it. This too is meaningless and a great misfortune. What do people get for all the toil and anxious striving with which they labor under the sun? All their days their work is grief and pain; even at night their minds do not rest. This too is meaningless. (2:17–23)

> What do workers gain from their toil? I have seen the burden God has laid on the human race. He has made everything beautiful in its time. He has also set eternity in the human heart; yet no one can fathom what God has done from beginning to end. (3:9–11)

The Teacher is looking back at his life with some pretty intense emotions.[2] He's finding a deep, spiritual futility to much of the labor he's given himself to over the course of his life. Now, at the end, he realizes several things important for our final reflections as well. First, his impact will ultimately be infinitesimally small. "What do I get from my labor?" he asks. Not much. The generations come and go, and eventually no one will even remember his name. Everything he's worked to achieve will be forgotten. And what about

2. C. L. Seow, *Ecclesiastes* (Yale University Press, 2008), 48.

the riches he amassed? Also meaningless. He will just hand them over to someone else, someone who didn't earn them.[3] To describe this existential angst he's feeling, he says that God "set eternity in the human heart" (3:11). Scholars have mixed views of this statement's exact meaning, but set against the discussion we've been having, it seems plausible to conclude that he means that humans go through life wanting something they can never have.[4] They want to leave a lasting impact, but the generations come and go. They want riches that last forever, but they must give them to others. They want to, in some sense, live forever, but ultimately everyone is just going to die. So: Meaningless! It's all a vapor.[5]

But the Teacher isn't suggesting that all labor is undignified, or that our work has no value or meaning. He is reminding us that having *everything* is impossible. You can't make that kind of impact. You can't hoard that kind of wealth. You can't exist for all eternity (at least in that way). You can't have everything. Going through life wanting it all will bring you to the end of your life with a deep-seated disillusionment and disappointment because you've been reaching for *everything*, and *everything* is always just out of reach.

Sounds like upward mobility. And, in fact, it is. The Teacher is describing the same set of values and aspirations that define those devoted to upward mobility today. He writes Ecclesiastes from the same place of dissatisfaction. He also provides the evidence of its falseness. In fact, scholars suggest the word we translate "meaningless" could be translated "deception," as in the promise of *everything* is a lie.[6] And here's where the writer flips the script: We come to find out that the dissatisfaction and disillusionment we feel isn't because *everything* is just out of our grasp; it's because we were never supposed to be reaching for it in the first place. Look at the conclusions the Teacher draws about what the good life actually is:

> A person can do nothing better than to eat and drink and find satisfaction in their own toil. This too, I see, is from the hand of God. (2:24)

> I know that there is nothing better for people than to be happy and to do good while they live. That each of them may eat and drink, and find satisfaction in all their toil—this is the gift of God. (3:12–13)

3. Seow, *Ecclesiastes*, 48.
4. William Brown, *Ecclesiastes* (John Knox, 2000), 43; Peter Enns, *Ecclesiastes* (Eerdmans, 2011), 54; Seow, *Ecclesiastes*, 173.
5. Seow, *Ecclesiastes*, 47. Literally "breath, puff, whiff, steam."
6. Julie Ann Duncan, *Ecclesiastes* (Abingdon, 2017), 2.

> This is what I have observed to be good: that it is appropriate for a person to eat, to drink and to find satisfaction in their toilsome labor under the sun during the few days of life God has given them—for this is their lot. (5:18)

> Whatever your hand finds to do, do it with all your might, for in the realm of the dead, where you are going, there is neither working nor planning nor knowledge nor wisdom. (9:10)

In the final calculus, the Teacher tells us that the good life will elude anyone grasping for *everything*, but it will find the one who embraces the profound ordinariness of their life and labor. This is the other option, the "alternative course."[7] The takeaway is that "the simple pleasures of eating, drinking, and, literally, 'seeing good in one's work.' These are the vestiges of joy. . . . The true pleasures are the most mundane."[8]

Upward mobility leaves a person eternally unsatisfied, but the Teacher invites us to see that contentment allows us to see the good gifts of life: food, drink, friendship, and ordinary work.[9] The Teacher knows that no one is called to some grand quest. Instead, we are all called to the work our hands find to do. It is into that labor we are called to put our full selves. And when we are done with the ordinary work of our hands, we can be satisfied. We can enjoy the fruit of that labor: ordinary food and drink shared in celebration of God's gifts with our families, friends, and communities. Instead of grasping for everything, embrace the very real limitations of our capacity. This is not a concession to our failure to achieve something as big as our dreams and aspirations. Rather, we chasten our aspirations because we are learning to recognize the ways they actually lead us astray from the good life God intends for us. This is real contentment—not settling for less but recalibrating what we understand to be enough.

Dissatisfaction with "our lot" leads us to take from others, to demean others in order to build ourselves up, to create hierarchies of value and worth, to make comparisons between those whose work we think matters and those whose work we think does not, to maximize profit at the expense of the less powerful; the list could go on. It is all in service of economic aspirations that betray a devotion to upward mobility instead of an abiding contentment with the good life God puts in front of us—a life that shares with others in the great divine abundance.

7. Duncan, *Ecclesiastes*, 82.
8. Brown, *Ecclesiastes*, 37.
9. Seow, *Ecclesiastes*, 50–52.

The discontent breeds resentment and anger. It tempts us to despair of lives that are not as well off as we'd intended and then demean others or compare ourselves to them as a way of managing the inner sense that the life we have is less than the life we could be living.[10] This could make us long for impact. But the Teacher says that impact is an illusion; the good life comes from embracing the smallness of our humanity and the ordinariness of our mark in the world. It could make us long for wealth. But the Teacher says that all your gains will go to others, so instead of pursuing wealth, simply feast on the bounty in front of you. It could make us idolize the protagonist and give in to the impulse to cast ourselves as the main characters in lives that we expect will be epic sagas. "But death will put an end to every aspiration," and everyone will forget your name someday, so spend your days loving and being loved by people you can embrace in the flesh and blood.[11]

Stanley Hauerwas, reflecting on the work of my favorite writer, James Rebanks, tells the story of Rebanks coming to terms with his life as a shepherd in England's Lake District. An Oxford-educated writer, Rebanks finds himself—reluctantly at first—tending sheep, mending fences, shoveling muck from barns, and tying his and his family's livelihood to the land and what his hands can produce. That is a journey that leads him ultimately to utter a line the Teacher of Ecclesiastes is after (for himself and for us): "This is my life. I want for no other."[12] Could we say the same about our lives?

What does this have to do with labor? Plainly, upward mobility is the enemy of ordinary toil. Disdain for ordinary labor disregards the working class. But the invitation is to cease our strivings for *everything* and to embrace the work our hands find to do. If we do that, we will begin to deepen our appreciation for work that builds and sustains communities—work that fosters sometimes-small expressions of the common good. We will reject the social hierarchy of labor and model alternative ways of life in its stead. We will be able to recognize the value of ordinary contributions and embrace the fact that, over time, the world flourishes through the many contributions of "unremarkable" folks. We will notice when the world gets this wrong at the expense of workers. Our senses will be more finely tuned to observe and respond when the dignity of the work of someone's hands is demeaned and devalued. We will be better able to see and celebrate the image of God bursting forth from someone's participation in our shared life together.

In other words, the church will have an answer to the labor question.

10. Stanley Hauerwas, "A New Search for the Good Life," https://reflections.yale.edu/article/spirit-and-politics-finding-our-way/new-search-good-life.

11. Seow, *Ecclesiastes*, 156.

12. Hauerwas, "New Search."

# INDEX